North America in Colonial Times

An Encyclopedia for Students

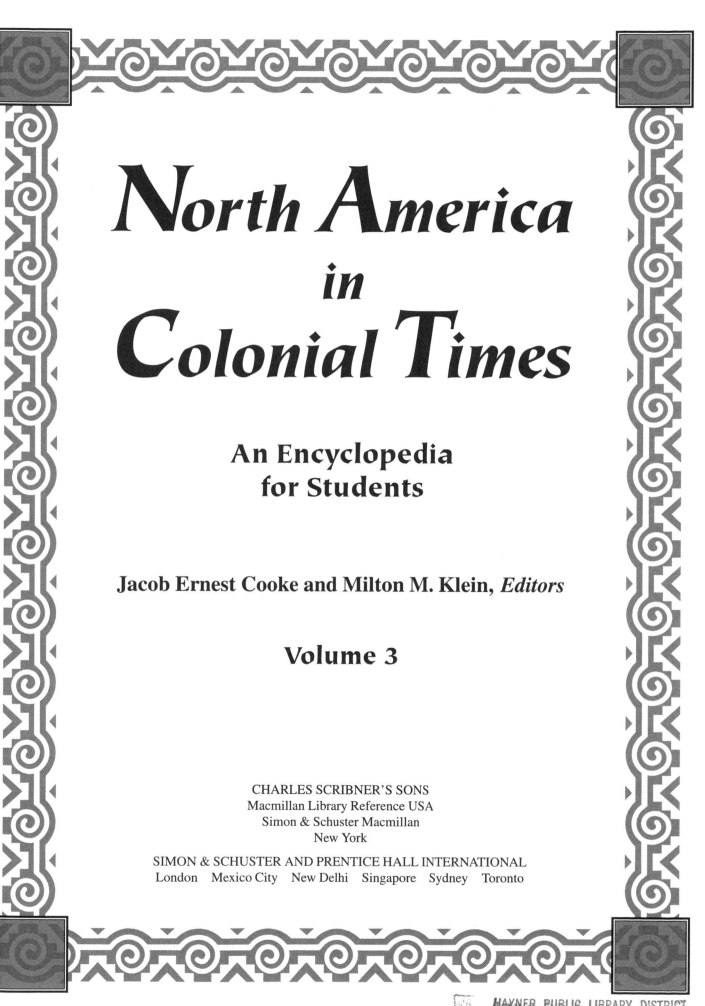

North America in Colonial Times

An Encyclopedia
for Students

Jacob Ernest Cooke and Milton M. Klein, *Editors*

Volume 3

CHARLES SCRIBNER'S SONS
Macmillan Library Reference USA
Simon & Schuster Macmillan
New York

SIMON & SCHUSTER AND PRENTICE HALL INTERNATIONAL
London   Mexico City   New Delhi   Singapore   Sydney   Toronto

Developed for Scribners by Visual Education Corporation, Princeton, N.J.

Library of Congress Cataloging-in-Publication Data

North America in colonial times : an encyclopedia for students / Jacob Ernest Cooke and Milton M. Klein, editors.
    p.   cm.
    Adaptation and revision of Encyclopedia of the North American colonies for young readers.
    Includes bibliographical references and index.
    Summary: An encyclopedia of the history of the American colonies and Canada, including Native Americans, Spanish missions, English and Dutch exploration, the slave trade, and the French and Indian War.
    ISBN 0-684-80538-3 (set : alk. paper).— ISBN 0-684-80534-0 (v.1 : alk. paper).— ISBN 0-684-80535-9 (v.2 : alk. paper).— ISBN 0-684-80536-7 (v.3 : alk. paper).— ISBN 0-684-80537-5 (v.4: alk. paper)
    1. Europe—Colonies—America—History—Encyclopedias, Juvenile.   2. North America—History—Encyclopedias, Juvenile. [1. North America—History—Colonial period, ca. 1600–1775—Encyclopedias.]   I. Cooke, Jacob Ernest, 1924– .   II. Klein, Milton M. (Milton Martin), 1917– .   III. Encyclopedia of the North American colonies.
E45.N65   1998
970.02—dc21   98-29862
                                            CIP
                                            AC

1 2 3 4 5 6 7 8 9 10

PRINTED IN THE UNITED STATES OF AMERICA

Time Line of North America in Colonial Times

ca. 20,000 B.C.   *The first human inhabitants of the Americas cross from Siberia into Alaska.*

A.D. 985   *Erik the Red establishes a Norse colony in Greenland.*

ca. 1000   *Leif Eriksson lands on the coast of North America.*

ca. 1420   *Prince Henry of Portugal establishes a school of navigation at Sagres, from which seamen set out and discover the Canary, Madeira, and Azores islands.*

1492   *Christopher Columbus, attempting to sail west to Asia, finds the "New World."*

1494   *The Treaty of Tordesillas divides the world between the Spanish and Portuguese empires.*

ca. 1500   *The French begin fishing off the coast of Newfoundland.*
              The Mohawk, Oneida, Onondaga, Cayuga, and Seneca peoples unite to form the Iroquois Confederacy.

1507   *Martin Waldseemüller calls the land explored by Columbus "America" in honor of Amerigo Vespucci, an Italian navigator who was the first to use the term "New World."*

1513   *Juan Ponce de León claims Florida for Spain.*

1518   *African slaves are brought to Hispaniola (Haiti and Dominican Republic) to work in gold mines.*

1518~1521   *Hernando Cortés conquers the Aztecs in Mexico.*

1519~1522   *Ships under the command of Ferdinand Magellan sail around the world.*

1524   *Giovanni da Verrazano explores the North American coast.*

1534~1536   *Jacques Cartier explores the Gulf of St. Lawrence and the St. Lawrence River as far as Montreal.*

1539~1543   *Hernando de Soto explores North America from Florida to the Mississippi River.*

1540~1542   *Francisco Vásquez de Coronado explores the Southwest as far as the Grand Canyon.*

1562~1568   *John Hawkins makes slave-trading voyages from Africa to the West Indies.*

1564   *France establishes Fort Caroline in Florida but quickly loses it to the Spanish.*

1565   *Pedro Menéndez de Avilés founds St. Augustine in Florida.*

1565~1574   *Spain sets up missions and forts between Florida and Virginia.*

1572   *Chief Powhatan unites Algonquian-speaking tribes in the Chesapeake region to form the Powhatan Confederacy.*

1578   *Francis Drake sails around South America and lands in present-day California.*

1583   *Sir Humphrey Gilbert leads an expedition to Newfoundland.*

1585~1590   *The English attempt twice to establish a colony at Roanoke Island. The second settlement mysteriously disappears.*

1598   *Juan de Oñate founds the colony of New Mexico.*

1602   *Bartholomew Gosnold explores the Atlantic coast from southern Maine to Narragansett Bay and transmits smallpox to his Indian trading partners.*

1604 Samuel de Champlain and Pierre du Gua de Monts establish a French settlement at Port Royal in Acadia (present-day Nova Scotia).

1606 James I of England grants charters to the Virginia Company and the Plymouth Company to colonize the Atlantic coast of North America.

1606–1608 The Plymouth Company establishes Saghadoc, an unsuccessful colony in present-day Maine.

1607 Colonists found Jamestown, the first permanent English settlement, in Virginia.
Massasoit becomes chief of the powerful Wampanoag of New England.

1608 Samuel de Champlain establishes a French settlement at Quebec.

1609 Henry Hudson explores the Hudson River as far north as present-day Albany.
Santa Fe is founded in New Mexico.

1612 New varieties of tobacco are planted in Virginia, launching a tobacco boom in the Chesapeake region.

1613 English forces destroy the Acadian town of Port Royal.

1614 Captain John Smith explores the New England coast.
New Netherland Company gains a monopoly on trade in the Dutch colony.

1616 Africans arrive in Bermuda, the first slaves in the English colonies.

1619 The Dutch bring the first blacks to Virginia.

1620 The Pilgrims establish Plymouth colony.

1622 Powhatan Indians fight the English in Virginia.

1624 Thirty families arrive in the Dutch colony of New Netherland.

1625 Jesuits arrive in Quebec.

1626 Peter Minuit becomes director general of New Netherland and buys Manhattan Island from the Indians.

1628 The English take over Acadia and Quebec, which are returned to France in 1632.

1630 The Massachusetts Bay Company establishes a new colony at Boston.

1630–1642 The Great Migration brings 16,000 settlers from England to the Massachusetts Bay colony.

1632 George Calvert, Lord Baltimore, receives a grant to found the colony of Maryland.

1633 French Jesuits establish Quebec College.

1633–1638 English colonists begin settling along the Connecticut River.

1636 Roger Williams founds the colony of Rhode Island.
Harvard College is established at Cambridge, Massachusetts.

1636–1637 In the Pequot War, English colonists in Connecticut destroy most of the Pequot tribe.

1636–1638 Anne Hutchinson challenges the authority of religious leaders in Massachusetts, is exiled, and settles in Rhode Island.

1638 Peter Minuit founds New Sweden on the Delaware River.

1639 North America's first hospital, the Hôtel-Dieu, is established in Quebec.

1641 The Bay Psalm Book, the first book printed in the English colonies, appears in Boston.

1642   *French fur traders establish a base at Montreal.*

1642–1649   *The English Civil War pits supporters of the monarch against Parliamentarians (mostly Puritans). King Charles I is executed in 1649, and England becomes a commonwealth.*

1643   *Massachusetts Bay, Plymouth, Connecticut, and New Haven colonies form the New England Confederation.*

1646–1665   *Iroquois Indians raid the Algonquin, Huron, and other neighboring tribes, driving refugees into Quebec and the Great Lakes region.*

1647   *Peter Stuyvesant becomes director general of New Netherland.*

1649   *Maryland passes the Act of Toleration establishing religious freedom for Christians; the act is repealed in 1654.*

1650   *Poems by Anne Bradstreet, the first published American poet, are printed in London.*

1652–1654   *First war between English and Dutch colonists.*

1653–1660   *England is ruled by Oliver Cromwell, Lord Protector of the Commonwealth.*

1654   *The first Jews arrive in New Amsterdam.*

1655   *Peter Stuyvesant conquers New Sweden, ending Swedish colonization in North America.*

1660   *The first Navigation Act requires all goods going into or out of the English colonies to be carried on English ships. The English monarchy is restored under Charles II.*

1663   *Louis XIV of France declares New France a royal province. Charles II of England gives eight proprietors a grant for the colony of Carolina.*

1664   *English naval forces capture New Netherland, which is renamed New York.*

1665–1667   *Second war between the English and the Dutch.*

1666–1667   *French colonial forces attack the Iroquois Confederacy and force it to accept French terms for peace.*

1668   *The English establish Charles Fort at the mouth of the Rupert River in present-day Canada.*

1669   *John Locke draws up the Fundamental Constitutions, a proposed plan of government for the Carolinas.*

1670   *The Hudson's Bay Company gains control of the fur trade in the Hudson Bay region.*

1672   *Royal African Company gains a monopoly on the English slave trade to America and the West Indies.*

1672–1674   *In the third war between the English and the Dutch, the Dutch temporarily regain control of New York.*

1673   *Louis Jolliet and Father Jacques Marquette explore the Mississippi River.*

1675–1676   *King Philip's War: Wampanoag leader Metacom, called King Philip, leads Indians of southern New England in an unsuccessful uprising against the English.*

1676   *Bacon's Rebellion: Virginia settlers, led by Nathaniel Bacon, seize control of the colony.*

1680   *Pueblo Revolt: Pueblo Indians drive Spanish from New Mexico.*

1681   *William Penn receives a charter to establish Pennsylvania from King Charles II of England.*

1682   *English colonists attack Quebec.*
René-Robert Cavelier, Sieur de La Salle, claims Mississippi River valley for France, calling it Louisiana.

1686~1689 King James II of England creates the Dominion of New England, which includes the colonies of New Hampshire, Massachusetts, Rhode Island, Connecticut, New York, and New Jersey. Sir Edmund Andros is renamed governor of the new province.

1687 Father Eusebio Francisco Kino establishes mission settlements in Pimeria Alta (modern Arizona).

1688 Protestant monarchs William II and Mary ascend the throne in England in what is called the Glorious Revolution.

1689~1691 Glorious Revolution in America: Colonists revolt against the Dominion of New England and receive new charters from William and Mary.

Leisler's Rebellion: Jacob Leisler seizes control in New York and is executed in 1691.

1689~1697 King William's War brings French and English colonies and their Indian allies into conflict.

1692~1693 Salem witchcraft trials: Nineteen people are hanged as witches in Massachusetts.

1693 The College of William and Mary is founded in Virginia.

1696 Carolina adopts the first slave laws in the British mainland colonies.

Spain reconquers New Mexico from the Pueblo Indians.

1699 Pierre Le Moyne d'Iberville founds the first French settlement in Louisiana.

1701 Anglicans create the Society for the Propagation of the Gospel (SPG) to convert Indians and Africans.

Yale College is established in New Haven.

Antoine de la Mothe Cadillac founds Detroit.

1702~1713 Queen Anne's War brings new conflict between French and English colonists and their Indian allies.

1707 The Act of Union unites England and Scotland into the United Kingdom of Great Britain.

1709 African and Indian slavery is legalized in New France.

1710 British forces conquer Port Royal in Acadia and rename it Annapolis Royal.

1711~1713 Tuscarora War: Carolina colonists join the Yamassee to defeat the Tuscarora Indians.

1713 Treaty of Utrecht: France gives up Acadia, Newfoundland, and Hudson Bay to Great Britain.

1715~1728 Yamassee War: Yamassee attack South Carolina towns and plantations and are defeated by British and Cherokee forces.

1718 Jean Baptiste Le Moyne de Bienville founds New Orleans.

1729 North and South Carolina become separate royal colonies.

1729~1731 Natchez Revolt in Louisiana.

1730 The Great Wagon Road is begun. It eventually stretches from Philadelphia to Georgia.

1731 Benjamin Franklin establishes a circulating library in Philadelphia.

1732 Franklin publishes Poor Richard's Almanack.

1733 James Oglethorpe founds Georgia as a refuge for British debtors.

British Parliament passes the Molasses Act, taxing sugar and molasses from the French West Indies.

1734–1735   *Clergyman Jonathan Edwards leads a religious revival in Massachusetts.*

1735   *The trial of publisher John Peter Zenger in New York promotes the principle of freedom of the press.*

1737   *"Walking Purchase": Delaware Indians sell the colony of Pennsylvania the entire Lehigh Valley.*

1738–1745   *Great Awakening: English preacher George Whitefield sparks religious revivals throughout the British colonies.*

1739   *Stono Rebellion: Slaves in South Carolina revolt and are stopped by the militia.*

1740s   *Eliza Pinckney begins indigo cultivation in South Carolina.*

1741   *Rumors of plots by slaves to revolt lead to arrests and executions in New York.*
Russian explorer Vitus Bering lands in Alaska.

1743   *Benjamin Franklin establishes the American Philosophical Society in Philadelphia.*

1744–1748   *King George's War: European war between Britain, France, and Spain spreads to North America.*

1746   *College of New Jersey (later Princeton University) is founded.*

1754   *French and Indian War begins when Virginia sends its militia, led by George Washington, to challenge the French in the Ohio Valley. France and Britain officially declare war in 1756.*

1755   *Britain expels French colonists from Acadia. Many Acadians migrate to Louisiana.*

1759–1760   *British forces under General James Wolfe capture Quebec. A year later, the French surrender at Montreal.*

1762   *Spain declares war on Great Britain.*

1763   *Treaty of Paris: Great Britain wins Florida from Spain and Canada and Cape Breton from France. Spain gains Louisiana. Britain issues proclamation forbidding colonists to settle west of the Appalachian Mountains.*
Touro Synagogue opens in Newport, Rhode Island.

1763–1766   *Chief Pontiac of the Ottawa leads an alliance of Indians against the British in the Great Lakes region.*

1764   *The Sugar Act imposes high import taxes on non-British sugar, leading to colonial protests.*

1765   *The Stamp Act provokes outrage and widespread protest in the colonies and is repealed.*

1766   *British Parliament passes the Declaratory Act to emphasize its "full power and authority" over the colonies.*

1767   *Jesuits are expelled from Spanish territories. Franciscans take over the western missions.*
In the British colonies, the Townshend Acts impose new taxes on certain imported items.

1769   *Junípero Serra founds the first Spanish mission in California at San Diego.*

1770   *Boston Massacre: British troops fire into a crowd, killing five colonists.*

1773   *Boston Tea Party: Colonists protest the tea tax by dumping a shipload of tea into Boston harbor.*
Publication of Poems on Various Subjects, Religious and Moral *by Phillis Wheatley, a slave in Boston.*

1774   Parliament passes the Intolerable Acts to strengthen British authority in Massachusetts.
In the Quebec Act, Parliament extends the borders of Quebec province southward and grants religious freedom to Catholics, angering American colonists.
The First Continental Congress meets in Philadelphia.

1775   Battles are fought at Lexington and Concord.
The Second Continental Congress assembles in Philadelphia.
George Washington takes command of the Continental Army.

1776   Thomas Paine's Common Sense is published in Philadelphia.
American colonists issue the Declaration of Independence to explain their separation from Great Britain.

1777   Under military pressure, Cherokee Indians yield their lands to North and South Carolina.
Vermont declares its independence from New York and New Hampshire.

1778   Captain James Cook explores the northern Pacific coast.

1779   Spain declares war on Britain and enters the American War of Independence.

1781   American troops under George Washington and French forces under General Rochambeau defeat British troops led by General Charles Cornwallis at Yorktown, Virginia, winning independence for the United States.

1783   Treaty of Versailles: Great Britain recognizes the independence of the United States of America. Florida is returned to Spain.

1784   New Brunswick province is established in Canada as a refuge for American Loyalists.

1789–1793   Alexander Mackenzie reaches the Pacific coast by traveling overland across Canada.

1791   Constitution Act: Britain divides the province of Quebec into Lower Canada (Quebec) and Upper Canada (Ontario).

1792   Captain George Vancouver explores the west coast of Canada.

1794   Slavery is abolished in French colonies.

1799   The Russian-American Company is chartered and given a monopoly to conduct trade in Alaska.

1800   Spain returns Louisiana to France.

1803   Louisiana Purchase: France sells Louisiana to the United States for $15 million.

1812–1841   The Russian-American Company maintains a base at Fort Ross, in northern California.

1819   The United States acquires Florida from Spain.

1821   Mexico declares independence from Spain.

1825–1832   Stephen F. Austin brings American colonists to Texas.

1833   Great Britain declares an end to slavery in all its possessions, beginning in 1834.

1840   The Act of Union reunites Upper and Lower Canada and grants them self-rule.

1867   The British North America Act establishes the Dominion of Canada.
Russia sells Alaska to the United States.

Literature

* genre type of literary or artistic work

* narrative story or description

$\mathcal{A}$lmost from the start, the Europeans in North America put pen to paper to describe their experiences in the colonies. While they often used the literary genres* of their homelands, colonists also developed their own styles. Histories, travel narratives*, letters, and diaries interested early settlers far more than works of poetry or novels.

Much of the writing of the colonial period served a practical purpose. Struggling to survive in a new land, early settlers had little time for creating literary works with an artistic purpose. They regarded writing as part of the duties of an explorer, a military officer, a governor, a minister, or a landowner—not as a career.

The literature of colonial North America also includes the oral traditions of African Americans and Native Americans. Stories, chants, and poems transmitted from generation to generation helped preserve the culture of these groups. Only recently have the verbal art forms of Native Americans and African Americans been recognized as literature.

British Colonies

As might be expected, British tastes and styles greatly influenced the literature produced in the North American colonies. Colonists imported a vast number of books from Great Britain, and American writers often imitated the techniques of British writers. In the early years, almost all books written in the English colonies were published in London. It was not long, however, before colonists began creating literature with a uniquely American point of view.

Regional differences emerged at an early stage. Broadly speaking, the literature of the New England PURITANS had a strong religious and moral voice. Scientific and rational* thinking characterized the writing of the middle colonies, which was home to people from a variety of backgrounds. The literature of the southern colonies tended to be more cosmopolitan* and elegant, reflecting the tastes of the upper-class landowners who lived there.

* rational based on reason

* cosmopolitan worldly, not provincial and narrow; having wide interests and knowledge

New England generally dominated colonial writing. Many Puritan leaders, especially ministers, felt a strong need to promote their religious views, and literature provided a means to do so. In addition, New Englanders had access to printing centers in Boston and Cambridge. By the time of the Revolutionary War, however, the literary capital had moved to Philadelphia—partly as a result of Benjamin FRANKLIN's influence. Moreover, political writing had become more popular than religious works as colonists engaged in heated debate over whether or not to break their ties to Great Britain.

Histories.　In the 1600s the English considered historical works second in importance only to the BIBLE. Colonists in North America began almost immediately, therefore, to record their experiences in the "New World." In 1608, a year after the establishment of the Jamestown colony, Captain John SMITH published his account of the colony's beginnings. He became the first author in English North America. Smith told the famous episode of his rescue by POCAHONTAS in his *Generall Historie of Virginia* of 1624. Another early history writer was William BRADFORD, governor of the PLYMOUTH COLONY in Massachusetts. He started his work, *History of Plimouth Plantation,* in 1630 and continued to update it until 1650.

Literature

Although prominent men in the southern and middle colonies also wrote accounts of discovery and settlement, Puritan writers in New England dominated the genre—both by the number and length of their histories and by the strong feeling with which they wrote. Puritans viewed themselves as God's chosen people and believed that their settlement in North America fulfilled a divine plan. They wanted to record their story to show how God was at work in their community. Puritan writers compared events in their settlement's history to biblical events, especially those in the Old Testament. They also focused on biographies of Puritan leaders, just as the Bible tells the stories of great individuals such as Moses and David. Cotton MATHER's *The Great Works of Christ in America* (1702) is a huge collection of biographies of Puritans and observations on religion.

Neither Puritans nor other colonial writers attempted to provide a factual account of their history. They tended to interpret events to show their colonies in the best light or to promote a point of view. In *The History and Present State of Virginia* (1705), Robert Beverley wrote in a plain style with realistic descriptions, but he criticized Virginians for being too dependent on England and urged them to show more loyalty to the young colony. *A True and Historical Narrative of the Colony of Georgia* (1741), written by a group of dissatisfied settlers, is actually a satire* on the administration of Governor James OGLETHORPE. One work that did attempt to report events in a factual manner is *History of the Colony of Massachusetts Bay* (1764) by Thomas HUTCHINSON, a Loyalist* and the last royal governor of Massachusetts.

Promotional Writing. Promotional writing—often in the form of pamphlets—attempted to convince Europeans to invest money in North American settlements or to immigrate. Colonial histories frequently served as promotional literature. In *History of Plimouth Plantation,* Bradford boasted about the fertile land and described the colony's need for honest, hardworking settlers. The VIRGINIA COMPANY OF LONDON hired ministers and other educated individuals to write glowing accounts of the Jamestown colony,

* *satire* humor that makes fun of something bad or foolish

* *Loyalist* American colonist who remained faithful to Britain during the American Revolution

Held captive by the Wampanoag and Narragansett Indians for three months in 1676, Mary Rowlandson wrote an account of her experience that became a very popular book.

hoping to attract investors to its colonial enterprise. This type of literature fascinated people back in England, especially if it included descriptions of North American wildlife.

Indian Captivity Narratives.

Among the most popular forms of literature in the British colonies were stories of white settlers being captured, tortured, and slaughtered by Indians. One well-known narrative described the Deerfield Massacre of 1704, in which the entire population of this Massachusetts community was killed or captured by Native Americans and the survivors taken to Canada. In another account of an Indian attack, Mary ROWLANDSON wrote movingly of seeing children killed by "a company of hell hounds, roaring, . . . ranting, and insulting." Less frequently told were stories of acts of cruelty committed by white settlers against the Indians, such as the 1637 slaughter of the entire PEQUOT tribe at Mystic, Connecticut.

Related to Indian captivity narratives were works discussing how best to control the Native Americans. Writers often portrayed Indians as demons and savages—an image colonists used to justify their inhumane treatment of Indians. A rare exception was Daniel Gookin, a Puritan who wrote two sympathetic accounts of the Indians in the late 1600s, much to the dismay of his fellow New Englanders.

Diaries and Journals.

Many British colonists kept DIARIES or journals, and the personal writings of prominent people were frequently published. New England Puritans used diary writing as a way of developing their spiritual life. They recorded their thoughts and feelings and examined their lives for signs that God had chosen them for salvation. In the *Diary of Cotton Mather, 1681–1708,* the famous preacher provided an account of his conversations and pleadings with God.

Unlike the inward-looking Puritan writers, William BYRD, a well-to-do Virginia landowner, wrote about the events of everyday life in a matter-of-fact, often humorous way. His journal of a surveying expedition, written in shorthand, contains stinging comments about other members of the group. The *Diary of Samuel Sewall, 1673–1729* combines both the sacred and the secular*. Sewall, a prominent Boston judge, had presided at the SALEM WITCHCRAFT TRIALS of 1692. His diary reveals the agony he felt as a participant in the cruel proceedings, but it also provides a glimpse into life in colonial Boston.

Sermon Literature.

Ministers in Puritan churches preached the word of God vigorously, boldly, and often—at least twice a week. An amazing number of these sermons found their way into print. Later Puritan sermons followed a format known as the Jeremiad, named after the Old Testament prophet Jeremiah who condemned the people of Israel for abandoning God's ways. In a Jeremiad sermon, a minister started with a biblical text, then discussed a Christian doctrine* derived from the text, and finally applied the doctrine to the congregation. Jonathan EDWARDS is perhaps the best-known author of sermon literature. His finely crafted sermon "Sinners in the Hands of an Angry God" (1741) used vivid images of fires and floods to illustrate his message about final judgment and salvation.

Prolific Preacher

The prize for producing the most writings during colonial times goes to Cotton Mather. The Puritan preacher produced an amazing 450 printed titles, including books, sermons, and pamphlets. Highly intelligent and immensely learned, Mather covered a great variety of subjects, including religion, history, politics, medicine, botany, and physics.

* *secular* nonreligious; connected with everyday life

* *doctrine* set of principles or beliefs accepted by a religious or political group

Poetry. The Puritans of New England published more poetry than did writers of the middle and southern colonies. As with other literary forms, Puritans used verse as a way of instructing people in the Christian life. Children learned Puritan doctrine and Bible stories by memorizing lines from Michael Wigglesworth's *The Day of Doom* (1662), the most widely circulated volume of poetry in colonial times. Wigglesworth's descriptions of the eternal damnation* that awaited those who fell to temptation frightened many young readers.

The work of Anne BRADSTREET, the colonies' first female poet, also dealt with Puritan morality and discipline. Her "To My Dear and Loving Husband" upheld the Puritan view of male authority in marriage. In "The Tenth Muse Lately Sprung Up in America" (1650), however, Bradstreet asserted her right to compose verse in a world dominated by male writers.

A very different type of poetry appeared frequently in colonial newspapers. Humorous, satiric poems were used to comment on political events of the day.

Biography and Autobiography. "Life writing," as biographies and autobiographies were called, offered another opportunity for presenting the Puritan view of the world. Puritan writers often portrayed the people they wrote about as "saints" and models of the Christian life. These biographies followed a formula, which included the individual's conversion experience at an early age and a lifetime of good works.

The most famous biography of colonial times, that of Benjamin Franklin, stood out in great contrast to the Puritan biographies. Franklin's *Autobiography* (1791), which covered his life in the first half of the 1700s, shows the new American dream that was developing toward the end of colonial times. While the Puritans believed that life was a journey toward a heavenly reward, Franklin emphasized achieving prosperity in the here and now. His *Poor Richard's Almanack,* first published in 1732, was one of the most popular BOOKS in the British colonies.

Dutch Colony

Established by the DUTCH WEST INDIA COMPANY in 1624, NEW NETHERLAND existed as a colony for only 40 years before the English seized it and renamed it New York. Much of the literature of New Netherland focused on the colony itself. Beginning with the notes of explorer Henry HUDSON, Dutch colonial writing attempted to describe the new land for the people back in the Netherlands. In periodicals, promotional books, and pamphlets, colonial writers described the landscape in detail and painted vivid images of the social life and customs. They tried to explain the unfamiliar by comparing it to things in the homeland. Familiar sayings, dialogue, allegory*, and verses were used to help get the writers' meanings across.

Adriaen van der Donck, a lawyer and New Netherland landowner, wrote the first book about the colony. Richly detailed and colorful, *A Description of the New Netherland* (1655) encouraged Dutch citizens to immigrate to the colony. This came a few years after he had written a piece complaining about the Dutch West India Company's mismanagement of the colony.

Dutch colonial poets also played a role in promoting the young colony. In "The Praise of New Netherland," Jacob Steendam stressed the colony's

* **damnation** condemned to dwell in hell eternally

* **allegory** literary device in which characters represent an idea or a religious or moral principle

Father Cats

The Dutch writer Jacob Cats was the most popular writer among the common people of New Amsterdam. Affectionately known as "Father Cats," he wrote clever verses and wise sayings that offered guidance in everyday life. First published in 1632, his *Spiegel* (meaning mirror), and the family Bible were the two most important books in Dutch colonial homes. Even in the early 1900s, people living in the Hudson River valley of New York still recited Cats's verses.

* *clergy* ministers, priests, and other church officials

* *masque* dramatic entertainment performed by masked actors

* *Jesuit* Roman Catholic religious order

abundant resources but made light of the dangers of living on the edge of the wilderness. Nicasius de Sille's poem "The Earth Speaks to Its Cultivators" featured a character named Adam who clears a new land—the poet's way of suggesting that New Netherland was a Garden of Eden.

Neither personal nor private, Dutch colonial diaries and journals were written for an audience in the Netherlands. The journal of David de Vries, a sailor and landowner, contained a wealth of practical information for new settlers. Jasper Danckaerts, a missionary, traveled throughout New Netherland looking for a suitable place to found a religious community. During his journey, he wrote detailed descriptions of the landscape and the people he met.

Letter writing provided another means of telling the people in the Netherlands about North America. The town council of NEW AMSTERDAM wrote reports to the Dutch government on the state of the colony. Letters from the clergy* described the condition of the church in New Netherland. There were also letters between business associates, such as those of Jeremias and Maria VAN RENSSELAER and their colleagues. Taken together, these letters form a body of literature that reveals much about social customs in the Dutch colony. They also show the varied and colorful personalities of the people who wrote them.

Even after New Netherland ceased to be a colony, Dutch prose and poetry continued to be produced by Dutch-speaking people in New York. The oral tradition of legends and tales survive in such later works as "Rip Van Winkle" and "The Legend of Sleepy Hollow" by Washington Irving and in the writings of James Fenimore Cooper.

French Colonies

Literary genres among French colonists included travel narratives and histories, geographical descriptions, sermons, satire, and letters. The period of French colonial literature ended in 1763, when the British gained control of NEW FRANCE and Spain took over the colony of LOUISIANA.

Travel Narratives. Travel literature was the most common form of French colonial writing. Narratives about voyages to faraway lands captivated the reading public in France. Explorers Jacques CARTIER and René-Robert Cavelier de LA SALLE provided the earliest descriptions of New France and Louisiana, respectively.

Early travel writing persuaded Marc Lescarbot to immigrate to North America. He created a cheerful picture of colonial life in his *History of New France* (1609). Because French writers of the time borrowed freely from one another, Lescarbot included the travel stories of Samuel de CHAMPLAIN and other explorers in the account of his own voyages. A well-educated man, Lescarbot also wrote a masque*, which is generally recognized as the first theatrical performance in North America.

Jesuit* missionaries in New France and Louisiana contributed greatly to French colonial literature. In 1616 Pierre Biard published a history of PORT ROYAL, an important French settlement in what is now Nova Scotia. Gabriel Sagard described a journey into the interior of New France, including encounters with Native Americans, in *The Great Voyage in the Land of the*

Huron (1632). The Jesuits also prepared annual reports of their work in North America. In one account, Father Paul du Poisson included a lively description of the ferociousness of the Louisiana mosquito.

Most French colonial travel narratives were written by newcomers to the continent. Pierre Boucher, however, provided the point of view of someone raised in New France. The leader of a thriving settlement in the St. Lawrence Valley, Boucher was sent to France to promote interest in the colony and to attract more settlers. At the suggestion of a government official, Boucher wrote *True History of Canada* (1664) on his return home.

Many travel narratives contained thrilling personal stories. In *Adventures of Sieur C. Le Beau* (1738), Claude Lebeau described his adventures hunting beaver with the Huron, living in Iroquois villages, being kidnapped by another Indian band, and much more. Some writers such as Mathieu Sagean, who described encounters with lions and leopards on his way to Montreal, got carried away by their imaginations. Their stories were sometimes almost pure fantasy. Travelers' tales became less popular after the mid-1700s, and writers began concentrating on factual accounts.

Authors of travel narratives wanted to tell about their experiences in the new land, but many also hoped to encourage settlement and promote their MISSIONS. In this respect their writings were successful. The French government approved colonization, and the ROMAN CATHOLIC CHURCH provided funds to support the work of the Jesuits.

Official correspondence—letters—formed a large body of writing in the French colonies. Personal letters such as those of Sister Marie-Madeleine Hachard, a nun in New Orleans, reveal a great deal about life in colonial times. After arriving in Louisiana in 1727, Hachard wrote regularly to her father in France, describing her new homeland and reassuring him that all was well.

Satire and the Burlesque.

In the mid-1600s, a genre known as burlesque became popular in France and soon appeared in colonial writing. Burlesque makes fun of serious events by exaggerating or imitating certain aspects. For example, a narrative poem might mock a disastrous military expedition by making it sound heroic. In New France, military life became a prime target for writers of burlesque, many of whom were unhappy army officers. Besides providing entertainment, burlesque was used as a way of criticizing people and institutions. One writer, Louis-Armand de Lom d'Arce de Lahontan, expressed his unflattering opinions of French authorities in *New Voyages* and *Dialogues* (1703).

Native Americans in French Colonial Literature.

Although much of French colonial literature contained descriptions of Indians as brutal savages, a new image emerged in the writings of the Jesuits. Well-trained scholars, the Jesuits viewed Native Americans with scientific interest and attempted to report on their origin, characteristics, and relationships. The Jesuit approach added substance to an idea popular in Europe in the 1700s—that the real nature of human beings could be found by studying simple, primitive peoples—and it contributed to the development in France of the myth of the "noble savage."

> **Remember:** Consult the index at the end of Volume 4 to find more information on many topics.

Spanish Colonies

Between 1521 and 1821, the Spanish explored and settled the Spanish Borderlands* and wrote about the regions's geography, people, and history. During this time the colonists developed a rich literary tradition, both written and oral. Although British colonial writing tends to receive more attention in the development of American literature, a close look at Spanish colonial literature reveals many important achievements.

Spanish Borderlands northern part of New Spain, area now occupied by Florida, Texas, New Mexico, Arizona, and California

Cartographic Narratives. Spanish explorers, soldiers, and settlers wrote of their experiences in reports, diaries, and journals. Many of the earliest accounts served a cartographic* function. The maps and descriptions of the land in these accounts helped chart unknown territory and served as a guide for later travelers. These reports also gave Spanish names to rivers, lakes, mountains, and other natural landmarks.

cartographic relating to map making

One of the best-known travel narratives is *Shipwrecks* by Alvar Núñez CABEZA DE VACA. The author described an astonishing eight-year journey that began in 1528, from Florida to the western coast of present-day Mexico. Cabeza de Vaca and three companions covered the distance on foot after their ships and most of the crew were lost at sea. The narrative is noteworthy for its respectful portrayal of the Indian tribes the four men encountered.

In the early 1540s, Spanish explorer Francisco Vásquez de CORONADO led an ambitious expedition into the interior of the continent in search of the SEVEN CITIES OF CÍBOLA. Although there were several written accounts of Coronado's unsuccessful mission to locate these fabled cities of gold, Pedro de Casteñeda's *Report of the Journey to Cíbola in 1540* was the most realistic. Casteñeda, who had been one of Coronado's foot soldiers, wrote his version 20 years after the event. In it he criticized the Spaniards for their brutality toward the Indians and their failure to recognize the possibilities of the land for settlement.

Soon after Coronado's expedition to present-day New Mexico, Texas, Oklahoma, and Kansas, the Spanish began exploring the California coast. In a journal of his 1542–1543 voyage, Juan Paez identified about 70 coastal points that proved useful for later exploration.

Early travel narratives served other functions as well. Adventurer Antonio de Espejo's *Relación* (1583) promoted New Mexico as a land ripe for permanent settlement. Rather than trying to lure settlers with promises of gold and silver, Espejo described the area's abundant game and fertile land. Fifteen years later, his writings influenced explorer Juan de OÑATE to lead over 500 colonists to New Mexico, where they established the first European settlement in the Southwest.

As the mapping of California, Texas, New Mexico, and other parts of New Spain's northern frontier neared completion, cartographic narratives became less useful. The final examples are the diaries kept during Juan Bautista de Anza's two expeditions into northern California between 1774 and 1776. As colonists settled into the new regions, official reports, commissioned by the Spanish government, took on new importance. These accounts provided specific information on topics such as resources, trade, Indian relations, and current events. The last narrative written during Spanish control

of the Borderlands was Luis Antonio Argüello's *Diário* (1821). Sent on an expedition to investigate rumors of a colony established by the United States in northern California, Argüello reported that he had discovered no American trespassers.

Mission Narratives. The Franciscans and Jesuits, two Roman Catholic religious brotherhoods, led or accompanied many expeditions into the Spanish Borderlands and established missions throughout the northern frontier. Their writings, sometimes referred to as "mission narratives," also form an important part of Spanish colonial literature.

Jesuit priest Eusebio Francisco KINO made more than 50 journeys on foot and on horseback into the interior of present-day Arizona between 1687 and 1711. His *Heavenly Gifts*—along with a diary, three reports, a few letters, and a map—provides a fascinating history of the settlement of Arizona. Likewise, Brother Francisco Palóu's *Notes on New California* (1776) described the missionary work of Franciscan Junípero SERRA in California.

Epic Poetry. In 1610 Gaspar Pérez de Villagrá published *History of New Mexico,* an epic* account of the heroism of Juan de Oñate and the 500 colonists who established the first settlement in New Mexico. Carefully crafted in poetic form by the author, the history included references to classical literature. As a captain and legal officer in Oñate's expedition, Villagrá was part of the events he described, which added authority to his writing.

Folk Literature. A strong oral tradition consisting of stories, poems, proverbs, and riddles circulated among the common people in the Spanish Borderlands. Colonists kept alive the oral tradition from Spain and also created new works based on written pieces. Local poets, singers, and storytellers drew inspiration from the old Spanish religious plays that were regularly performed in the Borderlands. A situation in a play might lead a troubadour—a wandering musician—to compose a song or poem.

Romances, or narrative ballads, formed a significant part of popular culture. Written in verse, these stories not only entertained people but also taught family and community values and responsibilities. The *romance* "The Unfaithful Wife," for example, reminded men and women of their marital duties. There were many *romances* on a variety of topics.

Telling *cuentos,* or stories, was a widespread and popular practice. There were hundreds of these tales, featuring enchanted young men and women, talking animals, devilish scamps, and witches and ghosts. *Cuentos morales,* or moral stories, like "The Three Brothers," attempted to instill values in young listeners.

African Americans

African Americans in colonial times managed to develop a literary tradition despite great obstacles. Most could not read or write, because slaveholders usually denied their slaves any schooling in order to keep them dependent. The few who did learn to read and write either taught themselves or were taught by a forward-looking, humane master.

* *epic* long poem about legendary or historical heroes, written in a grand style

Phillis Wheatley, a slave from Boston, was one of the first African American writers in the British colonies. In her poetry she called for an end to slavery.

See color plate 6, vol. 3.

* **ritual** ceremony that follows a set pattern

* **phenomenon** occurrence or fact that can be detected by the senses

* **supernatural** related to forces beyond the normal world; miraculous

African Americans also faced great prejudice. Most white colonists did not believe them intelligent enough to learn basic skills. Supporters of slavery argued that blacks were inferior to whites. A number of writings by European colonists helped keep these backward views of blacks alive.

Unable to read or write, slaves had to rely on oral communication to preserve their heritage. They passed along stories, myths, and folk tales from Africa by telling and retelling them. Most slaves also learned Bible stories from their masters. They particularly liked the one about God freeing the ancient Israelites from slavery in Egypt, a story with many similarities to their own condition.

Over time, so-called slave narratives developed as part of the oral tradition as well. These narratives consisted of a person telling the story, often based on personal experience, of an enslaved individual or group. The accounts included descriptions of brutal mistreatment by slaveholders and ended with a plea for freedom. By the end of the 1700s, the slave narrative had become an established written form as well.

The best-known of the slave writers, Olaudah EQUIANO described his sufferings eloquently in *The Interesting Narrative of the Life of Olaudah Equiano, or Gustavas Vassa, the African, Written by Himself* (1789). A self-taught writer, Equiano demonstrated the potential of blacks. Jupiter HAMMON, a black preacher, was the first African American to have his writing published in the British colonies. He produced several important works, including "Evening Thought: Salvation by Christ, With Penitential Cries." Other slave writings include a narrative by Briton Hammon (1760) and one by John Marrant (1785). These works emphasized the common belief among African Americans that God would someday deliver them from slavery.

One strong voice against slavery was that of the poet Phillis WHEATLEY. Born in Africa, she had been captured and sold to the Wheatley family in Boston, who raised her as a family member and educated her. "Liberty and Peace" (1784) and "On Being Brought from Africa to America" (1773) are two of her best-known poems. Although Wheatley was an accomplished poet, she struggled to gain recognition among educated white people. Even so, her poetry helped establish African American written literature in colonial times.

Native Americans

Unlike European colonists, who used the written word to record their histories, Native Americans relied on oral traditions to preserve their cultures. The Indians' verbal literature included prayers and texts from rituals*, such as the Plains Ghost Dance and Navajo Night Chant. Words to songs and narratives of various kinds were also important parts of the oral tradition.

Narratives were often performed by a storyteller. They ranged from myths to explain the beginning of the universe and stories about natural phenomena* such as thunder, lightning, and rain to histories of a tribe's wanderings. Tales of heroes illustrated a group's values and attitudes. Some narratives described events from the storyteller's life, such as hunting and fishing experiences, supernatural* encounters, or heroic acts in battle.

Many Native American stories feature a character known as "the trickster." The trickster—appearing in the form of a human or an animal, or even a

god—may be a villain who causes trouble or a fool who always gets into trouble. The most extensive collection of trickster tales, 49 episodes, comes from the WINNEBAGO INDIANS, who lived in what is now the Midwest.

Translations of or references to Native American narratives and other literary forms appear only occasionally in the writings of British colonials. Spanish explorers and colonists in Florida and the Borderlands preserved very little of the Indian literature. During colonial times, most Europeans did not consider oral narratives as literature. Moreover, many settlers mistakenly believed that Indian languages were too primitive for creating literature. The Puritans in New England recorded some descriptions of Native American narratives but only to illustrate their view that the Indians were in league with the devil.

Much of what is known today about Indian oral literature comes from the writings of the Jesuits, especially those who worked among the HURON and IROQUOIS in New France. The Jesuits took the Indians' traditions seriously. In their yearly reports to the church in Europe, the Jesuits attempted to translate Native American prayers, poems, and stories. These translations, of course, could not capture the meanings expressed by the performers' tone of voice, facial expression, and body language.

One aspect of Native American oral tradition that European colonists did admire was oratory, or speech making. Many Indian leaders were excellent public speakers. They developed their skills as they rose to positions of leadership within their tribes and sharpened them further in dealing with white people. During negotiations with the Indians, the colonists witnessed their speaking abilities, usually through translators. Tahgahjute (also known as James Logan), a Cayuga chief, delivered a famous speech that condemned the murder of members of his family by white settlers.

Some Indian groups did develop methods for recording oral literary texts. For example, the OJIBWA, who lived on the western shores of the Great Lakes, used drawings on birchbark to accompany songs. The pictographs—paintings on rocks—and petroglyphs—drawings carved in stone—of other tribes may have had some relation to oral literature. For the most part, however, Native American written literature in the European sense only began during the colonial period. Samson OCCOM, a Mohegan who converted to Christianity and became a minister, was the first notable Native American writer. His writings include sermons, hymns, and a history of the Montauk Indian tribe. (*See also* **Drama; Libraries and Learned Societies; Storytelling.**)

Livingston Family

Merchants, politicians, and statesmen

*T*he Livingston family of New York included wealthy merchants, judges, and prominent politicians. Along with the DE LANCEY FAMILY, the Livingstons controlled the colony's government in the 1700s. During the Revolutionary period, several members of the family served in the Continental Congress and in the new state and federal governments.

The first Livingston in North America, Robert (1654–1728) was the son of a Scottish Presbyterian minister. When the family moved to the Netherlands, young Robert learned to speak Dutch. In 1674 he immigrated to Albany, New York, where his fluency in Dutch and English and his good

Robert R. Livingston served as a delegate to the Second Continental Congress and helped draft the Declaration of Independence. He was often called Chancellor Livingston because of his position on New York's Chancery Court.

* *manor* large house

business sense soon made him a successful merchant. Through his marriage to Alida Schuyler Van Rensselaer, Livingston became part of the influential Schuyler and Van Rensselaer families and gained a place in upper-class society. His political connections helped him acquire a grant of 160,000 acres in New York, on which he built the Livingston manor*. From 1709 to 1725, he served in the provincial assembly. At the time of his death, Livingston was one of the wealthiest men in New York.

Robert's grandsons and great-grandsons inherited his business sense and his interest in politics. Grandsons Peter Van Brugh Livingston (1710–1792) and Philip Livingston (1716–1778) both made substantial fortunes through government contracts during the French and Indian War. Philip served in the First and the SECOND CONTINENTAL CONGRESS and signed the DECLARATION OF INDEPENDENCE. His brother William Livingston (1723–1790), a lawyer and politician, moved to New Jersey in 1772. He quickly gained support in his new home and became the state's first governor. A member of the Constitutional Convention in 1787, William helped persuade the New Jersey legislature to approve the Constitution of the United States.

Another of Robert Livingston's grandsons, Robert R. Livingston (1718–1775), greatly increased the family's land holdings through his marriage to Margaret Beekman. He was elected to the provincial assembly in 1758, became a judge on the New York Supreme Court, and served as chairman of the colony's COMMITTEE OF CORRESPONDENCE. One of his sons, Robert R. Livingston (1746–1813), became known as "Chancellor" Livingston because of his position as head of New York's Chancery Court.

A delegate to the Second Continental Congress, Chancellor Livingston served on the committee to draft the Declaration of Independence, although he missed its signing due to pressing political problems in New York. During the American Revolution, he played a key role on the congress's committees on financial, legal, and foreign affairs. Chosen to head the new American department of foreign affairs in 1781, Livingston helped negotiate peace with Great Britain. He also contributed to New York's first constitution and held the office of state chancellor for several years. In 1801 Thomas Jefferson appointed him minister to France. In this position, Livingston negotiated the purchase of the Louisiana Territory from France in 1803.

Locke, John

See *Enlightenment; Political Thought.*

Louisbourg

See map in New France (vol. 3).

*L*ocated on Cape Breton Island at the mouth of the St. Lawrence River, the French military town of Louisbourg served as a gateway to France's holdings in North America. Louisbourg played a key role in two wars between France and Great Britain, and its capture in 1758 opened the way for the British conquest of Canada.

In 1713 French settlers founded Louisbourg and named it after their king, Louis XIV. Construction on the fort began seven years later. Overlooking the Atlantic Ocean, Fort Louisbourg was built to guard the entrance into the St.

Louisbourg

* **citadel** stronghold or fortified place overlooking a city

* **siege** prolonged effort by armed troops to force the surrender of a town or fort by surrounding it and cutting it off from aid

See map in French and Indian War (vol. 2).

In 1758 during the French and Indian War, British troops laid siege to Fort Louisbourg. This view of the city was drawn "on the spot" by Captain Ince, an officer in the British forces.

Lawrence River and to protect France's interests in the profitable cod-fishing industry. It took 25 years to complete and cost so much money that the king wondered if the streets were being paved with gold. At the time the fort's citadel*, Château St. Louis, was the largest building in North America—365 feet long and three stories high.

In 1744, just as Fort Louisbourg was nearing completion, KING GEORGE'S WAR broke out between Great Britain and France. Colonists in New England viewed the fort as a threat to their safety, especially after the French attacked one of their fishing villages on neighboring NOVA SCOTIA. In 1745 the governor of Massachusetts organized a large expedition against Louisbourg with the support of the British navy. About 4,000 New England volunteers set sail from Boston in a fleet of 100 ships.

Despite the huge sums of money spent to build it, Fort Louisbourg had been badly designed and poorly situated. It was surrounded by low hills that provided excellent locations for enemy canons. After a 48-day siege*, the soldiers at Louisbourg surrendered.

The volunteer forces from New England rejoiced at their victory. But a few years later their joy turned to astonishment when Great Britain returned Louisbourg to France in the Treaty of Aix-la-Chapelle in 1748. Angry New Englanders began questioning Britain's commitment to their interests.

After regaining control of the fort, the French made it more secure by increasing their forces at Louisbourg to 1,500 soldiers. During this time, the town itself continued to be a fishing port and lively center of commerce. Tensions remained high between French and British colonists, even though the two sides regularly engaged in illegal trading activities with each other.

In 1756 France and Britain once again declared war on each other. The American part of this conflict—known as the FRENCH AND INDIAN WAR—was the final struggle between the two powers for control of North America. British strategy relied on taking control of the St. Lawrence River and then moving on to capture QUEBEC, the capital of New France.

Fort Louisbourg presented the first obstacle to this plan. Under the command of General Jeffrey Amherst and General James Wolfe, the British attacked in 1758 with a force of 16,000 soldiers and 150 ships. They captured the fort in seven weeks. The French had found Louisbourg impossible to defend without the support of a strong navy.

Wolfe used the fort as a base for the assault against Quebec. After the fall of Quebec in 1760, the British demolished Fort Louisbourg to prevent the French from ever using it again for military purposes. (*See also* **Forts.**)

See maps in European Empires (vol. 2).

tributary stream or river that empties into a larger river

At its largest, colonial Louisiana stretched the length of the MISSISSIPPI RIVER valley, from present-day Illinois to the Gulf of Mexico. Despite its vast size, the colony's population and economy grew slowly. The hot, wet climate and disease-producing mosquitoes of Louisiana's coastal areas discouraged settlers, and colonists avoided the inland areas because of conflicts with Native Americans.

The Spanish were the first Europeans to explore Louisiana. In the early 1500s, they probed northward from their bases in the Caribbean islands and Mexico, gradually mapping the Gulf of Mexico coast. Hernando DE SOTO led an expedition along the lower Mississippi River in the 1540s. But when the Spanish failed to find gold or silver in the region, they lost interest and established no settlements. Busy with activities in other parts of the continent, the European powers ignored the lower Mississippi for many years. Eventually France claimed Louisiana, but the colony changed hands several times before the United States purchased it in 1803. By that time, Louisiana's fertile Illinois territory had become an important grain producer, and its capital of NEW ORLEANS had emerged as a lively port with a unique culture.

French Louisiana. Almost 150 years after de Soto's expedition, René-Robert Cavelier, Sieur de LA SALLE, explored the Mississippi River for France. La Salle established France's claim to all the land drained by the Mississippi and the rivers that ran into it. He named this enormous territory Louisiana after King Louis XIV. La Salle did not know how large an area the Mississippi and its tributaries* occupied—his claim included almost a third of the present-day continental United States.

In 1684 La Salle attempted to found a colony at the mouth of the Mississippi, but he failed dismally. The French crown, however, believed that Louisiana could be useful—serving as a barrier to the growth of the English colonies on the Atlantic coast, as a base for attacking Spain's colonies to the west, and as a corridor linking New France to the Gulf of Mexico and the WEST INDIES. In 1698 the king gave the task of colonizing Louisiana to Pierre Le Moyne, Sieur d'IBERVILLE. Fulfilling this mission, Iberville built a fort on the site of what is now Biloxi, Mississippi, and another near the mouth of the Mississippi. His brother Jean Baptiste Le Moyne de Bienville founded Mobile, Alabama, and New Orleans. Still, by 1715 only about 300 Europeans lived in Louisiana and the Mississippi Valley.

The main economic activity of these colonists was trading with the Indians for deerskins, which they shipped to France in great quantities. Yet the

Louisiana

indigo plant used to make a blue dye

French also hoped to grow crops such as rice, tobacco, indigo*, and sugar cane for export. These crops required a large supply of labor, but colonists' attempts to force Native Americans to work the fields met with little success. Not only could the Indians escape by disappearing into the forest, but the practice of enslaving them also threatened France's relationship with its Indian allies. The French in Louisiana, like Europeans in the West Indies, turned to African slaves to meet their labor needs. The first slaves arrived in 1712.

To keep Louisiana from becoming a burden on the French crown, the king allowed several private developers to run it. The most ambitious of these firms was the FRENCH WEST INDIES COMPANY, which controlled the colony from 1717 until 1731. The company brought about 7,000 Europeans and an equal number of African slaves to Louisiana. The European settlers included convicts, prostitutes, and poor or homeless people sent by the government.

Conditions in Louisiana during the early years of the colony were primitive and at times desperate. In the words of a French historian writing over a hundred years later, "Numbers [of those who arrived in Louisiana] died of misery or disease, and the country was emptied as rapidly as it had filled." In 1730 the colony had a population of 5,300, consisting largely of African slaves.

By this time the French had come into conflict with some of the Native American tribes in the region. The CHICKASAW INDIANS, allies and trading partners of the British, often clashed with the French as tension between France and Great Britain increased during the mid-1700s. Even more troublesome were the NATCHEZ INDIANS, who resented the loss of their rich farmlands to the French and tried to drive the foreigners out. In 1726 French

The French colony of Louisiana was established around 1700 by Pierre Le Moyne d'Iberville. This 1720 print by Jeane Baptiste Michelle de Butox shows the fort that Iberville built at the site of present-day Biloxi, Mississippi.

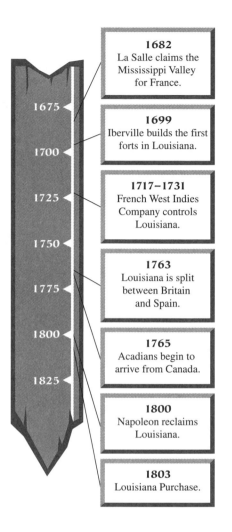

1682
La Salle claims the Mississippi Valley for France.

1675

1699
Iberville builds the first forts in Louisiana.

1700

1717–1731
French West Indies Company controls Louisiana.

1725

1750

1763
Louisiana is split between Britain and Spain.

1775

1800

1765
Acadians begin to arrive from Canada.

1825

1800
Napoleon reclaims Louisiana.

1803
Louisiana Purchase.

colonists moved onto land in a Natchez village that included a site sacred to the Indians. The angry Natchez killed 250 settlers. With the help of the CHOCTAW INDIANS, the French attacked Natchez strongholds. Within six months the Natchez were all but wiped out—killed, driven to take refuge with other tribes, or sent to the French West Indies as slaves.

The French defeated the Natchez, but the cost of the struggle crippled the French West Indies Company. The company's directors, seeing little chance of making a profit on the colony, returned Louisiana to the crown in 1731. Louisiana was a royal colony for the next 30 years. It never fulfilled its founders' hopes, remaining a poor, struggling region that drained money from the royal treasury rather than filling it. An exception was the Illinois territory. By the mid-1700s it had about 2,000 European inhabitants and 1,000 African or Native American slaves. French Illinois produced food for the settlements of the lower Mississippi.

The ROMAN CATHOLIC CHURCH and the colonial administration tried to shape Louisiana into a well-ordered society based on Catholic practices and French law. Yet most of Louisiana remained a frontier, where life was often disorderly, even crude. Pirates made it their hideout, and smuggling was an accepted part of the local economy. Louisiana also had a unique cultural and ethnic character. The relatively high number of marriages and relationships among Europeans, Indians, and Africans created a variety of mixed-race communities. By the late 1700s, Louisiana had emerged as a multiracial, multicultural society unlike anything else in North America.

Spanish Louisiana. The FRENCH AND INDIAN WAR, which ended in 1763, involved most of the nations of Europe and their American possessions. As a result of the war, France lost its North American colonies. Louisiana was divided—the territory east of the Mississippi River went to Britain, and the land west of the river, including New Orleans, fell under Spanish control.

News of the change in ruling powers caused widespread alarm in Louisiana. Most of the settlers were of French or French Canadian origin and had no desire to live under Spanish or British rule. In 1768 a group of New Orleans merchants, angered by Spanish trading regulations, organized a revolt against the new Spanish governor. To avoid bloodshed, the governor fled. The colony's leaders considered declaring Louisiana an independent republic, but Spain took steps before they could act.

General Alejandro O'Reilly, an Irish officer in the Spanish military, arrived in New Orleans in 1769 to restore order. Backed by 2,100 troops, he quickly ended the rebellion by capturing and hanging five of its leaders—earning himself the nickname "Bloody O'Reilly." He then reorganized the province's political and court systems to give the colonists more of a voice in their local government. From that time on, the French and Spanish inhabitants of Louisiana lived together in relative harmony. People of both French and Spanish descent held important administrative posts throughout the province.

Defense was the chief concern of officials in Louisiana. The British occupied the east bank of the Mississippi River, and British traders frequently crossed the river to deal with Louisiana Indians, cutting into the Spanish

Free Blacks in Louisiana

Not all the Africans in colonial Louisiana were slaves. The names of free black men and women appear in passenger lists from early ships. In addition, some Africans who arrived in the colony as slaves managed to gain their freedom. A man named Samba used his skill in French and several African languages to become an interpreter for the Superior Council, the highest court in the colony. With the job came freedom. Louis Congo, another African slave, volunteered to serve as the colony's executioner in exchange for freedom and land.

trade. Spanish officials built a string of forts along the river and ordered military boats to patrol its waters. During the Revolutionary War, Louisiana Governor Bernardo de GÁLVEZ helped the American cause by defeating British forces in several battles in the Southeast.

Under the Spanish, the focus of Louisiana's economic activities shifted from the Indian trade to plantation exports. By the 1780s the colony was shipping more indigo and tobacco than deerskins and furs. Plantations based on slave labor extended north along the Mississippi—the route for almost all travel and commerce within the colony.

Louisiana's population grew rapidly during these years, from about 9,000 in 1760 to 44,000 in 1790. Some of the new inhabitants came from Spain, but Louisiana welcomed non-Spanish settlers as well. The first ACADIANS arrived in Louisiana in 1765. These French colonists had been driven from their homes on the eastern coast of Canada by the British. After much wandering, they settled in Louisiana. More Acadians arrived in 1785 and established several communities near present-day Lafayette. The Acadians and their descendants, known as Cajuns, developed a distinctive dialect, music, and culture. The Spanish authorities also allowed some LOYALISTS fleeing the Revolution in America to live in Louisiana. Later they permitted Americans from Kentucky, Tennessee, and North Carolina to settle in the province.

Louisiana changed hands again in 1800, when the French ruler Napoleon Bonaparte forced Spain to return the territory to France. However, France was locked in a power struggle with Britain and did not really want Louisiana. Napoleon believed that a larger, more powerful United States would help keep Britain in check. He sold Louisiana to the Americans in 1803. That deal, known as the Louisiana Purchase, greatly enlarged the United States and opened the way for American expansion into the lands beyond the Mississippi. (*See also* **Race Relations.**)

Loyalists

During the 1770s, Americans had different views about their relationship with Great Britain. Patriots supported independence for the colonies, Loyalists wanted to remain part of Britain, and some Americans stayed out of the dispute. Historians estimate that about 20 percent of the colonial population—or one in every five people—were Loyalists. For these individuals, the AMERICAN REVOLUTION meant the loss of their homes, their property, their identity as British subjects, and sometimes, their lives.

Identity and Motives. Like the patriots, Loyalists came from all levels of colonial society. They included farmers, artisans, merchants, and planters. The majority of them lived in the middle and southern colonies. The issue of independence divided households—some families included both patriots and Loyalists. One of the greatest supporters of American independence, Benjamin FRANKLIN, had a son who remained loyal to Britain.

Patriots referred to the Loyalists as "Tories," a term intended as an insult. A Tory was a member of the British political party that supported the idea that kings received their right to rule from God. Few American Loyalists were actually Tories.

Loyalists remained faithful to Britain for a wide variety of reasons. Many had a genuine affection for the king and their British heritage. Some were members of the Anglican Church, the official religion of England, and felt bound to Britain by their religious connection. Other Americans favored the idea of independence but considered the patriots' use of force to be dangerous and unlawful. Quakers in particular refused to support the war because of their belief in nonviolence.

In many cases, self-interest was the motivation for Loyalists' allegiance. Predictably, a high proportion of royal officials stood by the British government, which had given them power and paid their salaries. Some Loyalists were wealthy merchants or large landholders who feared that war would harm their businesses or property. Other Loyalists supported the crown simply because they believed the colonies had little chance of defeating Britain's powerful army.

Most Native Americans remained neutral or sided with the British, who promised to limit the advance of settlers into their territory. This alliance proved to be disastrous for the Indians. After the war ended, Americans viewed them as conquered enemies and seized their lands.

Some African Americans joined the British as well, despite the fact that slaves caught aiding the enemy were hanged by patriots. British authorities hesitated to give guns and ammunition to the slaves, realizing that it might be difficult to return armed men to slavery after the war. But the British could not overlook a source of soldiers. In November 1775, the royal governor of Virginia offered freedom to slaves who took up arms against the rebellious colonists. The British did free some blacks, but they sold others to plantation owners in the West Indies.

* **confiscate** to seize private property
* **guerrilla** type of warfare involving sudden raids by small groups of warriors

The War Years. Considered traitors by the patriots, Loyalists experienced considerable hardship during the war years. Angry mobs sometimes harassed or tarred and feathered them. Special committees investigated anyone suspected of having British sympathies. States passed a variety of measures against Loyalists, including laws that prohibited their voting and confiscated* their property.

Loyalists never presented a real threat to the American cause. Differing widely in motivation, they did not form a unified opposition. But Loyalists did contribute to the British war effort. Some joined the British army, while others fought in guerrilla* bands along the frontier, often with Native American allies.

Between 60,000 and 80,000 Loyalists fled the colonies during or immediately after the Revolution. Some emigrated to the Bahamas, the West Indies, or Britain. In the early years of the war, about 19,000 of them moved to Florida, which was then British territory. In the late 1770s, some Loyalists settled in Spanish territory along the lower Mississippi River. A few simply sat out the war in the relative safety of rural areas far from the battlefields.

About half of the fleeing Loyalists ended up in Canada, which remained a British colony. To help the newcomers rebuild their lives, the British government provided them with land, items such as farming tools and seeds, and money. Many Loyalists settled in present-day Ontario, becoming the first sizable English-speaking community in the area. Others relocated to what is now the province of New Brunswick.

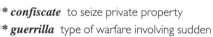

Tar and Feathers

Tarring and feathering—pouring hot tar over a person and covering the tar with feathers—dates back to the 1100s. It was used to punish wrongdoers in England. Although the practice was illegal in the colonies, mobs sometimes tarred and feathered an individual who violated the community's standards. A number of Loyalists suffered this treatment during the Revolutionary War. The practice died out in the late 1800s.

After the War. Many Loyalists who fled during the war returned home to find that their property had been seized by the government. Those who had remained throughout the Revolution received better treatment. By the 1790s public feeling against Loyalists had died down, and states lifted all remaining laws against them after the War of 1812. (*See also* **Independence Movements.**)

Lutherans

See *Protestant Churches.*

Madison, James

1751–1836
Political leader, author, and President

* *Anglican* of the Church of England

James Madison took a leading role in the politics of the Revolutionary period and the early years of the United States. He served in the Second Continental Congress, at the Constitutional Convention, and as the fourth President of the United States.

*J*ames Madison contributed greatly to American political thought during the Revolutionary War and the nation's early years. He was active in VIRGINIA politics, influenced the drafting of the U.S. Constitution, served in Congress, and became the fourth President of the United States.

Born in Port Conway, Virginia, Madison attended the College of New Jersey (now Princeton University), where he studied history and government. In 1776 he became a member of the Virginia convention, which wrote the new state constitution. There he defended the principle of FREEDOM OF RELIGION.

Beginning in 1780, Madison represented Virginia at the SECOND CONTINENTAL CONGRESS in Philadelphia. Three years later he returned to Virginia and was elected to the state assembly. He supported numerous laws to develop Virginia's economy, as well as legislation that ended state funding of the Anglican* Church—showing his commitment to the separation of church and state. In 1787 the states called a convention to revise the system of federal government then in place, and Madison attended as a member of the delegation from Virginia. From the beginning, he took a leading role, arguing for a strong central government. The Virginia Plan, proposed by the state's delegates, contained many of Madison's ideas and greatly influenced the final document—the U.S. Constitution. In fact, Madison has been described as "the father" of the document.

When the Constitution went to the individual states for approval, Madison devoted his energies to gaining support for it. Along with Alexander Hamilton and John Jay, he wrote a series of essays, known today as *The Federalist,* that explained the principles of the Constitution.

After the Constitution was approved, Madison served in the government he had helped create. He was elected to represent Virginia in the U.S. Congress, where he took an active role in shaping legislation and in foreign affairs. During this time, Madison became an ally of Thomas JEFFERSON, who believed the federal government should have less power.

In 1794 Madison married Dolley Payne Todd, and her popularity and charm greatly helped her husband's career. When Jefferson became President in 1801, he appointed Madison as secretary of state. In 1809 Madison succeeded Jefferson as President. He held the office for eight years, during which time he saw the new nation through its first major foreign war—the War of 1812.

Magellan, Ferdinand

See *Exploration, Age of: Spanish.*

Magic and Witchcraft

* **supernatural** forces beyond the normal world; miraculous

*I*n the 1600s, most people living in North America believed in some form of magic. In other words, they accepted the idea that under certain conditions, humans could use powerful supernatural* forces to control objects and events, break other "laws" of everyday life, or predict the future. Native Americans had their own beliefs about magic, or sorcery, as did the Europeans who colonized North America and the Africans who came to the colonies as slaves.

Christians and non-Christians alike also believed in the existence of witches—individuals with supernatural powers who performed evil deeds, often with the devil's help. In some communities, witch-hunts led to accusations, trials, and executions of those believed to practice witchcraft. The most famous example of colonial witch-hunting was the series of trials held in SALEM, Massachusetts, in 1692.

Magic, Witchcraft, and Religion. Over the centuries, magic has taken many forms, from simple superstitions to something related to science. The terms *low magic* and *high magic* described two sets of ideas about supernatural powers.

Low magic referred to the practices of ordinary, uneducated peasants and villagers who had faith in the power of good luck charms, spells to help people find lost objects, and fortune-telling. These beliefs were widespread in Europe and in the colonies. Healing was another kind of low magic. Most villages had a healer skilled in the use of herbal medicines, and people often credited the healer with magical knowledge or powers.

* **alchemy** study aimed at turning common metals into gold

High magic, studied by an educated few, included alchemy* and ASTROLOGY. Students of high magic hoped to gain hidden knowledge that would allow them to live forever or would give them extraordinary powers, such as the ability to turn lead into gold.

Magic also had a dark side. Magicians who had the power to heal might use that power to harm. To defend themselves against witches, many people used countermagic—spells or practices that would protect them from harm. One common custom was to nail a horseshoe over a door so that evil magic could not enter.

Ideas about the supernatural were closely related to religion. Some ancient magical beliefs, such as the notion of demons who cause human suffering, became part of Christianity. Magic and fortune-telling appeared in Christian teachings as miracles and prophecies. Yet all Christian faiths, Roman Catholic and Protestant alike, opposed the practice of magic.

The rise of Christianity changed the idea of witchcraft. Witches came to be seen as agents of the devil, sent to attack the orderly Christian community. In the 1500s, people began to believe that a witch's power stemmed from a pact, or agreement, with the devil. Those who had made such a pact would have a special mark, made by the devil, on their bodies. Eager witch-hunters might point to a mole or a birthmark as evidence of a pact. A witch who had dealt with the devil was guilty of the crime of heresy*, punishable by death.

* **heresy** belief that is contrary to church teachings

Magic and Witchcraft

Colonial ideas about magic were tied to beliefs about the power of evil spirits. This illustration from Cotton Mather's *On Witchcraft* shows a magician summoning a demon.

A wave of witch-hunting swept over Europe, reaching its peak in the 1600s. Most accusations sprang from the tensions and conflicts of rural life. People who quarreled with or who felt threatened by their neighbors might accuse them of being witches. Because most people accepted the existence of magic, they found it easy to blame a witch for misfortunes that occurred in the community. Charges of witchcraft became more serious when church and civil courts added the idea of a devil's pact. Many people accused of witchcraft confessed under the pressure of imprisonment, merciless questioning, and even torture. Those convicted were often hanged or burned to death.

The Supernatural in the Colonies.   Belief in magic was fairly widespread in the colonies. In the 1680s, Boston minister Increase MATHER criticized the practice of countermagic. His son Cotton MATHER, also a minister, warned people against astrology. Colonists who had earned reputations as healers or possessors of special powers were regarded by others with a mixture of respect and fear. A witness described one New England woman accused of witchcraft as "both a healing and a destroying witch."

Witchcraft played a part in the settlement of NEW MEXICO. In 1675 missionaries there, fearing the influence of the devil in Native American magic, whipped, jailed, enslaved, or hanged Indians suspected of practicing sorcery. In response the Indians staged the PUEBLO REVOLT, a violent uprising that overthrew Spanish rule. To the Spaniards, the Native Americans' success seemed the work of the devil. For years afterward, they blamed illnesses and deaths among the missionaries on Indian magic. In general, however, the Spanish colonial courts dismissed accusations of witchcraft. Such claims carried power among the Indians, however. Indians continued to execute other Indians suspected of sorcery into the 1800s.

In the colony of NEW FRANCE, missionaries worked to stamp out Native American magical beliefs along with the rest of Indian religious practices. Accusations of witchcraft occasionally surfaced among the French colonists, but there were no large-scale witch-hunts or executions. The severe shortage of women in New France may have played a role in this, for it was women rather than men who were usually associated with witchcraft.

Colonial Witch-Hunts. Witch-hunts may have reflected society's uneasiness with independent women. Women were expected to remain firmly under the control of men and to devote themselves to caring for their children. Many of the accused were older widows whose children had left home. Some of these women owned property. Others had reputations for arguing, scolding, or speaking their minds. The witch-hunts may have been the church's and society's way of punishing those who broke the patterns they expected women to follow.

More witch-hunts occurred in the British colonies than anywhere else. Nine people were tried for witchcraft in Virginia between 1627 and 1705. Authorities in the island colony of Bermuda hanged three women for witchcraft in the 1650s. The center of witchcraft and witch-hunting, however, was New England—the home of a large Puritan population that was constantly on the lookout for evil.

In the years between 1640 and 1700, perhaps 100 people—mostly women—faced accusations of witchcraft in New England. Most charges stemmed from local quarrels and simple dislike. As evidence, the accusers claimed that the "witches" had caused misfortunes, such as the deaths of livestock or young children. Accused witches were thought to have "familiars," or demon companions, in the form of cats, dogs, or other animals. Of course, in a rural, agricultural society, nearly everyone regularly dealt with animals, but that did not prevent people from believing in familiars.

A number of the New England witches were hanged. Others lived under suspicion for years, hounded from place to place, frequently in jail or in court. In two cases, a single accusation or confession unleashed a flood of similar claims. In Hartford, Connecticut, in the 1660s and again in the SALEM WITCHCRAFT TRIALS of the 1690s, a young woman's charge led to a wave of trials, convictions, and executions that spread to include a large part of the community.

The witch hysteria may have occurred for a variety of reasons. Perhaps it grew out of the adolescent accusers' desire for attention; general resentment of poor, troublesome, or outcast members of the community; social stress caused by wars with the Indians and with France; or simple mob panic. Even at the height of the witch-hunts, some authorities realized that many of the accused people were innocent and called for an end to the trials. By the 1700s the practice had died out.

Interestingly, African Americans were rarely accused of witchcraft by white Christians. However, blacks also believed in magic. According to the traditional African view, misfortune and illness resulted from evil spells cast by people possessing magical powers. Like many of the colonists, slaves commonly carried protective charms and had faith in fortune-telling. Most African Americans eventually adopted Christianity, but they kept many of their traditional beliefs about the supernatural.

See color plate 3, vol. 4.

Remember: Words in small capital letters have separate entries, and the index at the end of Volume 4 will guide you to more information on many topics.

Other forms of magical belief lingered in the American colonies. For example, during the 1700s some people used "seerstones"—rocks that supposedly had magical powers—to hunt for hidden treasure in New England. Unlike the witch-hunts, these practices had little or no effect on society at large. (*See also* **Religion; Women, Roles of.**)

Magna Carta

See *Great Britain.*

Mahican Indians

The Mahican Indians were Algonquian-speaking people who lived in the upper Hudson River valley region of New York in the early colonial period. Closely related to the DELAWARE INDIANS, they played an important role in the FUR TRADE during the 1600s.

The Mahican survived by farming, hunting, and gathering. Like the IROQUOIS, they lived in large rectangular buildings called longhouses that sheltered several related families. Their villages usually contained 20 to 30 longhouses surrounded by wooden walls. Mahican women had great influence in tribal matters, and male chiefs inherited their authority through the women of the tribe.

The first Europeans to come in contact with the Mahican were the Dutch, who began colonizing the Hudson Valley in the early 1600s. The Mahican traded furs to the Dutch and established close ties with them. Throughout most of the 1600s, the Mahican warred with the Mohawk Indians, an Iroquois tribe, over territory and control of the fur trade. In the mid-1600s, devastated by tribal warfare and European diseases, the Mahican began to sell their land to Dutch colonists.

See second map in Native Americans (vol. 3).

As colonization increased under the Dutch and later the English, the Mahican were forced to give up more land and to migrate to other areas. Some moved west, joined the Delaware Indians, and eventually settled in the Ohio region. Others went to western Massachusetts, where they joined other Indian groups in the 1700s and became known as the Stockbridge Indians. Most of the Stockbridge Indians moved to Wisconsin in the early 1800s.

Maine

Maine, the most northeasterly state of the United States, was visited by European explorers as early as the 1500s. Fishermen from England began sailing to the coast of Maine regularly in the early 1600s. During the colonial period, Maine became part of MASSACHUSETTS.

The name *Maine* comes from the term used by sailors and fishermen to distinguish the mainland from the many islands that dot the coast. The first settlements, established by the French in 1604 and the English in 1607, both failed after one winter. In 1622 two English gentlemen, Sir Ferdinando Gorges and John Mason, received a grant for all lands between the Merrimack and Kennebec rivers. Seven years later, the two divided their lands at the Piscataqua River, which meets the coast at present-day Portsmouth, New Hampshire.

See map in British Colonies (vol. 1).

* *feudal* relating to an economic and political system in which individuals give service to a landowner in return for protection and the use of land

Gorges received the eastern section, known as the province of Maine. He wanted to establish a feudal* society there but failed. After Gorges died, the Massachusetts Bay colony began to claim parts of Maine. In 1691 Massachusetts received a new charter that included control of Maine.

During the 1700s, Maine became a battleground as the French and British struggled for control of North America. Maine communities supplied soldiers for campaigns against the French during KING GEORGE'S WAR and the FRENCH AND INDIAN WAR.

In the years leading up to the AMERICAN REVOLUTION, the inhabitants of Maine strongly opposed British attempts to impose new restrictions and regulations on its colonies. The war's first naval contest occurred on June 12, 1775, when citizens of Machias, Maine, captured the British ship *Margaretta*. Months later, the British navy responded by setting fire to the town of Falmouth (now Portland, Maine), nearly destroying it.

After the war, the population of Maine continued to grow, with settlement expanding along the coast, up the rivers, and farther west. By 1819 a movement arose among the inhabitants to break away from Massachusetts. The following year, Maine became the nation's twenty-third state. (*See also* **New Hampshire.**)

Maize

This 1651 drawing by an artist named Bland of an ear of maize labels the grain "Indian wheat." Corn was as important a part of the diet of Native Americans as wheat was for Europeans. European colonists soon adopted maize as a basic crop and source of food.

Maize, or corn, is one of the oldest and most important crops of the Americas. First grown in Central America about 7,000 years ago, maize gradually spread throughout North and South America. It was a basic crop for Native Americans and later became an important source of food for European colonists.

Maize probably reached the present-day United States about 3,500 years ago, arriving first among the Indians of the Southwest. Within several centuries, the cultivation of maize had become the foundation of southwestern Indian life. It then spread to other parts of the continent.

Maize can grow in various climates, but its development is limited by temperature and rainfall. Indians living north of what is now the Canadian border did not have reliable results with the crop because of the cold climate. In dry areas such as the Southwest and Great Plains, Indians had to use irrigation and adopt special farming techniques to grow maize.

The cultivation of maize had a dramatic impact on Native American life. Many tribes that had wandered from place to place in search of food began to establish permanent settlements. Complex agricultural societies formed in many regions, and this contributed to the development of trade networks linking tribes across the continent.

Over the centuries, the Indians developed different kinds of maize, which were suited to various climates and served a number of purposes. Some varieties were easily ground into flour. Others could be stored for long periods of time. Sweet corn was good for eating before the plant matured. The most spectacular variety of maize was popcorn.

When Europeans arrived in North America, they learned how to grow maize from the Indians. Without this crop, early settlements such as Jamestown and Plymouth might not have survived. Maize soon became one of the

most important colonial crops. Easy to grow, it produced an abundant and dependable source of food. Like the Indians, the colonists ate sweet corn and ground maize into flour. They also fed maize to livestock and even used it to make whiskey. Europeans took maize back to Europe, and from there it spread to Africa and Asia. (*See also* **Agriculture; Economic Systems; Native Americans.**)

Manufacturing

See *Industries.*

Maps and Charts

*T*he explorers, conquerors, missionaries, traders, and settlers who sailed from Europe to North America in the 1500s and 1600s used a variety of maps and charts to guide them on their great journey to the "New World." After arriving, many of these travelers made maps that charted new territory or drew more accurate and complete maps of known lands.

The Americas did not appear on the maps that Christopher COLUMBUS carried on his famous voyage of 1492. The continents were still unknown to Europeans. But Columbus and other navigators of his time did possess fairly accurate world maps, which encouraged them to believe that Asia could be reached by sailing west from Europe.

The world maps were of little practical use in NAVIGATION. Instead, sailors relied on hand-drawn sea charts, called portolans or portolanos. These were detailed maps of known coastlines, with towns and landmarks and a web of lines that indicated sailing directions from point to point. Portolans were prized possessions, and sea captains were ordered not to let them fall into enemy hands. Mariners often sailed with the charts in lead boxes so that if their ships were captured, they could quickly sink the precious charts in the sea. There were, however, no portolans of regions beyond the Azores, islands in the mid-Atlantic.

After Columbus's first voyage to the Americas, mariners began producing sailing charts of American waters and coastlines. Columbus himself drew such charts, but only one survives—a map showing part of the coastline of the Caribbean island of HISPANIOLA. The first known world map to include the Americas is a portolan painted on animal skin in about 1500 by Juan de la Cosa, one of Columbus's navigators. Puerto Rico, Cuba, and Hispaniola are clearly marked on the map.

The voyages of Columbus and those who followed him revolutionized cartography, the art and science of mapmaking. Cartographers soon realized that the lands the explorers "discovered" were new continents, not part of Asia. In 1507 German mapmaker Martin Waldseemüller named those continents America, in honor of Italian navigator Amerigo Vespucci, who explored and mapped much of the coastline of South America. Other cartographers adopted the name and used it on their maps.

The first maps of the Americas appeared in the mid-1500s, the work of Italian cartographers. One of them showed a river running across North America into the Pacific Ocean. This imaginary waterway helped inspire the

Tracing the Gulf Stream

Benjamin Franklin, Philadelphia patriot, printer, and scientist, pioneered a new kind of scientific mapmaking around 1769. While studying Atlantic shipping, Franklin learned from sailors that a current of warm water flowed north along the American coast and then across the Atlantic Ocean to Europe. Ships sailing with the current traveled much faster than those going against it. Together with a sea captain named Timothy Folger, Franklin created a map showing this ocean current, known today as the Gulf Stream.

The coastline of the Americas was first mapped in the 1500s and 1600s. This 1585 map by Theodore de Bry shows a section of the region known as Virginia (present-day North Carolina), with notes indicating the locations of different Indian tribes.

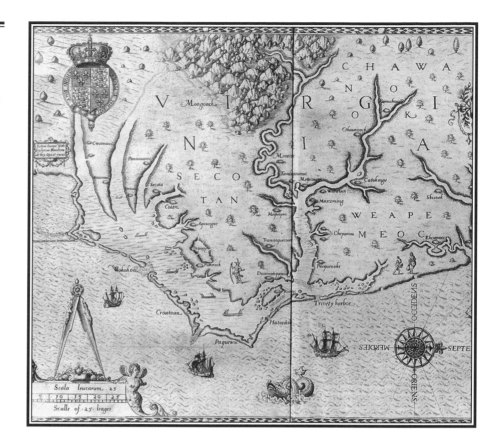

search for a NORTHWEST PASSAGE, which led many Europeans to explore and map the northern part of the continent.

The coasts of North America were mapped before its interior. Spanish, French, Dutch, and English explorers drew charts of the Atlantic coast in the early 1500s and 1600s. Spanish explorers began mapping the Pacific coast in the late 1500s. The French explorer Samuel de CHAMPLAIN created the first maps of the Great Lakes region, as well as the first accurate map of the northeastern Atlantic coast, in the early 1600s. In the following years, French JESUIT missionaries were tireless explorers and mappers of the interior regions of New France. The Spanish began charting the Southwest in the late 1600s.

The mapping of colonial settlements began in 1608, when a Virginia colonist sketched a plan of Jamestown. The first map to be printed in America was a woodcut of New England, carved from a block of wood by Bostonian John Foster in 1677. By the early 1700s, British colonists had produced a number of regional maps and charts, as well as maps that showed most of North America. In 1749 Lewis Evans created a map of the British colonies that included information about weather, resources, and wildlife. British, Dutch, and French maps of the time also featured illustrations of Indians, plants and animals, and colonial towns.

Maps were not simply visual representations of knowledge. They also had political meaning. European mapmakers of the 1700s took great pains to show their countries' territorial claims in North America. In this way, maps and charts helped Europeans divide up the continent as they explored it. (*See also* **Exploration, Age of.**)

Mardi Gras

*M*ardi Gras is a traditional day of celebration on the eve of Lent, the 40 days before Easter when many Roman Catholics in the past gave up certain foods. The name *Mardi Gras*—"Fat Tuesday" in French—probably refers to the custom of feasting on Shrove Tuesday, the day before Lent.

The celebration of Mardi Gras began in Europe during the Middle Ages or perhaps even earlier. Brought to North America by early French explorers and settlers, it gradually spread throughout the colonies of New France and Louisiana. The most notable tradition associated with Mardi Gras in the French colonies was questing or mumming—a good-natured form of fake begging.

In parts of New France, groups of men—disguised with blackened faces, red scarves, stockings over their heads, and Indian clothing or other costumes—would visit households during the day to perform songs and dances in exchange for refreshments or money. In rural Louisiana, bands of masked participants roamed the countryside singing songs and begging for the ingredients for a dish called gumbo. This dish was eaten before a masked ball that lasted until midnight of Shrove Tuesday.

Mardi Gras festivities reached new heights in the Louisiana city of NEW ORLEANS. Today its pre-Lenten celebration goes on for two weeks and includes masked balls, pageants, and parades sponsored by special societies called krewes. (*See also* **Festivals.**)

Maroon Communities

*M*aroon communities were settlements formed in North America by runaway slaves, also known as maroons. Appearing first in the slaveholding colonies of the West Indies and then in the mainland colonies, these communities encouraged other slaves to flee to freedom.

The maroons usually settled in isolated locations where they could find food and shelter. Many of them farmed, raised livestock, and hunted for food. Some also traded with settlers or raided towns for supplies. Most people in maroon communities sought a haven from SLAVERY and a chance to establish a new life. A few groups turned to violence and became a menace to the rest of society. The settlements were under constant pressure from authorities who viewed the maroons as a danger to public order and from plantation owners who considered them a threat to an economy based on slavery. As a result, most maroon villages did not last long.

Large, stable maroon societies existed on the Caribbean island of JAMAICA and in Brazil. By contrast, most maroon communities in the North American colonies were small. Runaway slaves sometimes joined up with fugitive whites, often indentured servants* who had escaped from their employers, and Indians. Some of the Indians had been captured by white settlers and had managed to run away, while others were survivors of tribes wiped out by disease or fighting.

By the mid-1600s, many groups of maroons were living in Virginia. In 1661 the colony passed a law forbidding white and black servants to run away together. Later another law set a reward for killing such runaways. North Carolina's backcountry also became home to many maroons. The largest group of maroons in the British colonies lived in the Great Dismal Swamp, along

* **indentured servant** person who agreed to work a certain length of time in return for passage on a ship to the colonies

the border between Virginia and North Carolina. The swamp was an ideal hiding place—outsiders needed a guide to explore its jungles safely—and it offered freshwater, game, and fish.

In the 1700s, many runaways headed farther west or south, and the number of maroons in South Carolina and Georgia soared. Others decided to leave the British colonies altogether and sought safety in Spanish Florida. During the AMERICAN REVOLUTION, many maroons sided with the British and staged attacks on colonists. (*See also* **Race Relations; Slave Resistance.**)

Marquette, Jacques

See *Jolliet, Louis.*

Marriage

*In some respects, marriage in the North American colonies resembled marriage today. It was a union between a man and a woman, recognized by the legal, religious, and social traditions of the community. It provided an orderly framework for sexual relationships and the raising of children and served as the foundation of the family. Because the majority of colonists lived and worked on family farms, marriage also created the main economic unit of society.

Colonial marriages differed from modern marriages in certain important ways, however. Practical concerns, such as the economic resources and social status* of the bride and groom, usually played a larger role than romantic love in choosing a mate. Moreover, marriage was viewed as an alliance between families—rather than just a union of individuals. As a result, decisions about marriage often involved whole families.

Although marriage was central to all colonial societies, various groups defined it in different ways. Laws and customs governing marriage grew out of particular traditions, religious beliefs, and ideas about GENDER ROLES. Marriage changed during the colonial period, as it has throughout history, to match people's changing needs, circumstances, and expectations.

* **status** social position

European Colonists

All Europeans in North America—whether they lived in the British, Dutch, French, or Spanish colonies—shared certain basic ideas about marriage. They believed that marriages and families should be patriarchal, that is, with the husband as head of the household. A religious as well as a legal institution, marriage was regarded as permanent. Couples who did separate could live apart informally, but churches did not readily grant divorces. Under church law, people who obtained divorces generally could not remarry.

Europeans believed that one of the most important purposes of marriage was to produce children who were legitimate—recognized as the legal heirs of their parents. Legitimacy was of vital importance because illegitimate children, those born outside marriage, could almost never inherit property. Marriage thus safeguarded the transfer of family property from one generation to the next.

A Woman's Dowry

A custom among European colonists was for a woman entering marriage to have a dowry—property or possessions that she brought to her husband. The woman's family generally supplied the dowry, although some girls who worked as servants earned their own. The dowry of a farm girl might consist of her clothes, a bed and some sheets, household utensils, and perhaps a cow or two. Upper-class families provided their daughters with large dowries to attract desirable husbands. These dowries might include land, money, or slaves. Some families brought financial hardship upon themselves in order to provide a daughter with an impressive dowry.

* *mate* marriage partner

* *annulment* formal action by which a marriage is canceled

In the 1600s and 1700s, people believed that marriage was the natural state of all adults. They regarded individuals who remained unmarried—by chance or by choice—as strange and unfortunate. In colonial America, nine out of every ten women married at least once. Those who did not wed generally lived and worked in the homes of relatives and had little status. Because such women spent much of their time making yarn at the spinning wheel, they were called spinsters.

British Colonists.   Because the colonies had far more men than women, a large number of men never married. The men competed for available mates* in places where women were scarce, such as the Chesapeake Bay colonies in the 1600s. This competition allowed women to choose husbands from a higher social class—for example, a servant girl might marry a landowner. When the balance between men and women was more even, individuals usually married within their own social class.

In the southern colonies, which had few women, girls tended to marry early, often while still in their teens. In contrast, the average age of marriage for women in New England was about 22. Men throughout the colonies generally married in their mid-20s, after they had learned a trade, saved money, acquired land, or otherwise gained the means of supporting a wife and family.

Colonists in New York and the Chesapeake and southern colonies adopted English marriage laws. These laws included the idea of marital unity: when a woman married, she gave up her legal identity as an independent person. As a wife, she could not own property or conduct business in her own name, and her husband had the right to manage the couple's property and make all decisions regarding their children. Yet women did have certain legal rights. Husbands could not dispose of land without their wives' consent, and they could not completely disinherit their wives.

The PURITANS of New England and the QUAKERS of Pennsylvania had somewhat different ideas about marriage. Their goal was to create new societies in America, not copy the traditions of England. They changed parts of the English marriage laws that they did not like, abolishing the laws that protected the rights of women in matters of land ownership. On the other hand, the Puritans made it easier for people to divorce and remarry. Even so, few marriages that failed ended in divorce. Desertion, usually by the husband, was much more common.

Dutch Colonists.   Women in the colony of NEW NETHERLAND enjoyed more rights and freedoms than those in the English colonies. Dutch people considered marriage to be something of a partnership, with the husband as the senior partner. Wives could own property and conduct business independently of their husbands, and they kept their own legal identities. Although rare, divorces or annulments* were granted to couples whose marriages had failed. When the English took over the colony in 1664, they gradually replaced Dutch marriage customs and laws with their own. By 1700 the notion that women had independent identities and rights had begun to fade.

French Colonists.   French authorities wanted to transform NEW FRANCE and LOUISIANA from wild frontier regions into settled, productive colonies.

This tapestry illustrates a New England wedding in the mid-1700s. Divorce and remarriage were easier in New England than elsewhere in the colonies. But married women there enjoyed fewer rights related to property.

Marriage was an important ingredient in their plans because it brought stable family life, which would help produce economic development and growth. Colonial officials encouraged marriage by offering cash rewards for marrying before certain ages. Parents whose children had not wed by those ages had to pay fines. The ROMAN CATHOLIC CHURCH, which considered sexual relationships outside of marriage a sin, also played a role in pushing French settlers to marry. The economic, religious, and social pressure led to very high rates of marriage and remarriage among widows and widowers in the French colonies.

Under French law, the men of New France had less authority over their wives than did men in the English colonies. Property was generally owned jointly by the couple, and a husband could not sell property without his wife's

* **Spanish Borderlands** northern part of New Spain, area now occupied by Florida, Texas, New Mexico, Arizona, and California

* **civil law** body of law that regulates and protects the rights of individuals

written consent. The law also ensured that part of a couple's estate—their total property and possessions—would go to the wife after her husband's death, even if he died in debt. When husbands died, their widows had the right to run businesses and manage their own estates.

Spanish Colonists. Marriage in the Spanish Borderlands* was defined by Spanish law and the rules of the Catholic Church. These two forces sometimes came into conflict. Civil law* supported the principle of parental authority, which gave parents the right to control their children's marriage choices. Parents used this authority to arrange matches that would bring the family wealth, status, and honor. The Catholic Church, however, claimed that true marriage required the consent of both individuals. Thus, priests sometimes married young couples whose parents wanted to keep them apart, and they might refuse to unite individuals who were being forced into marriage by their families.

The history of the Spanish Borderlands is full of stories of families torn by struggles between parents and children, elopements, and secret marriages. Only in the lower ranks of society did young people usually choose marriage partners on the basis of love. Lower-class couples might also live together without marriage, or perhaps until they could afford to marry. Servants and slaves, on the other hand, had little or no say in such matters. Their marriage partners were selected by the people they served.

Spanish law and church law also came into conflict over the principle of male authority. Church law granted husbands and wives nearly equal rights and obligations, including the responsibility for raising children. Under civil law, however, husbands had almost complete authority over their wives. A wife could own property, but her husband controlled it. She needed her husband's permission in most legal actions. Women also were held to a higher standard of sexual behavior than men. Civil law generally supported church law on the matter of divorce. The Catholic Church did not recognize divorce, but it did allow couples to separate and live apart.

Native Americans

Native Americans had a wide variety of marriage customs. As many as one-third of all Indian tribes may have been matriarchal societies, in which women acted as the heads of families. Other tribes practiced polygamy, a custom that allowed men to have more than one wife at a time. Many tribes regarded both marriage and divorce as matters of individual free choice. Divorce was more common among Native Americans than in European societies. In some northeastern tribes, for example, a husband or wife could end a marriage simply by choosing a new mate.

White colonists disapproved of Indian marriage customs such as matriarchy and polygamy because they conflicted with European traditions and beliefs. Some whites tried to encourage or force Indians to adopt European marriage practices. In the Spanish Borderlands, for example, the Indians who lived under the control of missionaries had to become Christians and marry according to Spanish law and custom. Some Indians accepted such changes, but others continued to practice their own ways.

Mixed-race relationships and marriages between Europeans and Indians were part of North American life from the beginning of colonization. They occurred most often in the Spanish and French colonies, where single men greatly outnumbered women. Faced with a shortage of women, many early settlers in these colonies chose Indian brides.

Priests and missionaries in New Spain, who believed that mixed-race marriages were better than sexual relationships between unmarried couples, performed many interracial marriages. This resulted in a large population of mestizos, people of mixed Spanish and Indian ancestry. In New France, authorities at first encouraged marriages between whites and Native Americans. They hoped that such marriages would help assimilate* the Indians and produce children who could be raised as French citizens. Officials soon realized, however, that French males who married Native Americans generally adopted Indian ways of life. Fearing that mixed-race marriages would divide the loyalties of settlers and make the colony harder to govern, officials tried to discourage or ban them. But Catholic priests continued to perform interracial marriages rather than allow couples to live together outside marriage.

* **assimilate** to adopt the customs of a society

African Americans

During the early years of colonization, slave traders brought far more African men than women to the Americas because plantation owners preferred male laborers. Not only did black men outnumber black women, but most slaves lived on small isolated farms and could not travel. This meant that African American men had little chance to form relationships or marry. In the 1700s, the black population increased, and more planters had large numbers of slaves. These growing plantation communities provided slaves with more opportunities to find partners.

All colonies had laws against the intermarriage of African Americans and whites. Free blacks could marry each other, and in New Netherland they could marry slaves. But European marriage laws and customs rarely applied to marriages between slaves. Some slaves entered formal marriages according to the traditions of their African homelands. Others joined in informal unions. As a way of increasing their slaveholdings, some planters encouraged their slaves to marry. Under the law, the children of such unions would be born slaves. At the same time, however, slaveholders were free to separate slave couples and families by selling the wife, husband, or children. Such involuntary separations seriously eroded the stability of African American marriages. (*See also* **Courtship; Family; Race Relations; Women, Roles of.**)

Maryland

Situated between the northern and southern colonies, Maryland helped link English settlements along the coast of North America. Early colonists in the region found fertile land and a network of waterways around CHESAPEAKE BAY with access to the Atlantic Ocean. These resources helped the colony prosper during the 1600s and 1700s. Maryland's early history also featured stormy periods. Founded as a haven for Catholics coming

Maryland

See map in British Colonies (vol. 1).

* **proprietor** person granted land and the right to establish a colony
* **charter** written grant from a ruler conferring certain rights and privileges

* **repeal** to undo a law

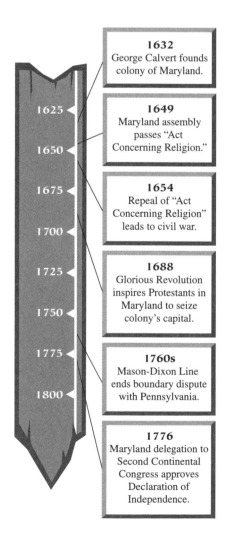

1632
George Calvert founds colony of Maryland.

1649
Maryland assembly passes "Act Concerning Religion."

1654
Repeal of "Act Concerning Religion" leads to civil war.

1688
Glorious Revolution inspires Protestants in Maryland to seize colony's capital.

1760s
Mason-Dixon Line ends boundary dispute with Pennsylvania.

1776
Maryland delegation to Second Continental Congress approves Declaration of Independence.

to North America, the colony faced almost constant religious tension and political turbulence until the end of the colonial period.

Early Settlement. Maryland was established by the CALVERTS, a prominent Catholic family from England. In 1632 King Charles I granted George Calvert about 10 million acres of land north of Virginia. Charles named the region Maryland after his Catholic wife, Henrietta Maria. He also gave Calvert the title Lord Baltimore.

Upon Calvert's death, his son Cecil became proprietor* of the colony. Cecil Calvert, the second Lord Baltimore, received a charter* for Maryland, granting him generous powers there and requiring him only to send the king "two Indian arrows of these Parts . . . every Year, on Tuesday in Easter-Week." Baltimore asked his brother, Leonard Calvert, to settle the colony and serve as its first governor. From the start, the Calverts declared that both Catholics and Protestants would be welcome in Maryland.

Leonard Calvert sailed from England with two ships, the *Ark* and the *Dove,* and about 200 settlers—mostly Protestants. Arriving in Chesapeake Bay in March 1634, the colonists purchased land from local Indians at the mouth of the Potomac River. There they established a community they called St. Mary's. Maryland's charter gave the Calverts complete control over land distribution in the colony, and they set up a headright system to encourage settlement. Under this system, the amount of land colonists received depended on the number of people they brought with them, including servants. Most of the settlers farmed their land. They also traded with the SUSQUEHAN-NOCK INDIANS, who lived north of Chesapeake Bay. The colonists formed a legislative assembly, although any laws they made had to have the approval of Lord Baltimore.

Religious Conflict and Civil War. The colony's early years were filled with conflict. Many of the early settlers in Maryland were Protestants, but the Calverts' promise of a religious haven also attracted a number of wealthy Catholics. Protestants in the area soon began to resent the Catholics, who owned large estates and held most of the leadership positions. The Calverts also had a problem with a Virginian named William Claiborne, who claimed ownership of Kent Island in Chesapeake Bay. He had set up a trading post there and refused to recognize the Calverts' right to the land. He remained a fierce opponent of the family for many years.

In 1645 Richard Ingle, a Protestant, led a rebellion that drove Leonard Calvert from the colony. After Calvert died in 1647, his brother Cecil, Lord Baltimore, took steps to restore peace. He appointed a Protestant governor, William Stone, and drafted the "Act Concerning Religion" (also known as the Act of Toleration), which guaranteed religious freedom for all Christians in the colony. The Maryland assembly passed it in 1649.

While Lord Baltimore tried to settle the problems in his colony, Puritans in the English PARLIAMENT had begun to rise up against Charles I. In 1649 they executed the king and took control of the government. This change encouraged the Protestants in the Maryland assembly to seek more power, and opposition to Lord Baltimore's rule increased. In 1654 the assembly repealed* the "Act Concerning Religion" and forbade Catholics to hold office in Maryland. The assembly's action led to civil war. The southern part of the colony defended Lord Baltimore and Governor Stone, and the northern part, aided by William Claiborne, supported the assembly. In March 1655, the rebels defeated the governor's troops in a battle at the Severn River, south of the city of Baltimore. The Protestants took over the government and appointed a new governor.

Lord Baltimore regained control of the colony a few years later, when the monarchy returned to power in England. In the 1670s, his son Charles, the third Lord Baltimore, became proprietor. As a result of the long-running dispute with William PENN over the border separating Maryland and Pennsylvania, Charles lost a section of the colony, which later became Delaware.

Meanwhile, tensions between Protestants and Catholics continued to simmer, both in Maryland and in England. By 1685 England had a Catholic king, James II. Three years later, James was overthrown and the Protestant monarchs William and Mary took his place. This event, known as the GLORIOUS REVOLUTION, inspired Protestant rebels in Maryland to seize the capital at St. Mary's and ask the new king and queen to take control of their government. Maryland became a royal colony, and Catholics were once again forbidden to hold office.

Economy. Throughout Maryland's political troubles, new settlers continued to come to the colony. Immigrants arrived from Europe, and residents of other colonies moved to the area in search of land. Most settled along the waterways, which they used to ship their crops to market. Some people who came to the colony as indentured servants* completed their period of service and obtained land to start their own farms. Located on Chesapeake Bay, the city of Baltimore became Maryland's largest settlement and a major port.

Farmers raised corn, fruits, vegetables, cattle, and hogs for their own use. Over time, however, TOBACCO began to play a larger role in the economy. Maryland farmers planted tobacco on much of their land, and in the 1680s, they began importing slaves to help with the crop. Large tobacco plantations replaced some small farms, and buying and selling slaves and tobacco produced much of the colony's income. By 1700 the population of Maryland reached about 32,000, including nearly 4,500 slaves.

Ships loaded with tobacco and other goods sailed between Maryland and Great Britain, making Chesapeake Bay a major shipping region. At the same time, shipbuilding became an important industry in Maryland. Damaging barnacles and shipworms, so common in salt water, did not survive in the less salty waters of Chesapeake Bay.

As the economy prospered, wealthy townspeople and plantation owners began to build substantial brick homes, replacing the wooden structures of the earlier settlers. By 1727 the growing colony had its first weekly newspaper, the *Maryland Gazette,* which published news and the political views of prominent citizens.

Revolutionary Era. The fourth Lord Baltimore, Benedict Calvert, became a Protestant, and his son Charles regained control of Maryland's government in 1715. Charles Calvert continued as the colony's proprietor until the AMERICAN REVOLUTION. Catholics were still barred from government and

* indentured servant person who agreed to work a certain length of time in return for passage on a ship to the colonies

See color plate 4, vol. 3.

forbidden to worship in public, but wealthy Catholics who had settled in the colony had considerable influence in Maryland society.

Further disputes with Pennsylvania over the northern border of Maryland led to a formal survey by Charles Mason and Jeremiah Dixon in the 1760s. They plotted a boundary—part of which is known as the Mason-Dixon Line—between the two territories. Both colonies accepted the boundary.

During this time, the British Parliament began to pass new trade and shipping laws, as well as to impose direct taxes, that affected the colonies. A movement opposing British rule gathered force in New England and soon spread to the Chesapeake region. Maryland's tobacco planters, dependent upon the merchants in Britain for the sale of their crops, objected to the trade restrictions and would not accept Parliament's right to tax them. They staged revolts against the STAMP ACT and the British tax on tea. In 1774, following the BOSTON TEA PARTY, Maryland patriots* burned a tea ship in the ANNAPOLIS harbor.

In July 1776, Maryland's delegation to the SECOND CONTINENTAL CONGRESS supported the decision to declare independence from Britain. That November the colonists finally brought Maryland's proprietary government to an end, writing a state constitution that set up a new government. Many residents of Maryland fought on the patriots' side during the American Revolution, although a few people, mostly from the eastern shore of the Chesapeake, remained loyal to Britain.

After the war, Maryland's delegates to the Continental Congress argued in favor of drawing clear western boundaries for states that, unlike Maryland, had claims to land beyond the Appalachian Mountains. When the congress agreed to this condition, Maryland accepted the Articles of Confederation*. The state also sent a delegation to the Constitutional Convention in Philadelphia. On April 28, 1788, Maryland approved the United States Constitution and became the seventh state of the Union. (*See also* **Acts of Toleration; Roman Catholic Church.**)

* *patriot* American colonist who supported independence from Britain

* *Articles of Confederation* plan approved in 1781 to establish a national legislature with limited powers

Mason, George

1725–1792
Virginia political leader

George Mason was one of the leaders of the American independence movement in the 1770s. A passionate defender of individual rights and liberties, he played an important role in shaping the government of VIRGINIA and of the new United States.

Mason was born into a wealthy Virginia family and received his early education from private tutors. He studied law on his own, using the extensive library of his uncle, who was a lawyer. As a young man, Mason inherited his father's estate near Alexandria, Virginia. In his late 20s, Mason became a member of the OHIO COMPANY, an organization formed to settle land along the Ohio River. In 1759 he served in the VIRGINIA HOUSE OF BURGESSES, along with George WASHINGTON, who became his friend.

Mason's most important political work began in the 1770s. In 1774 he wrote the Fairfax Resolves, later adopted by the Continental Congress as an explanation of the colonies' position in relation to the British crown. Two years later, as a member of the Virginia convention, he drafted most of the text for the state's new constitution. Even more significant was Mason's

Declaration of Rights, which served as a model for both the DECLARATION OF INDEPENDENCE and the Bill of Rights that later became part of the United States Constitution. At the same time, he influenced many political leaders of the day, including Washington and Thomas JEFFERSON.

After the American Revolution, Mason represented Virginia at the Constitutional Convention in Philadelphia. He spoke up frequently at the convention, fighting for provisions that he believed to be important. In the end, he objected to the document worked out during the summer of 1787 because it lacked a bill of rights and it did not adequately protect the freedoms of the states. Moreover, it gave official recognition to the institution of slavery. This approval was unacceptable to Mason, who considered the slave trade "diabolical in itself and disgraceful to mankind." For these reasons, he refused to sign the Constitution and campaigned forcefully against its ratification*. Many of George Mason's objections were dealt with in later years through Constitutional amendments. (*See also* **Political Thought; Revolutionary Thought.**)

* **ratification** formal approval

Massachusetts

* **dissenter** person who disagrees with the beliefs and practices of the established church

See map in British Colonies (vol. 1).

*M*assachusetts developed a tradition of self-government early in its history. Founded by English dissenters*, Massachusetts led the other colonies in protesting policies of the British government in the years before the American Revolution.

During the 1500s, the abundant codfish of New England's coastal waters drew French, Portuguese, and English fishing boats to the area. But the first recorded landing in Massachusetts did not occur until 1602, when English explorer Bartholomew Gosnold set foot on Cape Cod. Twelve years later, Adriaen Block from the Netherlands and John SMITH from England mapped the coastline of Massachusetts Bay. The name *Massachusetts* came from an Indian tribe that lived on the coast.

Early Settlement. English PILGRIMS established the first settlement in Massachusetts. Having separated from the Church of England and having suffered religious persecution, the Pilgrims wanted to find a place where they could worship in their own way. After wandering far north of their original destination, they landed at a place they called New Plymouth in December 1620.

The Pilgrims survived a difficult winter and, under the leadership of William BRADFORD, began building PLYMOUTH COLONY. An Indian named SQUANTO helped them plant corn, fish, and hunt. In the fall of 1621, the Pilgrims celebrated their first harvest—the first Thanksgiving feast—with the neighboring Wampanoag Indians.

As more colonists arrived and the Pilgrims established trade with the Indians, the settlement grew stronger. Meanwhile, English merchants were founding trading bases along the Massachusetts coast at Wollaston, Gloucester, and other spots. All these early settlements, however, were soon overshadowed by the Massachusetts Bay colony.

Massachusetts Bay Colony. In 1629 the English king Charles I granted a group of wealthy PURITANS title to a large area of land in Massachusetts.

Massachussetts

* **charter** written grant from a ruler conferring certain rights and privileges

This group, the Massachusetts Bay Company, also sought religious freedom in North America. Unlike the Pilgrims, the Puritans wanted to reform the Church of England rather than separate from it.

The company's charter* specified that a governor and an elected council would manage the colony. The Massachusetts Bay Company sent an advance group of 200 settlers to establish a base at a place called Salem while waiting for formal approval of the charter. The main group followed in 1630, under the leadership of Governor John WINTHROP. The Puritans' fleet consisted of 11 ships and about 1,000 colonists—the largest mass migration of English people to North America up to that time.

The group's leaders decided that Salem was unsuitable as the central location for the Massachusetts Bay colony. Instead, they chose a position that was easier to defend, farther south near the Charles River. The Puritans called the new settlement BOSTON. Because Boston did not have enough land or water for all the newcomers, other settlements developed around the Massachusetts Bay. Most settlers began farming as they had in England, and mills, shipyards, fisheries, and other industries soon sprang up.

The Massachusetts Bay colony was almost immediately successful. It faced almost no resistance from coastal Indian tribes, which had been greatly reduced by diseases brought by European fishermen. In addition, the Puritans had learned from the experiences of earlier settlers to bring enough livestock and tools with them. They were strengthened further by the belief that they were doing God's work. Winthrop and other Puritans believed that the Massachusetts Bay colony could serve as a model of a godly community and a pure church.

The colony drew thousands of immigrants fleeing religious persecution, difficult economic conditions, and social unrest in England. By 1640 the Massachusetts Bay colony consisted of 18,000 Puritans living in 30 towns, as compared with Plymouth's 3,000 settlers and 9 towns. The colony also

This painting, *View of Boston,* shows the Massachusetts capital in the early 1700s. The artist, John Smibert, was best known for his portraits of prominent Bostonians.

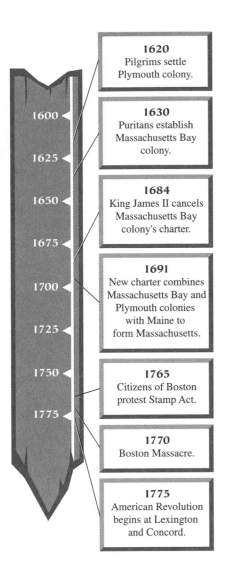

1620
Pilgrims settle Plymouth colony.

1630
Puritans establish Massachusetts Bay colony.

1684
King James II cancels Massachusetts Bay colony's charter.

1691
New charter combines Massachusetts Bay and Plymouth colonies with Maine to form Massachusetts.

1765
Citizens of Boston protest Stamp Act.

1770
Boston Massacre.

1775
American Revolution begins at Lexington and Concord.

1600
1625
1650
1675
1700
1725
1750
1775

* **Glorious Revolution** bloodless revolution in England in 1688 in which James II, a Catholic, was replaced as monarch by Protestants William and Mary

included Harvard, the first college in the American colonies, which was founded in 1636.

The founders of the Massachusetts Bay colony took advantage of the fact that the colony's charter did not require the company to keep its headquarters in England. Away from the prying eyes of the English government, the governor and his council had more freedom to make decisions. In time, the council grew into an assembly with two deputies from each town. The towns were allowed a considerable amount of self-government. Townspeople held meetings to discuss local issues and elected officials to run the town.

The Puritans' religious beliefs greatly influenced government in the colony. Settlers applying for a grant of land on which to build a town had to choose a minister and promise to build a church. As the best-educated person in most towns, the minister often had considerable political influence. Only adult males who were members in good standing of the church were allowed to vote. Finally, in their attempt to create godly communities, the Puritans passed laws prohibiting gambling, swearing, excessive drinking, and other forms of behavior they considered immoral. Those who disobeyed could expect severe punishment.

Changes in Government. During the 1650s, the English replaced the monarchy with a government led by Oliver Cromwell, a Puritan. Massachusetts enjoyed considerable independence under Cromwell's rule. When the monarchy was restored in 1660, the English government conducted a lengthy investigation of the colonies. The investigators found that Massachusetts was careless in enforcing English laws, especially those regulating trade, and that Puritans were persecuting religious dissenters. The colonists responded that they should not have to obey English laws because they were not represented in Parliament.

The Massachusetts Bay colony refused to send delegates to England to answer the investigators' charges, and in 1684 King James II canceled the colony's original charter. Two years later, he made Massachusetts part of a large province called the DOMINION OF NEW ENGLAND. From the beginning, the people of Massachusetts clashed with the new dominion governor, Sir Edmund ANDROS. His policies seemed to threaten their rights as citizens of England. When the Glorious Revolution* removed James II from the throne, the Bostonians rebelled against Andros and forced him to return to England.

The people of Massachusetts hoped that the new English rulers, William and Mary, would restore the original charter of the Massachusetts Bay colony. Instead, in 1691 King William issued the Massachusetts Province Charter, which combined the Massachusetts Bay colony, the Plymouth colony, and Maine into one royal colony with a governor appointed by the king. The charter allowed for an elected assembly and removed church membership as a requirement for voting.

Expansion and Growth. Indian wars and raids delayed the westward expansion of Massachusetts. After two wars—the PEQUOT WAR (1636–1637) and KING PHILIP'S WAR (1675–1676)—killed most of the Indians or brought them under control, settlers were able to move freely toward the Connecticut

River valley. Between 1700 and 1776, the number of towns in Massachusetts increased from 80 to more than 300.

Most of the new towns in the west were self-sufficient farming villages. Food, clothing, and tools were all produced locally. The larger, older towns along the eastern seacoast thrived on foreign trade. Boston became the principal seaport of the British colonies in North America, with fish and timber leading the list of exports. The eastern towns also relied more heavily on food and manufactured goods imported from Britain.

After 1700 the political influence of Puritanism declined in Massachusetts. New immigrants influenced the society's values, and many descendants of the early Puritans took more interest in acquiring wealth and possessions than in enriching their spiritual lives. In time a prosperous MERCHANT class emerged and assumed a leading role in the colony.

Massachusetts and the Revolution.   In the 1760s, Massachusetts—and Boston in particular—became the center of opposition to new British policies and regulations. In protest against the STAMP ACT of 1765, which imposed taxes on printed documents, a group of Bostonians known as the SONS OF LIBERTY attacked the homes of British officials, and Boston merchants refused to import British goods. Two years later, when Parliament placed taxes on British imports such as glass, lead, paint, and tea in the TOWNSHEND ACTS, the Massachusetts assembly persuaded the other colonies to boycott* these goods. British troops in Boston had several violent clashes with colonists, including the notorious BOSTON MASSACRE of 1770.

* ***boycott*** to refuse to buy goods as a means of protest

Samuel ADAMS, a political leader in Massachusetts, created the first COMMITTEE OF CORRESPONDENCE. This letter-writing network kept people in the countryside informed of patriot* activity in Boston. Adams's system spread to other colonies and became a powerful force in turning public opinion against the British government. After Parliament passed the TEA ACT in 1773, Adams led the Boston colonists in dumping a shipload of tea into Boston harbor to protest British control of the tea trade—an event that came to be known as the BOSTON TEA PARTY. This act of open rebellion against British authority led Parliament to pass the Massachusetts Government Act (1774), which canceled the colony's charter and abolished town meetings.

* ***patriot*** American colonist who supported independence from Britain

Angered by Parliament's actions, Massachusetts farmers formed companies of MINUTEMEN and began preparing for war. They stockpiled guns and powder in churches and drilled weekly. When British soldiers attempted to seize munitions* stored at Concord, Massachusetts, in 1775, the first shots of the AMERICAN REVOLUTION were fired. Two months later, the BATTLE OF BUNKER HILL was fought at Charlestown, across the Charles River from Boston.

* ***munitions*** weapons and ammunition

After these early battles, the people of Massachusetts saw little combat. British troops evacuated Boston in 1776, and the main battles of the Revolutionary War were fought outside New England. Massachusetts contributed money and supplies to the CONTINENTAL ARMY and supported the new American government. During the war, the people of Massachusetts adopted a new state constitution. Some of this document's features were later included in the United States Constitution. (*See also* **Glorious Revolution; Independence Movements.**)

Massachusetts Bay Colony

Mather, Cotton

1663–1728
Puritan minister

fellow member of a college

This portrait of Cotton Mather was created in 1727 by artist Peter Pelham. Mather was a prominent Puritan minister and the author of many books on a wide variety of subjects.

See *Massachusetts.*

One of the most influential religious leaders in colonial New England, Cotton Mather gained prominence in Massachusetts as pastor of Boston's Second Church. This position enabled him to voice his views on issues of the day. Mather reached an even wider audience through his writing, which included books on history, religion, education, politics, medicine, and music.

Mather was born in Boston into a distinguished PURITAN family. His father, Increase MATHER, and grandfathers, John COTTON and Richard Mather, had all been Puritan ministers. An eager student, Cotton Mather went to Harvard at the age of 12—the youngest student admitted to the college up to that time. After he finished his studies, he began helping his father, a pastor at the Second Church in Boston. When Cotton Mather was ordained as a minister in 1685, he continued to preach at the same church and remained there the rest of his life.

In addition to his preaching, Mather took an active interest in politics. In the 1680s he protested when the English king appointed a royal governor, Sir Edmund ANDROS, to reorganize the New England colonies. Mather openly opposed Andros and published a work explaining the colonists' objections to him. Mather supported the next governor, Sir William Phips, and wrote a biography about him.

Soon after taking office in 1692, Phips appointed a court to try several accused witches in the town of SALEM. Cotton Mather began to study the subject of witchcraft and discussed it in his speeches and writing. In *Wonders of the Invisible World* (1693), he commented on some of the witch trials, defending the court's guilty verdicts. Mather later changed his view and declared that some innocent people had been wrongly condemned in Salem. Nevertheless, his connection with the trials hurt his popularity.

Mather also devoted time to education and charitable work. He supported various community organizations and founded Indian missions and schools for slaves and the poor. Mather served as a fellow* of Harvard but eventually resigned from the position, believing that the college had lost its focus on Puritanism. He lent his support to a new college, Yale, and was offered its presidency but declined.

Mather's many books demonstrate the broad range of his interests. When smallpox struck Boston in 1721, his writings about preventing the disease helped introduce a program of vaccination. One of his historical works, *Magnalia Christi Americana* (1702; *The Great Works of Christ in America*), included a history of New England and biographies of many prominent colonists. He also published sermons and works about church music. In all, Mather wrote more than 450 books.

Mather's personal life was marked by misfortune. His first marriage ended with his wife's death in 1702, and his second wife died 11 years later. His third wife, who survived him, suffered from mental illness. He also saw all but 2 of his 15 children die during his lifetime. Yet in spite of these losses, Mather maintained his intense religious faith. (*See also* **Salem Witchcraft Trials.**)

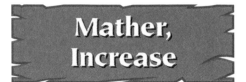

Mather, Increase

1639–1723
Puritan minister, politican, and author

* *fellow* member of a college
* *charter* written grant from a ruler conferring certain rights and privileges

*I*ncrease Mather, a prominent minister in MASSACHUSETTS, had considerable influence on the policies of the Puritan church. He also served as president of Harvard College and as an agent representing the views of the Massachusetts colony to the English government.

Born in Dorchester, Massachusetts, Increase Mather was the son of Puritan minister Richard Mather. He was educated as a minister and obtained a position at the Second Church in Boston. In 1674 he became a fellow* of Harvard, which later made him its president.

A political crisis in Massachusetts in the 1680s drew Increase Mather into politics. In 1686 King James II of England combined several colonies into the DOMINION OF NEW ENGLAND, suspended the charter* of Massachusetts, and sent Sir Edmund ANDROS to govern the region. Puritan churches in the colony opposed the move, and they sent Mather to England to present their views to Parliament and the king. In 1690 Massachusetts made Mather its official agent in England. Two years later he obtained another charter for Massachusetts from the new king, William III. The king allowed Mather to choose the colony's new governor.

Mather returned to Massachusetts during the SALEM WITCHCRAFT TRIALS. Along with several other ministers, including his son Cotton MATHER, he became worried about the type of evidence the court was using and believed that some of the people convicted of witchcraft might be innocent. Several months after the trials began, he published his concerns in a book called *Cases of Conscience Concerning Evil Spirits.* The book convinced the governor to suspend some of the sentences against the accused witches.

During the rest of his life, Mather pursued his political activities and continued his writing. He published more than 150 works on such subjects as politics, religion, and science. (*See also* **Glorious Revolution; Protestant Churches; Puritans.**)

Mayflower Compact

* *patent* permission to found a colony

A document signed by many of the original settlers of PLYMOUTH COLONY, the Mayflower Compact laid the foundation for a government that functioned for more than 70 years. Its democratic principles influenced other English settlements and American political thought in the following years.

In the early 1600s, a group of PILGRIMS obtained a patent* from the VIRGINIA COMPANY OF LONDON, a group of investors who financed settlements in North America. The patent allowed the Pilgrims to settle on land held by the company in Virginia. In return the colonists were required to send back to London most of the crops they raised for several years.

In September 1620, the Pilgrims set sail for North America on the *Mayflower.* The passengers included 35 Separatists—a group of English Protestants who chose to separate themselves from the Church of England—and 66 others. Rough weather and navigational errors caused the *Mayflower* to drift off course and arrive on the coast of New England, far north of its original destination. The Pilgrims decided to land in this area, but they realized that their patent would not be valid outside Virginia. Having lost the legal authority guiding their expedition, some passengers considered breaking away from the others after landing.

With the signing of the Mayflower Compact, the settlers of Plymouth colony agreed to form a united community, make laws by majority rule, and accept the authority of their governor. This agreement remained the basis of the colony's government until Plymouth became part of Massachusetts in 1691.

To keep the colonists together and to maintain order, Pilgrim leaders drafted the Mayflower Compact. On November 11, 1620, all 41 free men on board signed it before stepping ashore. In the document, the colonists agreed to act as a united group in organizing their community. They pledged to form a government and to obey laws made by the will of the majority and to accept the authority of the colony's governor. John Carver, one of the Pilgrim leaders, became the first governor and served until his death the following spring.

The Mayflower Compact remained the basis of the colony's government until 1691, when Plymouth became part of the Massachusetts Bay colony. For the Plymouth colonists—as well as many settlers who followed—the compact established important political principles, particularly the ideas of a self-governing community and majority rule.

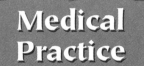

Medical Practice

*P*eople in colonial North America relied on a wide variety of medical techniques to treat DISEASES AND DISORDERS. Native Americans, European colonists, and African Americans all had their own ideas about what caused illness and how to treat it or cure it.

Some colonial medical practices were based on common sense—for example, allowing a sick person to rest in bed or keeping people with contagious illnesses away from others. Most colonial healers, whether European, Indian, or African, also made medicines from plants. Modern science has found that some of these old herbal remedies have real medical benefits, and a number of modern medicines are based on the same HERBS. For instance, a heart medicine called digitoxin is made from the foxglove plant.

People trying to treat illness or injury in colonial times lacked three of the most important elements of modern medicine. They did not have scientific knowledge of how germs—viruses and bacteria—affect the body, safe anesthetic drugs to make patients unconscious for major surgery, or an understanding of antisepsis, which means keeping wounds clean to avoid infection. For these reasons, people often died of illnesses and injuries that could be treated effectively today.

Colonial caregivers did the best they could with the knowledge and tools they possessed. When all else failed, they relied on the body's natural ability to heal itself. Many people in colonial America managed to recover from minor illnesses and injuries without any medical care.

Native American Medicine

Native Americans' ideas about sickness and medical treatment were linked to their beliefs about the spirit world, and their medicine was a religious as well as a practical matter. The Indians thought that the world was filled with unseen forces and spirits that could affect human lives, causing or curing illness. They also believed that certain individuals had special knowledge or powers that enabled them to communicate with the spirit world. People who used these powers to help others—by asking the spirits for assistance in healing a sick person, for example—were known as shamans*, or medicine men (or

* ***shaman*** person with spiritual and healing powers

Native American medicine was closely connected to religion. This illustration shows a group of Indians dancing as part of a ceremony to help heal a sick relative.

The relations of the sick person dancing

Medicine Societies

Many Indian tribes had special groups known as medicine societies that were responsible for safeguarding the health of the community. They cured sick individuals, performed ceremonies to please spirits and rid villages of evil, and rooted out sorcerers suspected of causing such troubles as disease and drought. The Zuni Indians of the Southwest, for example, had 12 societies devoted to curing and a group called the Bow Priesthood that was responsible for forcing sorcerers to confess to wrongdoing.

* *supernatural* related to forces beyond the normal world; miraculous

* *ritual* ceremony that follows a set pattern

women). Those who used their powers to cast evil spells or cause other harm were sorcerers, or witches.

Causes of Illness.   The Indians recognized that some health problems, such as injury from a fall or frostbite from exposure to extreme cold, had natural causes. Yet they believed that many ailments had supernatural* causes. A common explanation for illness was sorcery, which involved magic directed against human beings. The Navajo, Apache, and Pueblo Indians of the Southwest were especially afraid of sorcery. They believed that witches used images of their victims, items belonging to the victims, and poison made from dead bodies to cast spells and cause injury, illness, or death.

Another explanation for illness was the world of spirits. The Creek, Cherokee, and other Indians of the Southeast believed that animal spirits were an important cause of disease. If people did not treat animals with the proper respect, even when hunting and killing them, their angry spirits might bring sickness. The Creek associated specific ailments with specific animals—squirrel spirits caused swollen gums, turtle spirits brought on lingering coughs, and bear spirits produced fevers.

Many Native Americans believed that illness could result from the breaking of taboos, or forbidden acts. Among the Arapaho of the Great Plains, for example, it was taboo to speak about one's health, and an individual who did so could become sick. Every Indian tribe had a complicated network of taboos. Because it was almost impossible to go through life without breaking a taboo now and then, people could readily believe that such acts brought on their illnesses and misfortunes.

Indians thought that some illnesses came from troubled souls. The Huron Indians, for example, believed that people became sick when their souls did not get what they wanted. Shamans interpreted a sick person's dreams to identify the soul's desires and then arranged to provide feasts, dances, or gifts to satisfy the soul. Another possible cause of illness was that the sufferer's soul was lost outside the body, perhaps because the person broke a taboo or because the soul had been stolen by a sorcerer.

Medical Treatments.   Assuming that more than one cause might be involved in an individual's illness, Native Americans generally used more than one treatment. The first step was the diagnosis. A shaman identified the cause or causes of the illness, perhaps using dreams, prayers, religious ceremonies, or magic.

After making a diagnosis, the shaman employed one or more methods of healing, either privately with the patient or in community-wide ceremonies. These treatments might include chanting, singing, and various other rituals*. To deal with wounds or injuries, Indian healers resorted to a variety of surgical measures. They knew how to remove arrowheads from the body, set broken bones, pull teeth, and even perform amputations—the removal of a damaged arm or leg.

One of the shamans' most powerful tools was herbal medicine. Based on a knowledge of hundreds of different plants, they prepared medicines from roots, leaves, and flowers. Patients drank the remedies as teas, chewed them, inhaled them in steam, or mixed them with grease and rubbed them on the body. Among the plants Native American used as drugs were willow root, which contains the ingredient found in aspirin, and ginseng root, which the Indians used to treat fevers and shortness of breath.

Sweat baths were another form of treatment. Indians heated stones in a fire and then sat close to the stones, either while wrapped in blankets or crouched in small huts, until they sweated freely. Many tribes used sweat baths regularly to prevent illness and maintain good health.

Native Americans often took other measures to protect their health and prevent illness. They wore charms—objects thought to possess special powers—to guard against supernatural harm, ate certain foods to boost strength, and performed various ceremonies to ward off misfortune. Unfortunately, none of these measures protected Indians from the new illnesses that Europeans bought to America. Smallpox, measles, and other diseases devastated the Indians, who had never been exposed to the diseases and had no resistance to them.

European Medicine

European ideas about health and sickness were based on theories about the human body developed by the Greek physician Hippocrates in the 400s B.C. The general belief was that illness occurred because of an imbalance of four fluids in the body. These fluids, called humors, were blood, phlegm*, bile*, and black bile. Many medical treatments were aimed at restoring the balance of the humors.

phlegm mucus
bile liquid produced by the liver

According to this theory, disease could be triggered by external factors that affected the humors. The most common trigger was "bad air," which contained invisible, harmful particles. People in colonial times believed that bad air caused certain diseases—in fact, the disease malaria got its name from a phrase meaning "unhealthy air." They did not know that malaria actually comes from mosquitoes that carry tiny disease organisms. To protect themselves, colonists forced smoke through their homes, kept windows closed, and cleaned places such as outhouses and ditches that could breed bad air.

European colonists thought that climate played a role in disease as well. Yellow fever was associated with hot, humid weather, while pneumonia was linked to cold, damp weather. The colonists also believed that illness could be caused by natural disasters such as earthquakes, floods, or volcanic eruptions or by God as punishment for sin.

The settlers did recognize that illness could be the result of contact with sick people or animals or with disease-carrying objects. To prevent the spread of diseases believed to be contagious, patients with the illness, or people who might have been exposed to it, were kept apart for a period of time in quarantine.

Medical Treatments.   Colonists in North America used more than 200 different medicinal drugs to treat illness. Most were imported from Europe or the West Indies, although settlers also grew medicinal plants in their gardens. The colonists adopted surprisingly few plant remedies from the Indians. For the most part, they relied on traditional cures used in European medical practice.

In colonial times, most sick people were cared for in their homes. If home remedies failed, they would seek the help of a doctor. The physician shown here—"Dr. Gleason," as painted by William C. Chandler in 1785—is taking the pulse of a female patient, who remains behind the bed curtains.

Many drugs were considered effective because they made the patient discharge fluids that were thought to represent bad humors. Colonists regularly used potions that caused them to cough, spit, vomit, sweat, pass urine, or move their bowels. Among the most popular drugs were laxatives and tonics, believed to "tone" the blood vessels and nerves. Many tonics included Peruvian bark, or cinchona, which proved to be an effective treatment for malaria. Scientists now know that Peruvian bark contains quinine, an antimalarial chemical.

Narcotics, drugs made from opium, had many uses. The most common drug was laudanum, a mixture of alcohol and opium. Narcotics killed pain, controlled diarrhea, and helped people sleep. Mothers often gave them to crying babies to quiet them and make them sleep. The dangerous addictive properties of narcotics were little recognized at the time.

For patients with the most serious fevers or injuries, doctors had two drastic treatments: blistering and bleeding. In blistering, the doctor applied a lotion of alcohol and crushed beetles to the patient's skin to cause swelling and blisters. This was supposed to draw bad humors from the body and counteract fever. Doctors thought that bleeding, withdrawing blood from the patient's body, not only removed bad humors but also relieved pressure on the blood vessels. In the middle colonies and the South, they often bled patients by applying leeches, water-dwelling creatures that suck blood through the skin. Elsewhere in North America, doctors generally bled patients by cutting a vein.

Surgery in colonial America was generally limited to dealing with broken bones, taking care of open wounds, or draining fluid from swellings with a large needle. More complex operations, usually performed only by skilled surgeons, included amputating arms or legs, removing bladder stones, or operating on the eyes. Surgery of the chest and abdomen had to wait until the 1800s and the development of anesthesia and antiseptic techniques.

Caregivers. Colonial America had two levels of health-care providers. Most basic treatment took place in the home, perhaps with the help of a part-time medical practitioner. People consulted trained physicians, the second level of health care, only when home health care failed.

Women were the most important healers in the home. They took care of their families, servants, and farm laborers. In addition to healing techniques they learned from their mothers, women often consulted basic medical books. They often kept journals in which they recorded home remedies. Women grew herbs for medicines, bought drugs from apothecary* shops, and used prepared remedies such as Juniper's Essence of Peppermint or Daffy's Elixir, available in shops and taverns. Wealthy families often had medicine chests filled with a supply of the most frequently used drugs, scales for measuring ingredients for potions, and small sharp blades for bleeding.

* *apothecary* pharmacist

Outside the family, ministers, priests, and missionaries often provided medical treatment, even if they lacked formal medical training. Colonists paid for this assistance in labor, farm produce, or cash. The midwife—a woman who assists in childbirth—was another fee-for-service caregiver in most communities. Patients and caregivers were not separated by gender. Women who provided medical services cared for both male and female patients, and male physicians or ministers helped women deliver children.

The British colonies had about 3,500 trained physicians at the time of the American Revolution, but only 10 percent of them had earned professional degrees—either in Europe or at one of the two new medical schools in the colonies. Most of the rest had acquired their training informally, as apprentices. Although physicians generally saw between four and ten patients a day, many could not support themselves on the fees from their medical practice. They often earned additional income as judges, lawyers, farmers, or merchants, especially drug merchants.

Medical practitioners in New Spain and New France were licensed by the government and paid almost entirely on a fee-for-service basis. New France had two kinds of medical professionals. *Chirurgiens* were similar to modern general practitioners and treated common illnesses and everyday conditions. *Médecins* were specialists in certain ailments. Physicians in New Spain tried to avoid competition by limiting the number of new doctors who could enter and practice in the colony. The resulting shortage of doctors led many people to seek medical care from unauthorized healers who practiced a blend of Indian and European medicine.

The Spanish and French established the first HOSPITALS in North America in the 1500s and 1600s. The British colonies lagged far behind, building their first general-purpose hospital in Philadelphia in 1751. Before that time, they had only temporary clinics, usually set up to deal with epidemics.

African American Medicine

Like the Indians, African American slaves believed in a world filled with spirits that could affect human life, bringing sickness or curing it. To Africans, illness had both natural—that is, physical—and supernatural causes. They took medicine to treat the physical causes and turned to religion or magic to deal with supernatural causes. Yet the natural and the supernatural were closely intertwined.

Slaves often sought medical help from African healers called "conjure" doctors. These conjurers were both respected and feared, for it was believed that they talked to spirits and could cast spells as well as lift them. Their treatment generally consisted of secret rituals and charms for the patient to wear. During colonial times, the conjure doctors were important members of every black community. Their influence faded when the slave trade to North America ended in the early 1800s, cutting off direct contact with Africa.

Other African healers, called "root" or "herb" doctors, practiced a different kind of medicine. These healers believed that nature provided a cure for every illness, and though they lacked formal education, they knew a great deal about the medicinal properties of many plants. The herb doctors often acted as caregivers for the plantation and were consulted both by other slaves and by whites. Whites, however, were always a bit nervous about taking medicine provided by blacks, fearing that slaves might poison them. Among the plants African American healers used were garlic, sage, catnip, mustard weed, dogwood, pine needles, wild cherry bark, and raspberry leaves. They also used some less appealing substances, such as fried "young mice" and boiled cockroaches.

Another medical specialist who played a vital role in black communities was the midwife. Even in places where white slaveholders treated their slaves with European medicine, the business of childbirth was almost always left to black midwives. These women delivered the children of slaves and assisted with the births of white infants.

The disease pattern of African Americans differed from that of whites. Blacks seemed to have some resistance to certain tropical diseases, such as yellow fever, hookworm, and malaria, that severely affected European colonists. Yet African Americans suffered more than whites did from an illness called yaws. The poor diet of the slaves contributed to some of their health problems, especially pellagra and beriberi—illnesses caused by vitamin shortages. Blacks also suffered severely from smallpox, the leading cause of death in North America during the early colonial period. In Africa, however, some people had learned how to protect themselves from this deadly disease. It was from a black slave named Onesimus that the New England minister Cotton MATHER learned a method of inoculation* that was the first step toward controlling smallpox in North America. (*See also* **Health and Safety; Life Expectancy; Magic and Witchcraft.**)

* **inoculation** medical treatment involving exposure to a mild version of a disease to create resistance to it

Menéndez de Avilés, Pedro

1519–1574
Spanish colonizer

See map in Spanish Borderlands (vol. 4).

* **presidio** Spanish fort built to protect mission settlements

* **armada** fleet of warships

P edro Menéndez de Avilés, head of Spain's West Indies fleet, founded ST. AUGUSTINE in the area the Spanish called FLORIDA. He also built several forts that helped establish Spanish power in the region. Today St. Augustine is the oldest European settlement in the United States.

Spain's King Philip II appointed Menéndez governor of Florida in 1565. At the time, the Spanish saw France as a threat to its empire in the Caribbean Sea. In exchange for a large land grant and a title of nobility, Menéndez agreed to drive the French out of Florida and to settle the area for Spain at his own expense.

Menéndez arrived on the northeast coast of Florida in August 1565 with almost 3,000 Spanish colonists. He led an assault on France's Fort Caroline, near present-day Jacksonville. After destroying the fort and killing most of the French soldiers and settlers, the Spaniards moved about 50 miles to the south. There Menéndez founded the military base of St. Augustine on September 8.

In the late 1500s, Spain's claims for Florida included territory extending north along the Atlantic seacoast to Newfoundland and west along the Gulf coast. Menéndez was determined to establish Spanish settlements throughout the area. By 1567 he had set up a line of presidios* from Tampa Bay, on the west coast of Florida, to Parris Island, off the southern tip of present-day South Carolina. Menéndez also started a colony in Virginia and made plans to extend the string of military posts to Mexico.

The Spanish government called Menéndez home in 1572 to take command of its armada* and defend its coastal waters. Two years later he died. His settlements in Florida were eventually abandoned because of difficulties with the Indians. Only St. Augustine remained.

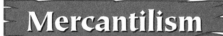

Mennonites

See **Protestant Churches.**

Mercantilism

A n economic theory and system, mercantilism was a driving force in European colonization from the 1500s to the early 1800s. It was based on the idea that governments should structure their economies to enrich and strengthen the state. According to this theory, a nation increased its power by accumulating valuable resources and by maintaining a favorable balance of trade—that is, exporting more goods than it imported. The establishment and development of colonies played a key role in mercantilism because colonies could provide parent countries with both resources for their industries and markets for their exports. To fulfill their mercantilist goals, European governments passed a series of laws that regulated most aspects of economic life, both at home and in their colonies.

Development of Mercantilism.
Mercantilism developed with the rise of strong, centralized nations in Europe in the late 1400s. These countries needed funds to finance their expanding governments and their armies and navies. European rulers hesitated to raise the money by increasing taxes,

fearing that such an action would provoke discontent and opposition in their countries. Instead, they turned to foreign trade as a source of revenue, collecting customs duties, or taxes, on imported and exported goods.

Following the "discovery" of the Americas in 1492, European nations saw an opportunity to acquire great wealth in the region. Spain was the first to take advantage of this opportunity. Its conquests of present-day Mexico and Peru brought vast amounts of GOLD and SILVER into the Spanish treasury. Other nations, envious of Spain's growing wealth, began trying to exploit* the riches of the Americas as well.

Competition among nations led to conflicts, and war became an inevitable part of mercantilism. Spain's empire began to decline in the 1500s as the commercial power of the Dutch increased. In the 1600s, however, the Netherlands lost a succession of wars with England and France, ending its role as a major European power. By the late 1600s and 1700s, mercantilist competition had shifted to England and France. Great Britain eventually won this struggle and, in time, ruled a vast, worldwide empire.

exploit to use for selfish reasons without regard to the consequences

Principles of Mercantilism.

According to the principles of mercantilism, a nation's economy should serve the interests of the state. For that reason, it was important to evaluate the usefulness of various economic activities. In some cases, the government needed to prohibit the production within the country of a particular item—such as tobacco—in order to encourage overseas trade in that product. Although this ban would hurt domestic producers, overseas trade brought revenue from customs duties, while domestic production did not.

European nations tried to structure their overseas trade to obtain the greatest benefits from it. At first, they focused on accumulating gold and silver because these precious metals increased the nation's wealth and power. The Spanish had considerable success in this area, extracting great riches from their American colonies. But precious metals were scarce in other colonial areas, and in time the Spanish colonies' supplies dwindled as well.

As a result, mercantilists' main effort shifted to expanding foreign trade, exchanging domestic manufactured goods for colonial agricultural products and raw materials. Exporting goods to their colonies helped European nations maintain a favorable balance of trade. The policies they created to protect this balance had a significant effect on the economies of the North American colonies.

Mercantilism and the Colonies.

European governments believed that their North American colonies existed only for the benefit of the parent countries. They attempted to shape the colonial economies through various laws and regulations that encouraged the export of goods such as furs and tobacco that were much in demand in Europe. To help the growth of manufacturing at home, European governments passed laws limiting the development of industries in the colonies. Colonists would have to buy manufactured goods from their parent country instead of producing them locally. Other laws attempted to discourage the colonies from trading with other countries by limiting colonial trade to ships owned by the parent country or the colonies and taxing goods coming into the colonies from other nations.

For their part, the colonists of North America tried to pursue economic policies that would benefit themselves. They generally participated in the trade-oriented economy encouraged by mercantilism, and some colonial merchants grew wealthy as a result of trade. But most colonists proceeded to raise the crops and manufacture the products they needed without regard to the wishes of the parent country.

As the colonies grew, their economic interests often clashed with those of the parent country, and opposition to mercantilism increased. In the British colonies, dissatisfaction with mercantilist laws such as the NAVIGATION ACTS contributed to the American INDEPENDENCE MOVEMENT. (*See also* **Colonial Administration; Economic Systems; European Empires; Industries; Money and Finance; Smuggling; Taxation; Trade and Commerce.**)

Merchants

*M*erchants were a vital link between the North American colonists and the rest of the world. Through a far-flung trading network, they brought all types of imported goods—from manufactured goods such as clothing and cookware to luxury wines and slaves—to the colonies. Merchants also shipped furs, fish, tobacco, corn, beef, wheat, timber, and other colonial products to markets in Europe and the West Indies.

Merchants in British Colonies. Colonial merchants ranged from large, wealthy firms with many ships to individuals who dealt in small cargoes of imports and exports and rented space on others' vessels. All merchants dealt primarily in foreign trade, that is, business outside the colonies. Some of this commerce took place with European countries or with people in Africa and Asia. Another important market was the West Indies, which traded sugar, molasses, salt, and cotton for agricultural products and manufactured goods from the American colonies.

Merchants bought and sold goods at wholesale* prices. Local storekeepers and peddlers, who were involved in retail* business within the colonies, purchased imported goods from merchants and then sold them—with an increase in price—to individual consumers. In the southern colonies, people called merchant-planters combined two roles. Besides owning and running plantations, they imported goods and sold them locally, either in stores they owned or to traders.

Like all colonists, merchants relied upon two features of the colonial economy: barter* and credit. Although some business deals involved gold or silver money, coins were usually in short supply. Instead, individuals bartered for things they needed. For example, a farmer might trade several hogs for a gun and ammunition. Merchants practiced barter on a larger scale, such as swapping a cargo of tobacco for a load of manufactured goods. Many of them also purchased items on credit, promising to pay the seller at a future date. A merchant might acquire a cargo of goods on credit in London, sell the items in the West Indies or North America, and then pay for them upon his return to Europe.

Merchants on the coast supplied the stores of the British colonies with a wide variety of imported goods. In the 1730s, one shop in rural Connecticut

* **wholesale** sale of goods in large quantities from one business to another, usually at a lower price than to the general public
* **retail** sale of goods to the general public

* **barter** exchange of goods and services without using money

50

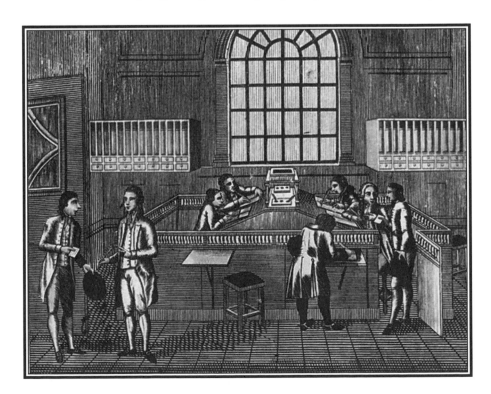

sold pepper, lace, gloves, gunpowder, drugs, pots and pans, needles, knives, molasses, rum, and hymnbooks from coastal merchants. Customers paid for their purchases with game, skins, livestock, or produce. The storekeeper then carted these goods to the coast to trade them to merchants for more products to sell in the store.

Merchants did not have to travel to distant ports to carry out their business. They relied on ship captains or local residents who acted as agents for information about the kinds of cargo to select, where to buy it, and how much to pay. The merchants obtained this information by promising a share of their profits. The success of a merchant depended on the use of clever, honest, and reliable captains and agents.

status social position

Successful merchants acquired wealth and the status* that went with it. In the British colonies, the richest merchants adopted the style of life of the British upper classes, with expensively decorated country estates and town houses that displayed their wealth. These men often rose to positions of importance and leadership in their communities. Although urban merchants were generally more interested in business than in politics, a large number of rural merchant-planters entered public service as magistrates*, judges, militia commanders, and other officials.

magistrate official with administrative and often judicial functions

Merchants in Dutch, French, and Spanish Colonies.

The colonies of the European powers offered various roles and opportunities for merchants. During the early years of the Dutch colony of NEW NETHERLAND, trade remained in the hands of the DUTCH WEST INDIA COMPANY, which ran the colony. Independent merchants had no opportunity to do business. In 1640, when the company stopped trying to control all of the colony's trade, the merchant community began to grow and prosper. By the time the colony came

Colonial merchants hired ship captains and other agents to carry out the actual work of acquiring and trading goods. Back in the home office, clerks kept track of the finances.

under English control in the 1660s, the merchant class dominated politics in the capital city of NEW AMSTERDAM, later New York City. These merchants continued to flourish under English rule.

In the French colonies, three different groups of merchants were involved in foreign trade: Roman Catholics, Huguenots (French Protestants), and government or military officials. Members of the third group dominated the trade in NEW FRANCE for most of the colonial period, conducting business on the side while carrying out their regular duties as royal officials, magistrates, and army officers. After a period of time, officials and full-time merchants alike generally retired to France, taking their profits with them—even those who had been born in North America.

Independent merchants got a late start in the Spanish Borderlands*. From the end of the 1500s to the early 1700s, MISSIONS AND MISSIONARIES supplied most of the goods needed by military posts and communities. The missionaries imported products from agents in Cuba or Mexico and sold them locally. They also controlled the crops and items produced by Native Americans. As the region's population grew during the 1700s, the missions lost much of their importance and influence, and merchants gained control of international, regional, and local trade. The Spanish crown gave responsibility for large-scale trading ventures to private merchants, some of whom were Scottish or French. A number of smaller-scale agents and traders—including a few women—traveled throughout the Borderlands, trading cloth, arms, ammunition, and liquor for deerskins and agricultural products. This border trade involved people of all races, contributing to the cross-cultural exchange of New Spain's northern frontier. (*See also* **Economic Systems; Money and Finance; Smuggling; Trade and Commerce.**)

* **Spanish Borderlands** northern part of New Spain, area now occupied by Florida, Texas, New Mexico, Arizona, and California

Mestizos

See *Race Relations*.

Metacom

ca. 1640–1676
Wampanoag leader

* *sachem* Indian chief

Metacom, known as King Philip by the English, led a Native American movement against English power in southern New England. He and his followers tried to drive away the white settlers, who had moved onto Indian lands. After a bloody struggle, the colonists overcame Metacom's forces, ending Indian resistance in the region.

Metacom belonged to the WAMPANOAG tribe. His father, Massasoit, was the sachem*, who had formed an alliance with the Pilgrims of PLYMOUTH COLONY. When Massasoit died in 1660, his son Wamsutta came to power. Two years later Wamsutta died as well, and Metacom became sachem. The tribe's territory, which lay between Plymouth, Rhode Island, and the Massachusetts Bay colony, faced constant pressure for land from the growing English settlements. Additional problems arose when English livestock strayed into the Indians' fields, destroying crops.

In 1667 Plymouth colony angered the Wampanoag by building the town of Swansea on land in the tribe's territory. Four years later, authorities from Plymouth and Massachusetts forced Metacom to sign a treaty placing his

people under the colonists' control. Metacom responded by preparing the tribe for war and forming alliances with other tribes in the region.

In 1675 the colonists executed three Wampanoag for killing an Indian who had been an English spy. The Indians responded by raiding English villages. The conflict, which became known as KING PHILIP'S WAR, continued for months. The powerful NARRAGANSETT INDIANS joined Metacom's forces, while the Mohawk, PEQUOT, and most Christian Indians supported the colonists. Both sides suffered heavy casualties* and the destruction of homes and crops.

* casualty person who is killed or injured

In the spring of 1676, Metacom's network of alliances broke down, and the sachem retreated to the Wampanoag homeland in Plymouth. In August, Metacom was killed by an Indian fighting for the English. His death ended the war and the independence of Native Americans in New England. (*See also* **Massachusetts; Native Americans.**)

Methodists

See *Protestant Churches.*

Mexican Independence

By 1800 dissatisfaction with Spanish colonial rule was growing in MEXICO, the most important region of NEW SPAIN. But the people of Mexico were far from united in their movement toward independence. Tensions ran high between *criollos,* or Creoles—people of Spanish descent born in the colony—and *peninsulares*—native-born Spaniards who lived in New Spain. The *peninsulares* controlled most high government offices, but the *criollos* wanted a larger share of the power.

Meanwhile in Europe, French emperor Napoleon Bonaparte invaded SPAIN in 1808 and deposed its king. The resulting confusion over control of Spain's North American colonies encouraged some Mexicans to launch an independence movement. A number of *criollos* began plotting to break away from Spanish rule. Hoping to attract Mexican Indians to their movement, they recruited Miguel HIDALGO Y COSTILLA, a Catholic priest who was popular with the Indians.

* mestizo person of mixed Spanish and Indian ancestry

The Spanish colonial government discovered the conspiracy in September 1810. Faced with possible arrest, Hidalgo gathered his followers on September 16 and urged them to revolt. Thousands of Indians and mestizos* answered his call. In the weeks that followed, they marched through the Mexican countryside, capturing town after town. The ragged army, made up largely of poor peasants, began looting the haciendas along the way. To protect their property and power, many of the wealthier members of society, including both *criollos* and *peninsulares,* joined together to crush the peasant revolt.

In late October 1810, the rebels suffered serious losses in clashes with Spanish troops in Mexico City, the capital of New Spain. Several crushing defeats followed, and Hidalgo was eventually captured and executed in 1811. The struggle for independence continued under the leadership of another priest, José María Morelos y Pavón. Morelos and his army of rebels fought against Spanish colonial forces for the next four years.

In the fall of 1815, Agustín de Iturbide, an officer in the Spanish colonial army, captured Morelos. The independence movement split into a number of separate rebellions, each under different leadership. The revolution began to strain loyalties, with *criollos* and Spanish troops frequently changing sides. Among those who moved to the opposite camp was Agustín de Iturbide.

In 1820 the viceroy* of New Spain ordered Iturbide to lead his troops against Vicente Guerrero, one of the rebel leaders. Instead of attacking Guerrero, Iturbide joined forces with him. Together they issued the Plan de Iguala, which called for an independent monarchy for Mexico, equality for *criollos,* and the preservation of the Roman Catholic Church.

The Plan de Iguala won broad support in Mexico. Iturbide and Guerrero organized a united military force under Iturbide's command. Faced with this powerful threat, and with Spanish troops exhausted by years of fighting, the viceroy chose to end the hostilities. On August 24, 1821, he signed the Treaty of Córdoba, which recognized Mexican independence. Officials in Spain rejected the agreement, but with political problems at home, they could do nothing to stop it. The new government of Mexico took over control of the Spanish territories to the north—Texas, New Mexico, Arizona, and California. (*See also* **Independence Movements.**)

* *viceroy* person appointed as a monarch's representative to govern a province or colony

Mexico

M exico had seen the rise and fall of several great empires before the arrival of Europeans in the early 1500s. The last of these empires, that of the Aztecs, controlled large areas of central Mexico. The arrival of the conquistadors, Spanish conquerors who sought treasure and territory in the Americas, brought an end to the great Aztec empire.

Spanish Conquest and Rule

Spain launched its conquest of Mexico from its colony of Cuba in the West Indies. The Spanish governor of Cuba sent out several expeditions to explore the mainland. One campaign, led by Hernando Cortés, landed on the Mexican coast in 1519. After founding the settlement of Vera Cruz, Cortés marched inland in search of the magnificent Aztec empire he had heard about from Indians on the coast.

Conquest of Mexico. Cortés pushed into central Mexico with about 500 soldiers, some horses and guns, and several thousand Indians who had joined him along the way. The expedition arrived at the Aztec capital of Tenochtitlán in November 1519. The Aztecs greeted the Europeans courteously, believing Cortés to be the god Quetzalcoatl mentioned in their legends.

Cortés then began his conquest of the Aztecs. He captured their emperor, Montezuma, and spent two years fighting the Aztecs, finally defeating them in the summer of 1521. Cortés named the conquered territory New Spain and sent soldiers out to extend Spanish power over nearby regions.

Rise of New Spain. The Spanish crown quickly established its authority in New Spain. In 1528 it created an *audiencia,* or royal court, and in 1535

See first map in Exploration (vol. 2).

See color plate 1, vol. 4.

This view of Mexico City was published in Montanus's *New World* in 1671, 150 years after the Spanish conquest of the Aztecs. However, the artist tried to represent the Mexican capital as it looked before the Spanish arrived.

* ***viceroy*** person appointed as a monarch's representative to govern a province or colony

appointed a viceroy* to rule over the new territory. Many of the conquistadors were rewarded with ENCOMIENDAS, estates that included the right to the labor of the Indians living on the land.

The crown divided New Spain into an assortment of provinces and municipalities, and it set up a complex system of colonial administration to govern them. Catholic missionaries, who came to Mexico to convert the Indians to Christianity, established MISSIONS and schools throughout the colony. The church had strong ties to the monarchy, and its influence helped strengthen royal authority. At the same time, however, the interests of the church and colonial authorities sometimes clashed, especially in matters concerning the Indians.

One missionary, Bartolomé de LAS CASAS, argued against the *encomienda* system because it enslaved the Indians. In 1541 Indians staged an unsuccessful uprising against the *encomiendas*, now known as the Mixtón War. The next year the Spanish crown passed laws severely restricting the system. The colonists who held *encomiendas* rebelled against this attempt to lessen their power. Spanish forces put down this revolt, and the *encomienda* system gradually declined. In its place came the *repartimiento*, a system of labor in which landowners could use Indians as workers only at important times such as the harvest. The *repartimiento* system was abolished in the 1600s.

The discovery of silver in the 1540s transformed New Spain. Over the next 100 years, the economy expanded rapidly, and a large network of commerce and trade developed. Centered on Mexico City, the colony's capital,

this network linked flourishing urban centers throughout New Spain. Large agricultural estates and ranches helped feed the growing population and provide products for export to Spain.

By 1600 Mexico had become the center and most prosperous part of Spain's vast colonial empire. Very few colonists enjoyed the region's new wealth, however. Mexican society consisted of several social and ethnic classes. At the top were *peninsulares,* native-born Spaniards who lived in Mexico. They dominated the colonial government and controlled most of the wealth. Next came *criollos,* people of Spanish descent who were born in Mexico. Mestizos* and other people of mixed ancestry occupied lower rungs on the social ladder, while Indians were pushed to the bottom.

*** mestizo** person of mixed Spanish and Indian ancestry

See first map in European Empires (vol. 2).

*** presidio** Spanish fort built to protect mission settlements

Period of Decline.

The economy of New Spain began to decline in the 1600s. This was due in part to decreases in the Indian population through disease and overwork. With fewer laborers, Spanish colonists had difficulty running estates, ranches, and mines. In addition, Spanish trade regulations hampered economic growth by limiting the development of colonial industry.

As the economy declined, the colonists of New Spain began to spread out in search of new opportunities. In the north, settlement expanded into the regions that became known as the SPANISH BORDERLANDS, which included parts of present-day Florida, Texas, New Mexico, Arizona, and California. As colonists established settlements in frontier areas, the government in Mexico City found it increasingly difficult to rule over the far-flung reaches of the colony. With weakened central control, many areas became more independent, both economically and politically. The weakening of the central government also led to increased political corruption and abuses of power by local officials.

From Rebellion to Republic

Attempts to solve the growing problems of Mexico and New Spain began in the early 1700s. At this time, the Bourbons, a new royal family, came to power in Spain and carried out a series of reforms. Aimed at revitalizing Spain's colonial empire, these new policies brought great change to Mexico and a new era in its history.

Bourbon Reforms.

The Bourbon reforms reorganized the colonial administration of New Spain, shifted political boundaries, and brought in more honest government officials. The reforms also relaxed trade restrictions, reduced taxes on imports and exports, and gave local administrations greater control over economic policies. To provide better defense for the colony, the crown created a colonial army to supplement Spanish troops, most of whom were stationed at presidios* in the Spanish Borderlands.

The Bourbon reforms led to a period of great growth and prosperity in Mexico. Mining and agricultural production expanded dramatically, and trade increased as well. However, a limited number of people benefited from the booming economy. While certain members of the upper classes gained greater wealth and power, the majority of people in Mexico remained poor and powerless. This led to conflicts and eventually rebellion.

Dawn of Mexican Civilization

Spain conquered and colonized Mexico more than 450 years ago. But the history of Mexico and its native peoples began long before that. Several great cultures existed in Mexico before the Aztecs, including the Olmecs, who date back as early as 1300 B.C. Recent archaeological work, however, has possibly uncovered the beginning of Mexican civilization. The discovery of squash seeds in caves in southeastern Mexico suggests that ancient people in Mexico may have grown plants for food between 8,000 and 10,000 years ago. These early ancestors of modern Mexicans may have been the first in a long history of peoples to occupy what is now Mexico.

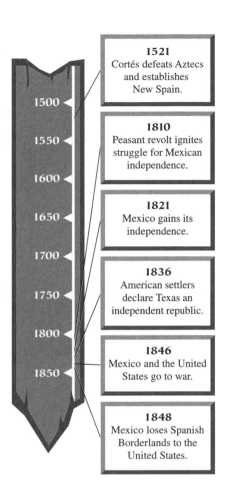

1521
Cortés defeats Aztecs and establishes New Spain.

1810
Peasant revolt ignites struggle for Mexican independence.

1821
Mexico gains its independence.

1836
American settlers declare Texas an independent republic.

1846
Mexico and the United States go to war.

1848
Mexico loses Spanish Borderlands to the United States.

1500
1550
1600
1650
1700
1750
1800
1850

* **autocratic** ruling with absolute power and authority

* **coup** sudden and often violent overthrow of a ruler or government

* **annex** to add territory to an existing state

Mexican Independence. By 1800 many Mexicans had become dissatisfied with Spanish colonial rule. *Criollos* wanted a greater role in government, which was controlled by *peninsulares*. Poor Mexican peasants wanted more economic opportunities and a better way of life. This discontent soon led to a movement for MEXICAN INDEPENDENCE.

The INDEPENDENCE MOVEMENT lasted for more than a decade and involved several different revolts against the Spanish colonial government. The first erupted in 1810 when a Catholic priest, Miguel HIDALGO Y COSTILLA, led a peasant uprising against the government. Hidalgo's rebellion was put down, but others soon followed.

The struggle for independence created conflicting loyalties for many Mexicans. *Criollos* and Spanish troops in particular changed sides many times during the course of the rebellions. Mexico finally achieved independence in 1821, when Augustín de ITURBIDE, a Spanish officer who had fought on the side of the colonial government, joined forces with the rebel leader Vicente Guerrero. Together they issued a declaration of independence and a plan of government and united their troops.

The combined armies of Iturbide and Guerrero soon gained control of Mexico. They forced the viceroy to sign the Treaty of Córdoba on August 24, 1821, officially ending Spanish rule of Mexico.

Mexican Empire and Republic. For a short time after independence, Mexico was organized as an empire, with Augustín de Iturbide as emperor. However, Iturbide failed to resolve the country's problems and ruled in an autocratic* manner. In 1823 military forces led by General Antonio López de Santa Anna overthrew the emperor.

Following the end of Iturbide's rule, Mexicans adopted a constitution reorganizing the country as a republic with an elected president and congress. The first two presidents were honest leaders, but they faced difficult economic, political, and social problems. In 1833 Santa Anna, the leader of the coup* against Iturbide, became president of Mexico. He continued to exert a powerful influence over Mexican politics for more than 20 years.

The so-called Age of Santa Anna was a difficult and turbulent time for Mexico. The president became increasingly autocratic, adopting a new constitution in 1836 that gave him almost unlimited power. The nation was still plagued with severe economic problems, including enormous domestic and foreign debt. In addition to domestic problems, Mexico faced several conflicts with other nations.

The most serious crisis occurred in TEXAS in the Spanish Borderlands. In the 1820s, the Mexican government had begun encouraging citizens of the United States to settle in Texas. In 1836, unhappy with Mexican rule, the American immigrants declared Texas an independent republic. Santa Anna led an army to put an end to the revolt. After an initial victory at the Alamo, Santa Anna and his troops met final defeat at the Battle of San Jacinto in April 1836.

The United States quickly recognized the independence of the Republic of Texas, but Mexico refused to do so. Then in 1845, the United States annexed* Texas, an act that led to war with Mexico. The Mexican-American

cede to yield or surrender

War, which lasted from 1846 to 1848, resulted in defeat for Mexico. According to the terms of the Treaty of Guadalupe Hidalgo, Mexico ceded* almost half of its territory to the United States, including most of the Spanish Borderlands. (*See also* **Colonial Administration; European Empires; Exploration, Age of; Government, Provincial.**)

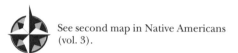

Miami Indians

See second map in Native Americans (vol. 3).

*T*he Miami Indians lived south of the Great Lakes. During the colonial period, they struggled to hold on to their lands as settlers began moving into their territory. The name *Miami* may have come from the Chippewa word *omaugeg,* meaning "peninsula people." It is not related to the name of Miami, Florida, which comes from another Indian tribe's word for "big water."

In the early 1700s, about 10,000 Miami Indians lived in present-day Indiana and Ohio. They built dome-shaped wigwams and raised corn that they traded with other tribes. Although the Miami formed an alliance with the French, they also exchanged goods with British traders. Contact with Europeans affected the way the Indians lived, and they began to dwell in log houses, wear some European-style clothing, and raise livestock.

Eventually, the Miami were caught between the French and the British in their struggle for control of territory in North America. In 1752 the French destroyed a Miami village that had been trading with the British. By the time of the Revolutionary War, American settlement had spread far into Miami territory, and the tribe joined the British effort to defeat the Americans.

When the war ended, the Miami resisted American control. Led by the war chief Little Turtle, they scored victories over American troops in major battles in the 1790s. However, in 1794 the American general Anthony Wayne defeated the Miami in the Battle of Fallen Timbers. After the victory, the Americans built Fort Wayne on the site of the former Miami settlement in Indiana. During the 1800s, the United States forced the Miami to sell much of their land in the region. Some members of the tribe remained in Indiana, while others left the area and settled in Oklahoma. (*See also* **French and Indian War; Native Americans; Ohio River Valley.**)

Micmac Indians

See second map in Native Americans (vol. 3).

*W*hen Europeans first arrived in present-day Canada, the Micmac Indians were one of the largest groups of Native Americans living there. As the French and the British competed for control of the region, the Micmac became involved in the struggle.

The homeland of the Micmac included what is now NOVA SCOTIA, Prince Edward Island, Cape Breton Island, and much of New Brunswick. The tribe, which spoke an Algonquian language, consisted of seven regional groups, each led by a chief. Together the chiefs formed the Grand Council, which spoke for the regional groups when dealing with other tribes. During the summer, the Micmac lived along the coasts, fishing and catching shellfish. When winter came, they moved inland and settled along lakes and rivers, where they built wigwams covered with bark or animal hides. They traveled

* *caribou* large deer, similar to reindeer

the waterways in bark canoes and hunted moose, caribou*, otter, and beaver. The Micmac were especially skillful at crafts such as basketmaking and decorating birch bark with beads or porcupine quills.

During the 1600s, the Micmac established trading relationships with French settlers, exchanging furs for European goods. Many members of the tribe converted to Catholicism, and some of the women married or lived with French traders and trappers. In the mid-1740s, the Micmac joined forces with the French to defend the region against the British in KING GEORGE'S WAR. The Indians fought the British in Nova Scotia in 1744, and the following year they raided British settlements in Maine, New Hampshire, and Massachusetts. After the British won control of Canada in 1763, they signed a peace treaty with the Micmac. As a result, the tribe was able to remain in its homeland in eastern Canada. (*See also* **Canada; Native Americans.**)

Middle Colonies

See *British Colonies; Delaware; New Jersey; New York; Pennsylania.*

Middle Passage

See *Slave Trade.*

Migration Within the Colonies

* *outpost* frontier settlement or military base

The first European settlements in North America were small outposts* on the edges of the continent. From these outposts, the Europeans spread across the land. Some who moved to the frontier regions were immigrants freshly arrived from Europe. Others were internal migrants—people moving from one part of North America to another. Internal migration played a major part in shaping America during the colonial period.

Not all movement within a region can be classified as internal migration. Some occurs as part of the normal pattern of life. For example, in colonial times, when young people married, they often left their parents' homes and settled in nearby villages or counties. Some laborers moved as their jobs changed with the seasons, spending summers in the countryside and winters in town. Migration, however, involved a relocation of individuals, families, or whole communities over distances that were great enough to break social ties with the families and friends they left behind.

In the first stages of colonization, the English and Dutch established settlements such as JAMESTOWN, PLYMOUTH, and NEW AMSTERDAM on the Atlantic coast. The French built QUEBEC and MONTREAL on the St. Lawrence River and PORT ROYAL on the east coast of what is now Canada. The Spanish founded ST. AUGUSTINE in Florida and SANTA FE in New Mexico. These communities became springboards from which people advanced into new territory, slowly extending the frontier until the original communities were part of a much larger, often continuous band of settled land. Shown on a map, the European population in North America would appear as a few scattered dots in the early years but in time would be represented by broad, filled-in areas.

Migration Within the Colonies

Native American Migration. The Europeans were not the only people migrating across North America in colonial times. The Native Americans, too, were in a state of almost constant movement.

For centuries before the Europeans appeared, limited migration was a way of life for many Indian tribes. Most moved to favored hunting grounds during the winter and to fishing stations in spring, but they remained for most of the year in villages near their farmlands. Every few years, they would shift their planting areas to allow the soil to recover.

The arrival of the Europeans brought a new kind of migration to the Native Americans. On the Atlantic coast, Indians were forced from their homelands and moved west, away from white settlements. These migrations began in the 1600s and increased greatly during the 1700s. Among the many tribes displaced by white settlement were the DELAWARE, who moved from the Delaware Valley to the Ohio Valley; the Seneca and Erie, who moved west along the Great Lakes; and the TUSCARORA, who left North Carolina for western New York. Native American migration was especially intense in the Great Lakes region. At least one-fourth of all the Indians living there in the late 1760s had recently arrived from someplace else.

The effect of white settlement on the Indians was far-reaching, like waves moving outward. Forced migration drove tribes into territory already occupied by other Indian groups. Often several dislocated tribes ended up living in the same territory. Sometimes they went to war. On other occasions, however, they formed new alliances to fight Europeans, as the SHAWNEE, Delaware, and MIAMI did in the Ohio Valley in the late 1700s.

Dutch and British Migration. English and Dutch colonists arrived in the coastal settlements, and those who did not settle there permanently usually stayed for a few months or years before moving inland. When they did begin to migrate, they followed rivers. The Dutch, for example, founded settlements along the Hudson River. During the 1600s, Europeans seldom settled much beyond two days' journey from the coast.

Many colonists moving to new regions loaded all their possessions in a Conestoga wagon—a large canvas-covered vehicle pulled by a team of horses.

Settling New Mexico

The province of New Mexico, the largest and most important center of settlement in the Spanish Borderlands, was populated almost entirely by migration within North America. For example, in 1692, 44 families from the capital city of Santa Fe, relocated and founded a new community called Santa Cruz. In Santa Fe, these families were replaced by other migrants from the settlement of Nueva Vizcaya to the south. Internal migration kept moving the population northward and outward. From time to time, Indian wars drove the settlers back to the south, but they always moved out again.

* **Spanish Borderlands** northern part of New Spain, area now occupied by Florida, Texas, New Mexico, Arizona, and California

* **New Spain** Spanish colonial empire in North America; included Mexico, the area now occupied by Florida, Texas, New Mexico, Arizona, and California, and various Caribbean islands

The level of migration within North America increased greatly in the 1700s. The defeat and exile of the Indians had opened up so much territory that colonists now expected to own large farms. They wanted to have enough land not only to feed their families but also to produce crops for sale and to provide farmland for their children. To achieve this goal, they had to migrate to frontier areas.

Colonists born in New York and New England tended to move north and northeast, up the Connecticut and Hudson River valleys, establishing new settlements in northeastern New York, western Massachusetts, and northern New England. Some people from this region also moved south, into the hills of northeastern Pennsylvania. Settlers in Pennsylvania or the southern colonies were more likely than their northern neighbors to move to locations more than 100 miles away. Migrants from southeastern Pennsylvania—many originally from Germany, Scotland, and Ireland—moved southwest along the Great Wagon Road that ran from the Susquehanna River into the mountain valleys of Maryland, Virginia, and the Carolinas.

Like the Native Americans, enslaved African Americans made forced migrations. When European colonists moved into the interior of the southern colonies to establish new tobacco and rice plantations, they took their slaves with them. Although many of these moves involved distances of less than 20 miles, they were deeply disruptive to black families.

French and Spanish Migration. Migration followed somewhat different patterns in the French colonies. For the French, one of the most attractive features of North America was the ease with which they could travel and relocate. As a result, they tended to move around a great deal. The St. Lawrence River led French explorers, traders, and settlers to the Great Lakes, which in turn led to many western rivers. The French quickly learned to use the bark of the white birch tree to make CANOES for river travel. In addition, the French generally maintained friendly relations with the Indians and did not drive them off their lands. Consequently, French settlers were able to migrate into Indian territory.

However, the best-known group of French migrants did not move voluntarily. These were the ACADIANS, driven out of their Nova Scotia homeland by the British in the 1750s. After long wanderings, many of them settled in LOUISIANA, where their descendants became known as Cajuns.

The European settlement of the Spanish Borderlands* took place very slowly, in a series of advances and retreats, between the late 1500s and the 1800s. It was achieved mainly by migrations within North America. Faced with hostile Indian tribes and rough terrain, the Spanish government organized expeditions from New Spain* to the Borderlands. Another type of migration in the region was the forcible relocation of Indians. Small-scale migration by individuals also occurred in the Borderlands, sometimes quite quickly. Word of a mining strike might lure scores of prospectors into an area, while Indian attacks or a spell of bad weather could push settlers to pull up stakes and move to a new location.

The various provinces of the Spanish Borderlands developed separately, with almost no migration from one to another. Each province's system of forts, missions, villages, and towns was linked to New Spain but cut off

from the other provinces, which lay hundreds of miles away across mountains and deserts. This meant that each province developed its own culture and economy.

Group Migrations. One important feature of internal migration in all the colonies was its communal nature. Despite the popular image of the pioneer family setting off alone to carve out a wilderness homestead, most people who moved to frontier areas did so in larger groups. Extended families, clusters of friends, and a number of people from the same community often relocated together. Sometimes they followed one another to new areas in a process called chain migration. Of the hundreds of migrants who moved from New France to the Illinois country in the 1700s, for example, almost half were following relatives who had already made the journey. The communal nature of migration meant that many new settlements were made up of people from similar backgrounds, who shared the same customs and beliefs. (*See also* **Immigration; Land Ownership; Transportation and Travel.**)

Military Forces

* *aristocrat* member of the highest social class, often nobility

* *pike* long sharpened pole used for stabbing

* *mercenary* hired soldier

From the start, the colonization of North America involved the military. The European powers that settled the new continent—England, the Netherlands, France, and Spain—used military force to gain land, to protect themselves from internal threats such as rebellions, and to settle the inevitable conflicts over territory and trading rights with NATIVE AMERICANS and other Europeans. The frequent clashes, ranging from small local disputes to full-scale wars, cast a constant shadow over colonial life, especially in the early days of settlement and on the FRONTIER.

In the 1500s—when Europeans first started to colonize the Americas—a great change was taking place in European warfare. For many years, wars had been controlled by aristocrats*, who fought with armor, horses, and a tradition of military honor that dated back to the Middle Ages. But European rulers had learned that an army of ordinary foot soldiers, or infantry, armed with swords and pikes* could defeat armored men on horseback. The monarchs increasingly relied on mercenary* armies to enlarge their territories, control rebellious aristocrats, and stamp out internal disturbances.

The growing use of infantry was one element that revolutionized warfare. Firearms were another. Unlike heavy cannons, a musket was light enough for one man to carry. Unlike a sword or pike, it could kill at a hundred paces.

During the colonial period, European warfare became the business of armies of regulars, or professional full-time soldiers. Yet no European nation could afford to maintain a large standing army in its colonies, except in emergencies. Without strong protection from the home countries, colonists took responsibility for their own protection by forming MILITIA units of armed citizens. If a colony had no regulars, the militia provided the military force needed. Militiamen also fought alongside the regulars when necessary to strengthen a colony's military force.

British Forces

The English colonies were private ventures with almost no formal military support from the English government. Yet many leaders in the first colonies—including John SMITH in Virginia and Miles STANDISH in Massachusetts—were experienced soldiers who trained and led armed colonists in war against the Indians. From the start, the colonists depended on themselves for military protection. Each colony—except Pennsylvania—established a militia that called on able-bodied men to be available for military training. Ministers, college students, and public officials were excused from service. At first the ranks of the militia included blacks and even some friendly Indians, but later laws limited membership to whites.

The militia system had many weaknesses. Men who could afford to do so simply paid a fine instead of reporting for service. Positions as officers sometimes went to popular or wealthy individuals who had no military experience. To make matters worse, officers who happened to be running in local elections might cancel militia duties to gain votes. As a result, some militia companies were disorderly and ill-trained groups.

Volunteer Armies.   Gradually, the colonies shifted to a system of voluntary military service. Instead of calling out the entire militia, colonial authorities decided how many men they needed and offered a small payment to volunteers. All others were excused from militia duty. Although in theory each male citizen was still supposed to be ready to fight when necessary, in reality the volunteers usually met the need. If more soldiers were required, the authorities forced men into the ranks. They targeted the poor and homeless—individuals described by some laws as "loose and strolling persons."

This engraving by an artist named Godefroy, dating from around 1784, shows the surrender of the British forces led by General Charles Cornwallis at Yorktown, the final battle of the Revolutionary War.

* ***indentured servant*** person who agreed to work a certain length of time in return for passage on a ship to the colonies

* ***privateer*** privately owned ship authorized by the government to attack and capture enemy vessels; also the ship's master

Communities formed new volunteer units each year, generally disbanding them in the winter. There was little continuity from year to year, and each spring the officers had to train new volunteers. The only year-round military units in the English colonies were the small groups of paid scouts and rangers hired for their experience and skill. Ranger groups that patrolled the frontiers included some of the best fighters in the colonies.

Not all volunteers in the 1700s came from the enrolled militia. Some were runaway indentured servants*. Blacks and Native Americans were accepted both in volunteer army units and aboard the ships of the American privateers*, a volunteer naval force that attacked the ships and ports of Britain's enemies. Volunteers had no uniforms and wore only the clothes in which they had left home. They carried muskets and blankets. They also possessed an independence not found in regular army soldiers, for they knew that if military service became too unpleasant, they could simply walk away. Colonists often gave sympathy and shelter to deserters, and desertion was a serious problem at all times.

Regular Armies.   The high point of the volunteer system came in 1745, when an army of 3,000 New Englanders raised by Governor William Shirley of Massachusetts captured the mighty French fortress at LOUISBOURG. But in the mid-1700s, the growing tension between the French and the British prompted Great Britain to reinforce its American colonies with regular army units, or Redcoats as the Americans called them because of their red jackets.

In 1754 there were fewer than 1,000 regulars in British North America. But during the FRENCH AND INDIAN WAR against France (1756–1763), thousands of British regulars crossed the Atlantic. The British army and navy dominated the fighting, aided by small bands of Indians and colonial rangers. For the most part, the American volunteer units were limited to the routine work of warfare, such as building roads and guarding supplies.

After winning the war, Britain decided to keep a large force of about 7,500 regulars in North America—possibly to defend the colonies against hostile Indians or to control rebellious colonists. Parliament passed part of the cost of maintaining the troops on to the colonists, who protested vigorously. Conflict over the presence of Redcoats in the colonies and the taxes that colonies had to pay to support them was a leading cause of the AMERICAN REVOLUTION.

Dutch Forces

Soldiers were a constant presence in the 40-year history of the colony of NEW NETHERLAND. Dutch troops sailed to North America with the first colonists in the 1620s and looked on from the walls of the fort in NEW AMSTERDAM as the colony's governor surrendered to the English in 1664. None of these soldiers belonged to a national army, however. They were professional fighting men employed by the DUTCH WEST INDIA COMPANY, which ran New Netherland under a charter* from the government of the Netherlands. The number of company troops in the colony increased from about 150 in the 1620s to about 550 in 1664. Approximately half of them were Dutch. German, Swedish, Danish, English, Scottish, Irish, and Swiss mercenaries made

* ***charter*** written grant from a government conferring certain rights and privileges

Press Gangs

Many soldiers and sailors in Europe's armies were poor, landless, unemployed, or possibly convicts. Even a grim life of military service looked good to some of these men. But when too few individuals volunteered, the military turned to other means. Armed recruiters called "press gangs" bullied or forced men into enlisting. At times they simply kidnapped people, using the excuse that the country needed their services—a practice known as impressment. In 1747 a Boston mob rioted to protest the British Royal Navy's habit of impressing American sailors. This practice provided another reason for the growing tension between American colonists and the British.

up the rest. All the soldiers had enlisted for terms of three or four years. They lived in barracks inside the colony's forts. Many were rough individuals, given to drinking, brawling, gambling, and fighting with knives when off duty. Those who broke discipline while on duty faced severe physical punishment—usually a whipping.

The company soldiers generally relied on three weapons: a musket, a half-pike—a stabbing weapon used for close-in fighting—and a dagger. Most of their battles involved hand-to-hand combat with Native Americans rather than the organized field maneuvers of European warfare. In colonial fighting, skill with hand weapons often meant the difference between victory and defeat.

The West India Company kept troops in New Netherland to defend the colony from foreign conquest and Indian attacks. In reality, though, the soldiers' principal military activity was against Indian villages. Some of these raids turned into brutal assaults on women and children. The only successful European-style military operation in New Netherland's history was the 1655 conquest of New Sweden, a short-lived Swedish colony on the Delaware River.

French Forces

The French colony of NEW FRANCE was run at first by trading companies, which were unwilling or unable to pay for major military forces. When French settlers suffered devastating attacks from the IROQUOIS CONFEDERACY in the 1630s and 1640s, militiamen fought side by side with the colony's few soldiers.

The colony came under royal control in 1663, and the French king Louis XIV sent troops to force the Iroquois to a peace settlement. Some of those soldiers returned to France at the end of this mission, but about 400 remained in the colony as settlers. France later sent additional forces from the army and the marines, a body of troops trained by the navy. The marines formed the center of New France's military force until the 1750s. About 2,000 were stationed in Canada, the province along the St. Lawrence River. The fort at Louisbourg and the colony of LOUISIANA each had several thousand marines.

Officers in the marines performed a wide range of functions beyond strictly military duties. As commanders of forts and trading posts, they were deeply involved in negotiations and relationships between the French government and Indian tribes. They also kept an eye on the fur trade and undertook many journeys of exploration into the interior.

As tension grew between France and Great Britain in the 1750s, both nations sent troops to reinforce the military strength of their North American colonies. By 1757 there were nearly 5,000 regular infantry soldiers in New France. Friction arose between the new army soldiers and the marines. Most army officers were haughty French-born aristocrats, while a growing number of marine officers considered themselves North Americans and felt at home in the wilderness and comfortable in their dealings with Indians and local militiamen. The marines were especially angry that the army troops received much higher pay. Quarrels broke out frequently.

The basic weapon of all the French troops was the musket. With the attachment of a short stabbing blade called a bayonet, the musket became a

weapon for hand-to-hand fighting as well as a firearm. The French soldiers wore distinctive blue-and-white woolen uniforms. But the marines had difficulty getting replacements from France and eventually adopted the clothes worn by the Canadians or the Indians, which were generally more comfortable and durable than uniforms. The regulars continued to wear their uniforms for some time. They had a better supply system—until the British navy began seizing supplies sent to them from France.

One important piece of French colonial military history was the development of a new way of fighting called *la petite guerre* (the little war)—better known by its Spanish name of guerrilla* fighting. Inspired by the Indians, the French learned to use small-scale, lightning-quick raids and attacks. Guerrilla parties, often made up of French marines and their Indian allies, could cover long distances, strike swiftly, and then disappear before the enemy could counterattack. Guerrilla warfare broke lines of communication, destroyed supplies, and confused and terrorized the enemy population. This powerful and effective technique would eventually be used by forces around the world. However, neither guerrilla fighting nor large-scale, European-style battles could save the French from defeat by the British in 1763 in the French and Indian War.

Spanish Forces

For three centuries, from 1550 to 1850, the Spanish Borderlands* was a vast territory dotted with isolated frontier outposts*. Spain viewed this region of mountains, deserts, and hostile Indian tribes not as a prized possession of its empire but as a buffer zone* to protect the central, settled areas of NEW SPAIN from invasion. The Spanish developed two institutions to govern the Borderlands. One was the MISSION, which introduced the Indians to Christianity and controlled their labor. The other was the PRESIDIO, the frontier military base. Military life in the Borderlands centered on presidios.

The nature of Spain's military forces changed over time. In the 1500s, a typical military outpost might consist of four or five soldiers, perhaps accompanied by their families. Outnumbered by the Indians, these soldiers counted on their firearms, their knowledge—however limited—of military maneuvers and techniques, and the support of the local militia. Gradually, the armed forces became larger, better organized, and more professional. By around 1600, a typical military outpost had perhaps 25 men led by a captain. Over time the presidio officially increased to 50 soldiers, but it was common for a base to have as few as 10. If the commander needed more troops, he would recruit them from the local militia. In addition to the soldiers, the presidio might house a civilian population of crafts workers, missionaries, and officers' family members.

Army organization was simple at the bottom but more complicated at the top. Enlisted men, or *soldados,* were either foot or mounted soldiers. Sergeants, responsible for discipline, supply, and training, led companies of soldiers. The top officer of a presidio was a captain, but sometimes a captain could be outranked by an individual known as a sergeant major. This was a civilian administrator such as a lieutenant governor or a mayor who had received military rank and privileges as part of the benefits of his civil office. Spanish society

* *guerrilla* type of warfare involving sudden raids by small groups of warriors

* *Spanish Borderlands* northern part of New Spain, area now occupied by Florida, Texas, New Mexico, Arizona, and California

* *outpost* frontier settlement or military base

* *buffer zone* neutral area between two enemy areas

This print by Josephus Ximeno, published in 1821, shows Spanish soldiers defeating "rebels" in Mexico. Clashes with the Indians occurred throughout the history of the Spanish colonies.

* *status* social position

attached a great deal of status* to titles, some of which had little real meaning and were handed out as honorary awards. When a captain and a sergeant major both claimed authority over the same presidio, the personalities, popularity, and past achievements of the individuals involved determined who really ran the base and issued orders.

Men who could afford a better life did not become soldiers—being assigned to a presidio was hard and boring and, from time to time, dangerous. Indians sometimes overran and destroyed small, remote presidios. The Spanish usually responded with attacks on rebellious Indian communities. In some parts of the Borderlands, the cycle of violence continued for years, with the military abusing the Indians and the Indians revolting against the Spanish. Occasionally, Native American resistance broke out into large-scale, open

warfare, such as the PUEBLO REVOLT of 1680. This uprising, which drove the Spanish out of New Mexico for a time, made Spanish military commanders aware of the limitations of their small, isolated military bases. After the revolt, militia enrollments increased throughout the Borderlands.

The 1700s brought reforms to many aspects of Spanish colonial administration, including the military. The presidios began to change from community centers to fully military forts staffed by professional soldiers and commanded by officers who were separate from local governments. By the late 1770s, traveling military inspectors reported regularly on the condition of each presidio. Officers and soldiers whose conduct did not meet military standards could face charges in court. Sloppy, lazy, once-neglected frontier outposts began to change into more professional fighting organizations. The Borderlands military still did not have enough men, and many of those it had were poorly trained and equipped. Yet it was able to keep control of the Borderlands and protect settlers as they moved into new areas. (*See also* **Continental Army; Warfare and Diplomacy; Weapons.**)

Militia

* *parish* church district

* *Spanish Borderlands* northern part of New Spain, area now occupied by Florida, Texas, New Mexico, Arizona, and California

During the colonial period, European settlers in North America needed armed forces to defend themselves against various dangers—Indian attacks, clashes with rival nations, and rebellions from within. However, European powers found that keeping regular army units in North America was expensive. Besides, they often needed their troops for wars in Europe. The solution, rooted in an old tradition of part-time soldiering, was for the colonial governments to create militias—bodies of citizens who could take up arms in case of war or emergency.

Each European power in North America had some form of militia. Unlike regular soldiers, members of the militia did not enlist in the army. Instead, these citizen-soldiers formed companies by town, county, or parish*. In most cases, prominent men in the community, such as judges, prosperous farmers, or merchants, served as militia officers.

In the Spanish Borderlands*, ranchers, merchants, and miners formed militia units to help the regular soldiers in their frequent clashes with Native Americans. The Spanish crown employed a *maestre de campo,* or field marshal, to head each militia company. These marshals often paid for the equipment used by the militiamen serving under them.

Militia service was obligatory in the French colony of NEW FRANCE—all healthy men between the ages of 15 and 60 had to be prepared to serve. However, only a portion of the available men served at any one time, leaving the others to work their farms and tend their businesses. The colony could also call on citizens to provide labor for military-related activities, such as building forts and roads and transporting supplies.

In the Dutch colony of NEW NETHERLAND, citizen-soldiers took part in all military operations. They fought beside the colony's regular troops in Indian wars, stockpiled weapons, practiced maneuvers in case of war with English colonists, and helped build and repair forts.

Militiamen made up the British colonies' primary defense against Indian attacks and internal revolts such as BACON'S REBELLION. Every colony but

Pennsylvania required able-bodied adult white males to belong to a militia, though they excused ministers and certain other individuals. In some cases, the governor or legislative assembly appointed officers, while in others the militiamen chose their leaders. Officers were supposed to assemble and train their men several times a year.

As war with Great Britain approached, patriots* gained control of the militia. Militiamen made up nearly half of the colonial troops fighting for independence in the AMERICAN REVOLUTION. (*See also* **Military Forces.**)

* **patriot** American colonist who supported independence from Britain

Mining

See *Industries.*

Minuit, Peter

See *New Netherland; Swedish Settlements.*

Minutemen

* **patriot** American colonist who supported independence from Britain

Although the term *minutemen* came into use as early as 1756, it will forever be associated with the patriots* who took up arms at the beginning of the AMERICAN REVOLUTION. These men, who claimed they could be ready to fight with only "a minute's warning," faced the British at the historic Battles of LEXINGTON AND CONCORD that launched the War of Independence.

In 1774 the colonists were moving closer to war with Great Britain, and nowhere were tensions higher than in Massachusetts. Patriot leaders decided

Massachusetts minutemen fought in the first skirmishes of the Revolutionary War. This woodcut, based on a work by Felix O. C. Darley, depicts minutemen setting out to strike "the first blow for liberty" at the Battle of Concord.

* *militia* army of citizens who may be called into action in a time of emergency
* *Loyalist* American colonist who remained faithful to Britain during the American Revolution

See color plate 7, vol. 4.

to reorganize the Massachusetts militia* units because some of them were controlled by Loyalists*. They asked Loyalist officers to resign and then divided the colony's three militia regiments into seven new regiments. One-third of the militia forces would be minutemen, supporters of the patriot cause. Over the next year, Massachusetts developed a double system of regiments, some of minutemen and some of regular militiamen—many of whom were also patriots.

In April 1775, minutemen and militiamen joined forces against the British troops marching on Concord. Minutemen fell to British bullets in Lexington, and men from the two groups attacked the British as they marched back to Boston. In June the SECOND CONTINENTAL CONGRESS organized an American army to fight for independence from Britain. Both minutemen and militiamen from Massachusetts joined the new CONTINENTAL ARMY, commanded by George WASHINGTON. The militia remained active and often fought alongside the army on a regional basis. The minutemen ceased to exist in Massachusetts, but a few units of minutemen were formed in Maryland, New Hampshire, and Connecticut to aid the army on special brief assignments. (*See also* **Independence Movements; Loyalists.**)

Missions and Missionaries

From the time Europeans began exploring North America, the majority of their expeditions included missionaries to convert the Indians to Christianity. Most of the missionaries came from France or Spain. As part of their work, they often created communities for the converted Indians. The purpose of these missions was to protect the converts and to strengthen their new faith by isolating them from old ways and from nonbelievers.

Missionaries in North America had a strong desire to bring salvation to the Indians. Most sincerely believed they were helping the Native Americans, but their work often aided European conquest instead. Convinced of the superiority of European culture, many missionaries required Indians to change their way of living as well as their religion. In this way, missionaries contributed to the destruction of Native American social systems, values, and customs.

British

Few British missionaries worked among the Indians. The British colonies contained far more white settlers than the Spanish Borderlands* or the French colonies, and the colonists' religious needs came first. In addition, the number of Indians living along the Atlantic coast declined, as many died in wars with colonists and the survivors moved farther west. With the notable exception of the Catholic priest Andrew White, who lived among the Piscataway Indians of Maryland, British Protestants conducted all missionary work.

New England Colonies. According to the charter of the Massachusetts Bay colony of 1630, one reason the PURITANS came to North America was to

* *Spanish Borderlands* northern part of New Spain, area now occupied by Florida, Texas, New Mexico, Arizona, and California

convert the Indians. Many Puritans, however, regarded Native Americans as subhuman—even demonic—and incapable of conversion, and they made almost no attempt to Christianize them.

One Puritan minister who did make the effort was John Eliot. In 1646 the "Apostle to the Indians," as Eliot became known, began preaching to a group from a Massachusetts tribe. Besides preaching to Indians in their native tongue, Eliot also translated the entire Bible into the Algonquian language.

Eliot established 14 towns in the Boston area where his Indian converts could live like white people. The "Praying Indians," or "red Puritans," put fences around their land, raised farm animals, and read their Bibles in church on Sunday. English colonists regarded these communities as models of successful missionary work. Even so, during the anti-Indian hysteria of KING PHILIP'S WAR (1675–1676), colonists falsely accused the Praying Indians of treason and sent them to camps, where many died from cold or malnutrition.

Another notable New England missionary was Eleazar WHEELOCK. A Congregationalist minister in Lebanon, Connecticut, Wheelock developed a new approach for spreading Christianity. He believed that the Native Americans themselves would make the best missionaries, and in 1754 he began training Indian youths in his preparatory school. Except for one pupil, the famous Indian preacher Samson OCCOM, Wheelock's idea failed—his Indian students had become too "European" and were not accepted by their own people. Wheelock later moved his school to New Hampshire, where he founded Dartmouth College, an institution originally intended for the education of Indians.

Middle and Southern Colonies. The Church of England conducted missionary work in the middle and southern colonies. In 1701 the Reverend Thomas Bray, the church's representative to the colonies, founded the Society for the Propagation of the Gospel in Foreign Parts to organize and support evangelism* among Indians and African slaves. During the 1700s, more than 300 missionaries from the society traveled up and down the Atlantic coast. They usually paid short visits to various Indian tribes, but some, such as John Brainerd and Samuel Kirkland, lived among the Indians.

evangelism spreading and preaching the Christian gospel

French

The JESUITS, a religious brotherhood of the ROMAN CATHOLIC CHURCH, carried out almost all missionary work in the colony of New France. In 1625 the first three Jesuit volunteers arrived in Quebec, and others soon followed. The Jesuits worked mainly in the St. Lawrence River valley and the Great Lakes region and primarily among the HURON, IROQUOIS, OJIBWA, and ILLINOIS INDIANS. After the British conquest of Canada and the Spanish acquisition of Louisiana, French Jesuit missionary work in North America declined markedly.

The Jesuits brought a unique perspective and distinct principles to their work among the Native Americans. Above all, they respected the Indians' languages, symbols, and beliefs. They sought to convert Native Americans to Christian beliefs and values while at the same time preserving important aspects of their culture. The independent-minded Jesuits refused to tie

Missions and Missionaries

Not all missionaries in the French colonies were men. The nuns who lived at the Ursuline Convent in Quebec (detail shown here) worked as nurses and teachers, helping Indian converts as well as French settlers.

Christianity to European ways. In other words, Indians did not have to become like white people in order to be Christians.

Besides bringing Christianity to specific Indian groups, the Jesuits made other notable contributions—many with far-reaching effects. In their travels to bring the word of God to Indians, the Jesuits explored lakes, rivers, and valleys and helped open the wilderness to trappers, traders, and settlers. Jesuit mission communities at Detroit, Pittsburgh, St. Louis, and many other places became the sites of future settlements. In addition, the Jesuits served as peacemakers between Indians and Europeans and often prevented armed conflicts. Their annual reports home, called *Relations,* provide an invaluable source of information about native populations in North America during colonial times.

Jesuits in Huron Territory.

Under the leadership of Jean de Brébeuf, the Jesuits achieved great success among the Huron Indians, who lived in present-day Ontario. By 1648, after 15 years of missionary work, Brébeuf and his associates had baptized 3,000 Hurons.

Following the custom of the Jesuits, these missionaries lived quietly among the Hurons. They spent years learning the Native Americans' language and customs. As much as possible, they followed Indian ways of doing things, including developing a taste for the wild game that the Hurons cooked over open fires. Rather than dressing in native style, however, the Jesuits maintained their traditional black cassocks*. For this reason, the Indians often referred to the Jesuits as "the blackrobes."

By sharing in their everyday life, the Jesuits gained the trust of the Hurons, which helped their missionary cause considerably. Instead of criticizing Huron

* *cassock* ankle-length garment with tight sleeves

beliefs, the Jesuits pointed out similarities between Christian teachings and the Indians' ideas. For example, the Hurons already worshiped a female deity named Aataentsic, who had a son, Iouskeha. The Jesuits compared this goddess and her son to the Virgin Mary and Jesus.

At first Huron converts continued to live among their people rather than in separate mission communities. After a while, though, the new Christians began to form their own groups within villages. This separation made the Hurons vulnerable to attack, a fact that the Iroquois Indians used to their advantage. In 1648 the Iroquois launched a ferocious war against the Hurons, killing most of them or driving them from their homes. The Iroquois executed Brébeuf and another priest. The remaining Jesuits, along with Huron survivors, fled to Quebec. Eventually they started a Christian town named Jeune Lorette—all that remained of the Jesuit missionary work among the Hurons.

Jesuits in Iroquois Territory.

The Iroquois lived to the south of the Hurons in present-day New York State. The Jesuits had less success in converting the Iroquois, primarily because of Jesuit ties to the Hurons, bitter enemies of the Iroquois. Allied with the British, the Iroquois also hated the French.

One Jesuit who attempted to bring the gospel to the Iroquois was Isaac Jogues. In 1646 Jogues negotiated a peace agreement between French government officials and the Mohawk Indians, one of the five tribes of the Iroquois Confederacy. Thinking peace had been established, Jogues entered Iroquois lands to begin missionary work. A few months later some Iroquois Indians killed him, believing he was responsible for recent sickness and poor harvests.

Jesuits and Western Indians.

Western Indians included the Ojibwa, Illinois, and many other tribes who inhabited present-day Michigan, Wisconsin, and Minnesota. Claude Jean Allouez, one of the most effective Jesuit missionaries in the French colonies, worked among the western Indians for 25 years. Traveling thousands of miles in the wilderness, he contacted at least 20 different tribes. Allouez, known as the "Apostle of the West," reportedly baptized 10,000 Indians.

Allouez arrived in the western region in the mid-1660s. In 1665 he built a bark chapel—La Pointe du Saint Esprit—on the western end of Lake Superior. Dozens of tribes traveled through the area, and soon a small number of converts began to settle around the chapel, forming a unique intertribal community of Christian Indians.

When Allouez left to work in Green Bay on Lake Michigan, Jacques Marquette continued efforts at La Pointe. Marquette eventually moved the mission to an island between Lakes Michigan and Huron to escape the rampaging Dakota Indians. The mission, called St. Ignace, flourished. Marquette became a well-known explorer, accompanying Louis JOLLIET in 1673 on an expedition that proved the Mississippi River flows south to the Gulf of Mexico, not west to the Pacific Ocean. Along the route, Marquette encountered Illinois Indians and set up a mission among them.

Jesuits in Louisiana Territory.

Jesuit missionary activities in the lower Mississippi River valley faced many difficulties. First, the Indians in

Remember: *Words in small capital letters have separate entries, and the index at the end of Volume 4 will guide you to more information on many topics.*

the area resisted the Jesuits' efforts. The Jesuits also lacked the support of important Catholic religious authorities in the region. Without money to build missions, many Jesuits instead served as chaplains to white settlers. Except for Fort Rosalie on the site of present-day Natchez, Mississippi, the Jesuits established no significant mission communities in the region.

Spanish

Another Catholic brotherhood, the Franciscans, conducted most of the missionary work in the Spanish Borderlands. They first came to North America with Spanish expeditions of exploration. The friar* Juan Suárez, for instance, accompanied conqueror and explorer Pánfilo de Narváez into Florida in 1528. Francisco Vásquez de Coronado's famous journey throughout the Southwest in 1540 included four Franciscans. One of them, Juan de Padilla, was killed by Indians and became the first missionary martyr* in North America.

The Franciscan way of doing missionary work differed considerably from that of the French Jesuits. Rather than acting independently, they cooperated closely with Spanish government officials and the military, and

* **friar** member of a religious brotherhood

* **martyr** someone who suffers or dies for the sake of a cause or principle

The establishment of missions in the Spanish Borderlands was the first step in colonization. Numerous present-day cities in California, New Mexico, Arizona, and Texas developed around the sites of these mission settlements.

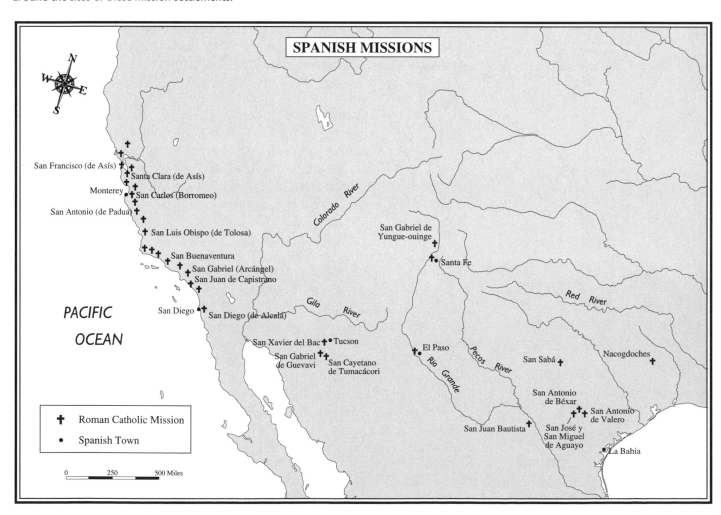

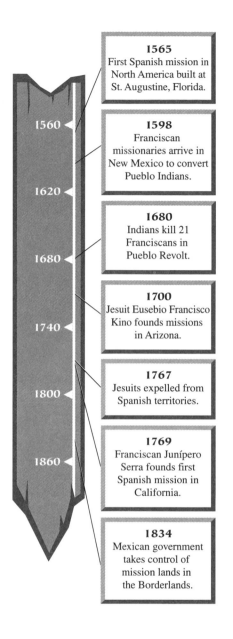

1565
First Spanish mission in North America built at St. Augustine, Florida.

1598
Franciscan missionaries arrive in New Mexico to convert Pueblo Indians.

1680
Indians kill 21 Franciscans in Pueblo Revolt.

1700
Jesuit Eusebio Francisco Kino founds missions in Arizona.

1767
Jesuits expelled from Spanish territories.

1769
Franciscan Junípero Serra founds first Spanish mission in California.

1834
Mexican government takes control of mission lands in the Borderlands.

* *presidio* Spanish fort built to protect mission settlements

* *outpost* frontier settlement or military base

they played a large part in Spain's colonizing efforts. The Franciscans believed that Spanish culture and Christianity went hand in hand. In their view, Indians had to accept the authority of the Spanish king and adopt Spanish customs before becoming Christians.

Along with Spanish mission settlements came the presidio*. The soldiers not only protected the settlement but also, at times, used force to persuade Indians to convert to Christianity. Missions and presidios served as the first outposts* of Spanish colonization in the Borderlands.

Franciscans in Florida. In 1565 the Spanish built ST. AUGUSTINE on the northeast coast of Florida. Now the oldest European settlement in the United States, St. Augustine contained a mission as well as a fort. The Franciscans intended to use the military post as a base for missionary expeditions into the Florida peninsula and beyond. Though the mission had some success converting Indians in the early years, it suffered from attacks by hostile Indians, interference from English colonists to the north, and lack of money. It eventually closed down.

Franciscans in New Mexico. Twelve Franciscans accompanied the 1598 expedition of Juan de OÑATE to establish a Spanish settlement in what is now NEW MEXICO. Besides ministering to the 500 colonists, the Franciscans wanted to Christianize the PUEBLO INDIANS, which would bring them under Spanish control and make future colonization easier. At that time, the Pueblo consisted of about 80,000 people, living in more than 100 towns. They had one of the most advanced civilizations of all North American Indian tribes.

The Spanish—particularly the Franciscans—failed to recognize the strengths and achievements of the Pueblo people. They looked down on Pueblo culture and disapproved of the Pueblo religion. Unlike the Jesuits in New France, who used native beliefs to explain Christianity, the Franciscans in New Mexico believed they had a sacred responsibility to crush the Pueblo religion and replace it with Christianity.

The Franciscans ignored Pueblo languages and made no attempt to translate the Bible or prayers into native tongues. Instead, they expected Native American converts to learn Spanish. They also believed Indians who attended church should understand the Latin terms used in worship.

Usually no more than 40 Franciscans served at any one time—a small number considering the vast territory of New Mexico. They traveled from town to town, never staying in one place very long. While this policy allowed the missionaries to cover more territory, it also prevented them from forming close bonds with members of their congregations and learning about Indian culture.

Despite Franciscan attitudes and methods of operation, thousands of Pueblo converted to Christianity. Raised to be cooperative, Pueblo people often converted—or seemed to convert—simply to be polite. At other times, threats of violence by Spanish soldiers convinced them to accept Christianity.

Over time Pueblo anger over their treatment by the Franciscans built up. The missionaries publicly burned Indian masks and other religious items and whipped those caught worshiping Pueblo gods. In addition, repeated crop

failures and an outbreak of disease caused many Indians to believe that they had made a mistake in accepting the new religion. Open rebellion finally erupted during the PUEBLO REVOLT of 1680. An alliance of Pueblo people from all over New Mexico attacked more than 30 Spanish settlements, driving out the colonists. The real target of their rage, however, seemed to be the Franciscans. While killing relatively few colonists, the Indians murdered 21 of the 33 friars and burned their churches.

The Spanish government quickly set about restoring order. It took more than 15 years, however, before government troops reclaimed all the lost territory and extinguished the last sparks of the revolt. In the process, they slaughtered thousands of Indians, drastically reducing the Pueblo population to 14,000. The Spanish government blamed the Franciscans for the revolt, and as a result, the friars lost much of their power. The Franciscans themselves decided to change their methods. After 1700 they began relying more on persuasion than force to win converts.

Franciscans in Texas.   The Franciscans made several attempts to establish missions in Texas, but they experienced frequent misfortunes and setbacks. The fiercely independent APACHE and COMANCHE made the missionaries' work especially frustrating and dangerous. As a result, the Franciscans produced few lasting results in the vast region named after the Teja Indians. The best known of their early missions is San Antonio de Valero, or the Alamo.

Kino in Arizona.   The Franciscans were not the only missionary group in the Spanish Borderlands. Spanish Jesuits, such as Eusebio Francisco KINO, also took part in the campaign to spread Christianity in the Southwest.

Working among the PIMA and TOHONO O'ODHAM Indians, Kino and his associates established more than 20 mission communities in present-day Mexico and Arizona. Kino introduced wheat, cattle, and other livestock to his missions so that they became, in effect, self-supporting cattle ranches. These Christian ranches also supplied beef to other settlements.

Kino's mission communities had other unique features. A firm believer in the intelligence and capabilities of Native Americans, Kino recruited Christian Indians to serve as missionaries among their own people. This wise and gentle "Apostle of Sonora and Arizona" traveled thousands of miles on mule and on horseback, personally baptizing about 4,000 Pima Indians.

The Jesuits' tendency to set up self-governing missions that preserved Indian culture clashed with the master plan of the Spanish government and the Catholic Church. In 1767 the government expelled the Jesuits from Spanish territories and turned their missions over to the Franciscans.

Franciscans in California.   Missionary work in California got under way in the late 1700s, when Spain began colonizing the region. Junípero SERRA, director of missions, skillfully guided the establishment of Franciscan missions along California's coast. He founded the first mission, San Diego de Alcala, in 1769 and eight others in the following years.

The Franciscans of the 1700s still linked Christianity with Spanish culture, and they worked closely with the military. As in New Mexico, they

Mission Life

Life in a California mission was peaceful and stable. Mission compounds generally contained a church, a convent, dormitories, a school, storerooms, and workshops. Surrounding the mission were orchards, gardens, and fields that provided food for the inhabitants. A typical day at the mission included prayers, meals, work in the fields or craft shops for the adults, and school for the children. The routine of mission life helped Indian converts to Christianity feel safe, strengthened their faith, and introduced them to European ways.

See
color plate 7,
vol. 1.

frequently resorted to physical punishment, causing resentment among the Native Americans. Thousands of mission Indians died from epidemic diseases and poor nutrition. Many ran away and joined inland groups in raids on the missions. During his administration, Serra did obtain permission from the pope to confirm Native Americans as full church members, an indication of some change in attitude toward the Indians.

Mission communities in the 1700s had changed as well. Besides instructing the Indians in Christianity, the Franciscans taught them European skills such as carpentry, masonry, and blacksmithing. They also showed Native Americans how to live like Europeans by constructing permanent houses, planting and harvesting crops, and ranching.

When Serra died in 1784, Fermín Francisco de Lasuén carried on his work for the next 18 years, adding 9 more missions. By 1823 a total of 21 Franciscan communities—with adobe walls and red-tiled roofs—dotted the California coast. The glory days of the missions were soon to end, however. As Spain's power began to fade, financial support for the missions diminished. Then in 1834, an independent Mexican government seized almost all mission lands, greatly reducing the influence of the Franciscans. (*See also* **Protestant Churches.**)

Mississippi River

tributary stream or river that empties into a larger river

*T*he Mississippi River has played an important role in American history since colonial times, providing a passageway into and out of the heart of the continent. The mighty river served as a highway for explorers and settlers and as a boundary between the territories of different nations. The Spanish, French, British, and Americans used the Mississippi and competed for its control. On more than one occasion, people almost went to war over it.

From its source in Lake Itasca, Minnesota, the Mississippi flows south for more than 2,300 miles to empty into the Gulf of Mexico. It is the longest river in North America and the third longest in the world—only the Nile and the Amazon rivers are longer. The Mississippi begins in the north as a clear, rapid stream. The river's center stretch, swollen by water from many tributaries*, is more than a mile wide in places. At the southern end, the Mississippi becomes a delta, branching into a maze of channels that wind among islands to the Gulf of Mexico. The Missouri and Ohio rivers are among the many tributaries that flow into the Mississippi, forming a vast navigation network.

Long before Europeans arrived in the Americas, Native Americans flourished along the central and southern part of the Mississippi River. Scholars refer to these early Indian societies as the Mississippian culture. The NATCHEZ INDIANS who lived in the region were descendants of this group.

The European exploration of the Mississippi River began with Hernando DE SOTO, the Spanish conqueror who led his troops to its banks in 1541. More than a century passed before the arrival of other Europeans was recorded. In 1673 the French explorers Louis JOLLIET and Father Jacques Marquette went as far south as the point where the Arkansas River enters the Mississippi. A few years later, René-Robert Cavelier, Sieur de LA SALLE, journeyed south along the river to the Gulf. His trip established France's claim to the river and the land around it, but he failed in his attempt to establish a colony at the

mouth of the river. In 1718 Pierre Le Moyne, Sieur d'IBERVILLE, founded a French colony at NEW ORLEANS. Other French settlements, such as St. Louis, appeared in the years that followed.

The French controlled the river until 1763, when they were defeated by the British in the FRENCH AND INDIAN WAR. For the next 20 years, the Mississippi was the border between British territory on the east bank and Spanish territory on the west. Under the 1783 treaty that ended the American Revolution, the territory of the United States extended to the Mississippi, and Americans had the right to use the river for shipping. However, the Spanish controlled the port of New Orleans at the river's mouth, making it difficult for Americans to exercise this right. Conflict developed between the Spanish and the Americans over the use of the river. The tension continued after Spain transferred Louisiana to France in 1800. When the United States purchased Louisiana from France in 1803, Americans finally gained full and unlimited use of the Mississippi. The river soon became one of the major shipping waterways of the world. (*See also* **Transportation and Travel.**)

Mississippian Culture

See *Native Americans: Early Peoples of North America.*

Mohawk Indians

See *Iroquois Confederacy.*

Molasses Act (1733)

*P*arliament passed the Molasses Act in 1733 in an attempt to protect sugar growers in the British WEST INDIES. The act placed high taxes on sugar, molasses, and rum imported into the North American colonies from non-British islands.

Molasses—a by-product of sugar manufacturing—was an important item in the colonial economy because it was used to make rum, a popular alcoholic drink. Most of the rum producers were located in New England and the middle colonies, particularly in the cities of Boston, Newport, Philadelphia, and New York. These distillers sold some of the rum within the colonies and shipped the surplus to Africa, where it was sold to European slave traders in exchange for slaves. The ships that had brought the rum sailed to the West Indies, loaded with slaves, who could be sold or traded for more molasses. The ships then carried the molasses back to New England. This three-way trade benefited the sugar planters in the islands, the slave traders in Africa, and the distillers in the American colonies.

Some of the sugar-producing islands in the West Indies were controlled by the British, while others belonged to the French and Dutch. American colonists purchased molasses from both British and foreign islands. In the 1730s, British sugar planters complained to Parliament about the purchase of foreign sugar products. Although the colonists protested that the British islands could not produce enough molasses for their needs, the sugar planters persuaded Parliament to pass the Molasses Act.

The act was not very effective in protecting the British sugar trade from foreign competition. Rather than pay the high taxes, the colonists began SMUGGLING molasses from Dutch and French islands. In the 1760s, the British revised their policy, lowering the taxes to such a point that smuggling was no longer worthwhile. (*See also* **Rum Trade; Sugar Act of 1764; Trade and Commerce.**)

Montcalm, Marquis de

See *French and Indian War; Quebec.*

Money and Finance

** **barter** exchange of goods and services without using money*

*T*he money and financial systems of the English, Dutch, French, and Spanish colonies shared certain characteristics. All the colonies relied on a combination of coins, paper money, and barter* to pay for goods and services. All the colonies also suffered from a chronic shortage of coins and, to a lesser extent, of paper currency. For this reason, they relied on the use of credit to carry on their business. In addition, colonial currencies generally had no fixed value and might vary greatly in different places and times. The lack of a stable currency together with European economic policies made the colonies dependent on their parent countries.

Barter.   Barter played a significant role as a medium of exchange in North America. But barter was useful only if each party involved in the exchange could offer something the other wanted. Many goods—including tobacco and grain—were used in barter. Furs were an important item of exchange in the early colonial period. Their value depended on the quality of the fur and the demand for a particular type.

In the Dutch colony of New Netherland, one of the most important barter items was WAMPUM—colored shells that the Indians traditionally used as a form of currency. The Dutch set up a barter system that involved the exchange of cloth, liquor, and firearms for the wampum of coastal tribes. They traded this wampum for furs of inland tribes. As the supply of wampum increased, its value began to decline. Dutch officials tried to stabilize the value of wampum by establishing an official exchange rate in 1650.

Coins.   Most of the money circulating in colonial America was in the form of metal coins. Coins were widely accepted and could be exchanged easily and promptly. Colonists normally kept a small supply of them to pay for everyday purchases, but few people, even the very rich, kept large amounts of money in their possession.

Coins of GOLD and SILVER were the most valuable, but copper, tin, and other metals were also used for coinage. Aside from Spanish America, most colonial regions lacked gold and silver. Spanish silver dollars were very popular in the British colonies and became the model for the coinage system developed in the United States after the American Revolution. Each dollar coin could be divided into eight pieces called *reales;* a quarter of a dollar was therefore "two bits"—a term still heard occasionally in the United States today.

Money and Finance

The British Parliament would not allow its colonies to mint* their own coins. Nor would it permit British coins to be exported to the colonies except to buy military supplies or to pay soldiers' wages. As a result, the British colonies relied heavily on foreign coins. Spanish gold and silver coins provided the bulk of coinage. French, Portuguese, and Dutch coins also were common.

The French government shipped gold and silver coins to its colony of New France on a regular basis to pay for military activities and the colonial administration. But the coins soon returned to France to purchase French manufactured goods, causing a shortage of currency in the colony. The situation was made worse because many colonists melted down the gold and silver coins to make jewelry, church ornaments, and other valuable objects. The French colony used Spanish coins—often obtained through illegal trade—to make up part of the shortage. Low-value French coins of copper and bronze were common as well.

Despite the abundance of precious metals in the Spanish colonies, most of their gold and silver was shipped to Europe. Spanish gold and silver coins also found their way to other European colonies through trade. As a result, even the Spanish colonies faced shortages of valuable coinage.

Paper Currencies. To supplement their supply of coins, the colonies relied on various types of paper currency. The value of paper currency varied even more than that of coins.

In some regions of the British colonies, farmers received paper certificates for tobacco or other crops. These tobacco certificates circulated widely as a medium of exchange and were the only form of paper money in circulation in Virginia until the 1750s. Bills of exchange, issued and backed by colonial governments for amounts ranging from 1 shilling to 20 pounds, were another type of money used in the British colonies. Most bills had a relatively small value, which made them useful for everyday financial transactions. Although each colony had its own bills, the money often circulated across colonial borders.

The Dutch colony of New Netherland also used bills of exchange, primarily for long-distance trading. In the Spanish colonies, wealthy merchant houses and individuals issued bills of exchange for cash. The bills could then be traded for goods. The person who received the bill could either present it for payment to the merchant who had issued it or give it to another person as part of a separate financial transaction.

Because of the shortage of gold and silver coins, many colonies issued their own paper money. The value of New Hampshire's five-shilling note was given as one-third of a Spanish dollar, a coin common in the British colonies.

Insuring Against Loss

Insurance is a service that helps protect people against the loss of their property or possessions. The first successful insurance company in North America, the Philadelphia Contributorship for the Insurance of Houses from Loss by Fire, was organized by Benjamin Franklin in 1752. Home owners paid a certain amount each year into a shared fund, receiving money if their homes suffered damage in a fire. If the fund ran out of money because of severe losses, all members would have to pay an additional amount. The company employed firefighters to combat blazes that threatened the insured properties.

* ***New Spain*** Spanish colonial empire in North America; included Mexico, the area now occupied by Florida, Texas, New Mexico, Arizona, and California, and various Caribbean islands

* ***collateral*** possession pledged to guarantee the repayment of a loan

Paper currency first appeared in New France in the late 1600s and early 1700s. Faced with a shortage of coins, royal officials gave a cash value to playing cards and then signed them. This "card money" was frequently issued to deal with financial emergencies. During the French and Indian War, a flood of card money appeared, causing its value to decline drastically.

Credit. Colonial economies relied heavily on credit—the ability to make a purchase and pay for it later. Credit developed in response to the chronic shortages of coins and paper currencies, as well as seasonal or temporary shortages. Farmers, for example, typically purchased supplies on credit and then paid the debt after harvesting and selling their crops. Merchants and shopkeepers often offered credit because it helped them sell their goods. Credit arrangements between merchants stimulated economic growth by promoting the flow of goods throughout the colonies and overseas.

Networks of credit developed throughout the colonies. In the British colonies, the use of credit increased steadily throughout the 1700s. The entire British colonial economy became linked through chains of credit that extended from domestic and foreign merchants and manufacturers to individual storekeepers and customers in remote areas.

In New Spain*, credit became the primary medium of exchange. Powerful merchants in Mexico City, the capital, extended credit to local merchants and various colonial officials. They, in turn, gave credit to individuals throughout New Spain, including the frontier regions to the north known as the Borderlands.

Financial Policies and Institutions. All the North American colonies were dependent on the financial policies and institutions of their parent countries. MERCANTILISM—the idea that colonies existed to increase the parent country's wealth and power—had an overwhelming impact on colonial finances. For example, most of the gold and silver mined in Spanish America had to be sent to royal treasuries in Spain, causing shortages of money in the Spanish colonies. In addition, the colonies generally traded cheap raw materials and products for expensive European manufactured goods. This meant that more money flowed out of the colonies than flowed into them, resulting in money shortages.

The British colonies issued paper currency whenever they needed money. Doing so, however, often increased the supply of currency so much that its value decreased. Parliament tried to stabilize the situation by passing laws that prohibited the colonies from issuing new paper currency. Many colonists resented this interference in their domestic affairs, and the issue contributed to growing tensions between the colonies and Britain.

Banks, as they exist today, did not develop in North America until after the colonial period. Financial affairs were handled by various governmental offices, businesses, and individuals. In the British colonies, the government set up public loan offices known as land banks, which made loans primarily for agricultural improvements or other business purposes. Property was used as collateral* for the loans.

In New Spain, large merchant firms, wealthy individuals, and the Catholic Church provided bank services. They not only made loans but also

safeguarded money and issued bills of exchange. Colonial officials, wealthy landowners, and missions offered similar financial services in the more remote Spanish Borderlands.

By the mid-1700s the British colonies had made great progress in developing systems of money and financial institutions independent of Britain. By contrast, Spain moved in the 1770s to link the finances of its colonies more closely to its own economy. (*See also* **Economic Systems; Taxation.**)

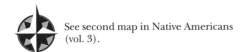

Montagnais Indians

See second map in Native Americans (vol. 3).

*T*he Montagnais Indians inhabited the woodlands north of the Gulf of St. Lawrence in what is now CANADA. During the 1600s, the French began settling this region, and their arrival greatly affected the lives of the Montagnais.

The name *Montagnais* comes from the French word for "mountaineers." Like their closely related neighbors, the Naskapi, the Montagnais spoke an Algonquian language. The tribe consisted of small groups of related families who spent winters inland and summers in camps along rivers and lakes. They built birch-bark wigwams, traveled by canoe and sled, and hunted and fished for food.

In 1603 a party of French explorers, including Samuel de CHAMPLAIN, met a group of the Montagnais at Tadoussac on the ST. LAWRENCE RIVER. The French soon established fur-trading posts and MISSIONS in the region. They also formed an alliance with the Montagnais and other tribes against the IROQUOIS CONFEDERACY. When the Iroquois attacked Montagnais communities in the 1600s, the French often intervened, startling the advancing Iroquois with the sound of their firearms.

The French gained from the alliance as well. During the 1700s, they faced increasing competition from the British for trade routes and land in North America. The Montagnais continued to work with the French, even raiding British settlements bordering the French colony. Today groups of Montagnais still live in this region of Canada. (*See also* **French and Indian War; Fur Trade; Native Americans.**)

Montesquieu

See *Political Thought.*

Montour, Madame

ca. 1684–ca. 1752
Interpreter

*M*adame Montour acted as an interpreter between Indians and British colonists in North America. For many years, she assisted the colonial authorities in New York and Pennsylvania during negotiations with the IROQUOIS CONFEDERACY.

Madame Montour may have been the daughter of a French colonist and an Indian woman. She claimed that she had been taken captive by Iroquois Indians when she was a child and that she had lived among the Iroquois for some time. Her impressive knowledge and abilities suggest that she had some formal education. She was married twice, both times to Indian men.

Madame Montour began her work for the colonists in 1711, when she served as interpreter at a conference between Governor Robert Hunter of New York and the chiefs of the Iroquois Confederacy. The following year she assisted Colonel Peter Schuyler of New York. He was meeting with the Iroquois to urge them not to join the war begun by the TUSCARORA INDIANS of North Carolina.

In 1717 Madame Montour moved to Pennsylvania. There she continued her work, acting as interpreter for the colony's governor during discussions with the Iroquois in the 1720s and 1730s. She was so successful in maintaining good relations between the Indians and the British that the French colonial authorities tried several times to convince her to work for them instead.

Montreal

palisade fence of stakes forming a defense

See map in New France (vol. 3).

outpost frontier settlement or military base

patriot American colonist who supported independence from Britain

Montreal was one of the principal towns in NEW FRANCE, the French colony in present-day CANADA. The center of the French FUR TRADE in North America, it was also the starting point for French exploration and colonization in the interior of the continent.

When French explorer Jacques CARTIER sailed up the ST. LAWRENCE RIVER in 1535, he traveled as far as the Indian village of Hochelaga. It was located on an island with a mountain in its center, and Cartier named the mountain Mont Real, or Mount Royal. Samuel de CHAMPLAIN, another French explorer, visited the island in 1603. The Indian village had disappeared, and the island soon became a gathering place for French traders. The first permanent settlement appeared in 1642, when missionaries built a fort and started a community on the island. They built palisades* around the town as protection against attacks by Indians of the IROQUOIS CONFEDERACY, enemies of the French.

Montreal grew slowly from a village of about 200 in 1650 to a town of 3,500 in 1710. During the 1720s, Montreal became an important economic center as the home of French fur-trading companies. Explorers, trappers, and traders gathered at Montreal to organize their expeditions into the *pays d'en haut,* the "upper country," as the remote Canadian interior was called.

In 1760, during the FRENCH AND INDIAN WAR, Montreal fell to an enemy for the first time. The British and the French were at war in Europe and in North America, and conditions were desperate in the French colony. QUEBEC, the other major town of New France, had already been taken over by British troops. The fate of Montreal depended on winds and tides—both a French and a British fleet were headed toward the city. The British arrived first and surrounded the city, ending French hopes of a victory. On September 8, the governor of New France surrendered Montreal to the British, along with all of France's remaining outposts* in Canada. After the war ended in 1763, the treaty of settlement confirmed that Montreal and all but two tiny islands of New France belonged to Great Britain.

During the AMERICAN REVOLUTION, some American patriots* attempted to strike a blow against Great Britain by attacking Canada. Ethan ALLEN of Vermont tried and failed to capture Montreal in September of 1775. Two months later, an American force under General Richard Montgomery advanced on the city. Guy Carleton, the governor of Canada, believed that Montreal could not be defended. He fled the city, allowing the American troops to

Monts, Pierre du Gua, Sieur de

This view of Montreal appeared in a 1768 collection called *Scenographia Americana*. At that time, the former French city had been in British hands for eight years.

capture it without a fight. Benjamin Franklin was part of a group of Americans who visited Montreal in an effort to persuade the Canadians to join them against the British. The Americans failed. Learning that a British army was marching on the city, the Americans withdrew, and the British reclaimed Montreal in June of 1776.

During and after the American Revolution, Montreal attracted many of the LOYALISTS who left former British colonies. The city flourished under British rule and remained an important fur-trading center for many years.

Monts, Pierre du Gua, Sieur de

See *Exploration, Age of: French.*

Moravians

See *Protestant Churches.*

Morgan, Henry

1635–1688
English buccaneer

*H*enry Morgan was one of the most famous of the English "brethren of the coast," sailors who preyed on England's enemies in the Caribbean Sea. The Spanish called Morgan a PIRATE, but to the English he was a PRIVATEER, an independent captain authorized to attack England's foes. Morgan and other privateers weakened Spain's authority, bringing some Caribbean islands under English control.

Morgan was born in Wales and probably came to the West Indies in 1655 as a soldier in the English campaign that won JAMAICA from Spain. By 1666 Morgan was sailing with Edward Mansfield, one of the leading buccaneers of the Caribbean. When Mansfield died, the crew chose Morgan as its leader. With the support of the English governor of Jamaica, Morgan launched a series of daring raids against Spanish strongholds around the Caribbean. He

captured large amounts of treasure and spread alarm and confusion among the Spanish.

The crowning achievement of Morgan's career came in 1670–1671, when he led 2,000 men from the Caribbean coast of Panama across the mountainous, jungle-covered isthmus* to the Pacific Ocean. Morgan's forces attacked Panama City, the port where the Spanish fleet took on shipments of silver from Peru. Although Panama City was destroyed in the fighting, the Spanish had taken away much of their treasure before the attack. Morgan's followers later accused him of cheating them out of their share of the loot.

Unfortunately for Morgan, Spain and England had made peace while he was at sea. As a result, authorities in Jamaica arrested Morgan as a pirate and sent him to London. Relations between the two countries soon worsened, however, and King Charles II of England not only pardoned Morgan but made him a knight and the lieutenant governor of Jamaica. The former buccaneer spent his remaining years as a planter and well-respected figure on the island. (*See also* **West Indies.**)

* **isthmus** narrow strip of land connecting two larger land areas

Mound Builders

See *Native Americans: Early Peoples of North America.*

Music and Dance

*D*uring the colonial period, music could be heard in many different places and situations in North America—from the hymns of thanksgiving offered by grateful PILGRIMS in New England to the work songs of enslaved Africans in the southern tobacco fields, from the piping flutes and pounding drums of military marches to the tender love ballads of the Spanish Borderlands*. In worship, mourning, courtship, work, and celebration, people expressed themselves by singing and dancing.

Colonial music and dance sprang from many different sources. The music and dance of Native Americans had sacred origins. Africans arrived in North America with their own heritage of singing, drumming, and dancing. European settlers brought along the musical traditions of their particular regions. In North America, settlers combined elements of these traditions to create new forms.

* **Spanish Borderlands** northern part of New Spain, area now occupied by Florida, Texas, New Mexico, Arizona, and California

Colonial Religious Music

In the period between the founding of the first English settlements along the Atlantic coast and independence from Great Britain, sacred music in the English colonies developed from a religious ritual* to an art form. Although church music of the late 1700s still emphasized religious meaning, it had come to be valued for its beauty as well.

* **ritual** ceremony that follows a set pattern

English Sacred Music. In England sacred music was produced in grand cathedrals by huge organs and trained choirs. The early colonists lacked both organs and choirs for their churches, and in any case, they had little use for this type of music. In New England the chief musical form was psalm singing,

Music and Dance

* **Anglican** of the Church of England

in which every member of the congregation joined in singing the poems from the Book of Psalms in the Bible. PURITANS allowed only psalms in their worship services, though other hymns could be sung at home. Other Protestant churches had their own selections of approved sacred music, as did the ROMAN CATHOLIC CHURCH.

Early Puritans practiced a traditional style of singing known as "lining out." Congregation members did not sing from written notes as few of them could read music. Instead, a clerk or other church official recited a line of the psalm, and then each member of the congregation sang the line according to his or her own idea of the way it should sound. This free-spirited approach to group singing did not lead to harmony. One listener complained that the singers sounded "bad beyond expression."

In response, singing schools began appearing in communities in the 1720s. They attracted many young people, drawn as much by opportunities to socialize as by the desire to read music. These schools produced an ever-growing body of young men and women who knew something about music and who could sing together harmoniously. For music, they used collections of hymns and sacred songs imported from England and works of the few colonial composers such as William BILLINGS, who also ran a singing school.

The popularity of these schools and the resulting increase in the number of trained voices brought about changes in church services. Gradually, ministers began allowing the trained singers to sit together in a certain part of the church. Before long these groups led the musical part of the worship service—the beginning of the church choir. Yet "lining out" did not disappear overnight. Conflicts arose between the students of "new singing" and supporters of the "old way." Many churches adopted compromises—the trained singers might present one psalm, and the next would be "lined out" for the congregation. Hundreds of churches struggled with the question of whether to open music schools and whether to continue "lining out" the psalms.

In some churches, choirs eventually performed the musical part of the service, and congregations became audiences. Not all churches followed this pattern, however. Many retained the custom of having the choir sing some songs and the congregation others.

The introduction of musical instruments was another development in British colonial sacred music. Anglican* churches purchased organs as soon as they could afford them. But most Protestant churches believed that only the human voice should be used in worship. As singing techniques became more sophisticated, however, singers wanted bass viols—stringed instruments similar to violins—and other instruments to support and accompany their voices. This disturbed some traditional church members, who called the viols "devil's fiddles." Nonetheless, by the late 1700s, organs, flutes, violins, and other instruments appeared in many churches.

Spanish Sacred Music. The sacred music of the Spanish Borderlands, like all other aspects of culture in the region, had two sides—the formal and the informal. Formal religious music included official programs of church and government and closely followed European styles and models. Informal, or folk, religious music contained Native American influences and reflected the values of the local people.

The Roman Catholic Church believed that music was a valuable tool for teaching Native Americans about Christianity and encouraging them to convert. In 1523 missionaries in New Spain founded the first formal music school in North America. There Indians learned to read and play music in the European style, using instruments such as viols. They also became skilled at making their own instruments. The sacred music played in cathedrals and large churches of the Spanish colonies, though often performed by Indians, remained almost identical to the music of Spain.

The folk tradition of religious music emerged on the frontiers of settlement and touched the lives of everyone in the Borderlands. It included *villancicos,* or Christmas carols, and the *alabado,* a ballad-like hymn in the form of calls and responses among different singers. Missionaries in the Southwest developed religious plays with music and songs to teach the story of Christ. One play tells about the shepherds who travel to Bethlehem to worship the infant Christ and contains some of the most memorable melodies in Hispanic folk music.

Colonial Secular Music

* *secular* nonreligious; connected with everyday life

Not all colonial music was religious. Secular* music and dance helped liven up many colonial gatherings. Most settlers in the British, French, and Spanish colonies knew many traditional tunes, songs, and dances. Some owned instruments and written music. They shared their music and dances with their neighbors in America and passed them along to their children.

* *satiric* referring to humor that criticizes or makes fun of something bad or foolish

Ballads, poems set to music, were popular traditional songs. Ballads told emotional stories of love, betrayal, and tragedy and recounted the lives and deaths of long-ago kings, queens, and heroic figures. People also created new ballads—often humorous or satiric*—about current politics or other local affairs. These songs often spread quickly throughout a community or region, appealing to all classes of people. As a young man, Benjamin FRANKLIN wrote a number of popular ballads, but his father considered this activity undignified and discouraged it.

Although often portrayed as serious, strait-laced folk who disapproved of all music and dancing, many Puritans actually enjoyed the latest love songs and dances. The famous Puritan minister Cotton MATHER once wrote worriedly that "the minds and manners of many people" were being damaged by "foolish songs and ballads."

In New York and Pennsylvania, colonists sometimes held private concerts for their friends. There were few professional musicians until the late 1700s, but amateurs pitched in eagerly to sing or to play the harpsichord—a stringed instrument similar to a piano. A steady stream of instruments, new music, and the latest dance books from London arrived at colonial ports. In the southern colonies, people who had left their plantations to attend court or legislative sessions in the colonial capitals enjoyed several weeks of concerts, dances, and balls.

Secular music in the Spanish Borderlands often took the form of special songs that celebrated important events such as weddings, funerals, and coming of age. Sometimes humorous, these verses contained traditional wisdom and common sense. One song offered advice to newlyweds:

Music and Dance

Many dances of the colonial era, such as the minuet and cotillion, were popular with both French and British colonists. This watercolor by George Heriot shows a dance at the Château St. Louis in Quebec.

Marriage isn't for a moment
nor a day or two;
it is for eternity
as long as you both shall live.

Borderland ballads celebrated honor, commemorated local victories over the Indians, and related comic stories of animals to entertain children.

Military music was also a part of colonial life. European armies used horn players and drummers to send signals and to create a marching rhythm, and colonial armies continued this practice. In the British colonies, the military hired civilian musicians rather than using soldiers. They provided music for special occasions such as social events and public ceremonies involving troops. Enlisted men with drums and fifes—flutelike instruments—played the signals, marches, and other tunes that were part of everyday military life.

Colonial Dance

American colonists enjoyed many kinds of dancing, most of them borrowed from Europe. Some involved a set pattern of steps, known as composed dances. Other more casual dances allowed participants to invent new variations.

The minuet, a slow and dignified composed dance, involved much bowing and resembled a ceremony or ritual. Upper-class colonists performed the minuet at formal affairs. It was especially popular in New France because of its association with the French royal court. The cotillion was a French dance generally performed by four couples in a square. The earliest mentions of cotillions in the British colonies appear in the 1770s. The English country dance, another composed dance, involved couples standing in a line with partners facing each other.

British colonists of the lower classes enjoyed free-form jigs and hornpipes for one or two people, reels for three or four people, and traditional folk

dances for larger groups. Jigs and hornpipes allowed dancers to display their skill and creativity. Each performer invented a personal routine, often involving skipping. For reels, dancers stood in a line and alternated bits of solo dancing with moving around each other in figure-eight patterns. These dances developed into the traditional New England art of contra dancing—the ancestor of American square dancing.

In the Spanish Borderlands, weddings served as an occasion for many traditional dances. For centuries these community dances—called *fandangos* in California—were a lively aspect of frontier life. In the *marcha,* a special wedding dance, men formed a line behind the groom, and women formed one behind the bride. The two lines passed each other, and then, through a series of circlings, men and women formed couples and eventually merged into a single line. The dance represented the way in which, by joining into couples and marrying, individuals become part of a united community.

The dance of the *matachines,* which appeared in Mexico and the American Southwest during the colonial period, tells the story of the conquest of the ancient Mexican religion by Christianity. The dance contains many elements from the musical culture of Native Americans. Performers wearing shawls, ribbons, and masks dance to the music of drums, violins, and guitars. The singers repeat their words in a style much like Indian chanting. Both Indians and Hispanics perform the dance of the *matachines,* but each community has its own version.

The movements of the *cuadrillas,* a set of dances descended from French square dances, were very intricate. Only those who knew the dances well dared to join in. Easier to learn was the *cuna,* or cradle dance, from New Mexico. Two couples faced each other, joined hands, swung under each other's arms, and formed a rocking cradle out of their intertwined arms.

African American Music

Some blacks, both slave and free, gained wide recognition in the colonies as skilled musicians. They played not only for gatherings of other Africans but also for parties given by their white masters or employers. Many newspaper notices offering rewards for runaway slaves mentioned the runaways' musical talents, which were greatly valued by the slaveholders.

Black musicians quickly learned to play the European instruments and compositions favored by white colonists, but their own musical heritage remained separate and alive. Torn from their homelands and families, subjected to the sufferings and misfortunes of slavery, African Americans clung to familiar music and dances as sources of comfort in a hostile new environment.

Music from all parts of western and central Africa shared certain common features. Singers and players often used antiphony—call and response—in which individuals or groups answered phrases sung or played by others. Unlike European music, which stressed the melody, African music emphasized the rhythm, or beat. The principal means of establishing the beat was the drum. But many southern colonists feared that the slaves might use drums to send secret messages about revolts and attacks on white people. During the late 1600s and the 1700s, some areas outlawed the use of drums by slaves.

An All-American Instrument

A small stringed instrument that produces a twanging sound when its strings are plucked, the banjo is an essential part of American folk music. The banjo descended from the banjer or banjar—a West African instrument brought to the colonies by black slaves in the 1600s. In 1775 a white minister described one as "a large hollow gourd, with a long handle attached to it, strung with catgut." Aside from the drum, the banjo was the most widely used African instrument in America.

Music and Dance

Black slaves in the British colonies struggled to preserve their African heritage by performing traditional songs and dances. African music emphasized rhythm; musicians used drums, tambourines, or rattles to set the beat.

Africans sometimes shook tambourines and rattles to provide the beat, or they struck together sticks or bones. They also used their bodies as instruments—hand clapping, foot stomping, and "patting juba," a complex pattern of hand clapping mixed with slaps on the thighs. These uses of the body to mark rhythm showed the close link between music and dance. Listeners expressed their connection to the music by bobbing their heads, moving their bodies, and dancing, perhaps in lines or circles. White colonists adopted versions of some African dances, such as the Virginia jig, in which a man and a woman danced around the room while others watched. When a second woman—or a second man—stood up to join the dance, the first woman—or man—had to sit down.

Whether expressing joy or sorrow, African songs tended to display strong emotions. Singers and listeners alike might punctuate the song with shouts of excitement or cries of misery. These emotions gave power and intensity to the spirituals—songs of suffering, endurance, and hope of Christianized Africans. The spirituals began to appear by the end of the colonial period but developed more fully in the 1800s.

For Africans, music was a community affair. Their religious rituals almost always involved music and dance. Nonreligious forms of music also played a role in bringing the members of the community together and strengthening their social bonds and shared values. Even in the grim circumstances of slavery, African Americans continued to express their emotions and form bonds through song. On the slave ships in shackles, they sang songs of grief and longing for their homes. They also sang as they labored in the fields. Work songs provided more than emotional comfort. They also set a rhythm for repetitive tasks such as bending over to plant rice or pick tobacco.

Over time African music in North America changed as it began to include some features of European and West Indian music. The spiritual, for example, combined elements of African songs and Christian hymns. African traditions also influenced later American music forms, such as blues, jazz, rock, rap, and hip-hop.

Native American Music

Native Americans believed that music was a gift from powerful spirits. For them, music created a link between the human and spiritual worlds. Indians often sang during religious rituals, ceremonies, and festivals. Some of these events lasted for several days and nights and involved hundreds of special songs.

Native American music emphasized singing. Songs were poems made up of both words and sounds. Singers sometimes chanted or repeated sounds or words many times. Within a tribe, some songs belonged to particular people or could be performed only at certain times. Only healers could use healing songs, and only the people who belonged to societies within tribes knew the secret songs of these groups. Indians also passed along "ownership" of songs through inheritance, trade, or gift giving.

Believing that music came from supernatural sources, some tribes used dreams and visions to ask the spirits for songs. Others performed only old songs and did not believe individuals could compose new ones. In other tribes, special groups of people worked together to create new songs. Indians also adopted songs from other tribes or communities.

Indians did play musical instruments but generally only to accompany the singers. The two most common kinds of instruments were drums and flutes made from wood or bone. By blowing across or into the holes of the flute, players produced whistling notes.

Tribes in different regions of North America developed varied musical styles and instruments. Eastern Indians beat out rhythms with drums, rattles, and striking sticks. They also used flutes and whistles. Indians of the Eastern Woodlands were the only ones to use the calls and responses of antiphony.

PLAINS INDIANS developed a musical style known as falsetto singing, in which people used unnaturally high voices. They also produced unique sounds by singing through their noses. Each singer in a group played a large bass drum, their principal instrument. In the Southwest, PUEBLO INDIANS tended to sing slowly, while other tribes favored fast-paced songs. All of them used drums and rattles. In addition, some southwestern Indians played an instrument known as the Apache fiddle—the only stringed instrument used by Native Americans.

Muskogee Indians

See *Creek Indians.*

Narragansett Indians

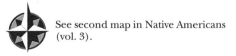
See second map in Native Americans (vol. 3).

When English colonists began to settle in present-day RHODE ISLAND, the large and powerful Narragansett tribe occupied the land to the west of Narragansett Bay. For many years the Indians had friendly relations with the colonists, but eventually they went to war with the white people.

An Algonquian-speaking people, the Narragansett raised corn, beans, and squash and also hunted and fished for food. The abundant shellfish along the coast provided them with food as well as shells for making WAMPUM—strings or belts of shells that were used as currency.

After the English settled in southern New England in the 1620s, the Narragansett began trading with them. They developed a prosperous trade, using wampum to obtain furs from other tribes and exchanging the furs for tools, clothing, and weapons from the Europeans. Roger WILLIAMS, who had been banished from Massachusetts, arrived in Rhode Island in 1636. He bought land from the tribe and founded the settlement of PROVIDENCE.

The Narragansett assisted the English in fighting the war against the PEQUOT INDIANS in 1636–1637. This close relationship did not last, however. In 1645 several New England colonies declared war on the Narragansett, hoping to gain the tribe's land. Though no fighting took place, relations between the Indians and the English settlers remained tense. The Narragansett joined other Native Americans against the colonists in KING PHILIP'S WAR (1675–1676). The tribe suffered heavy losses in the war. Afterward, many Narragansett fled their homeland and settled in Canada and elsewhere in New England. Most remained in Rhode Island, where their descendants still live today. (*See also* **Fur Trade; Native Americans.**)

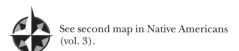

Natchez Indians

See second map in Native Americans (vol. 3).

Before 1700 the Natchez Indians were the largest and strongest tribe in the southern Mississippi River valley. They made their home near present-day Natchez, Mississippi. However, in the early 1700s, warfare with French colonists destroyed the Natchez people.

The Natchez shared a way of life with other tribes in the region, such as the CREEK, CHOCTAW, and CHICKASAW. They lived in agricultural villages, raising primarily MAIZE, and they were expert potters and weavers. Like the other tribes of the region, they worshiped the sun with fires that burned continuously. Natchez priests conducted religious services at a magnificent temple built on an earthen mound.

The Natchez social system, however, did not resemble that of any other American Indian tribe. Natchez society was divided into rigid classes. There were three ranks of nobles—Honored Men, Suns, and the Great Sun—and commoners, known as "stinkards." As the name implies, a stinkard received little respect in Natchez society. Children became part of the class of their mother rather than that of their father. A noblewoman's

The Natchez Indians called their chief the Great Sun. In 1758 a Frenchman named Le Page du Pratz made this sketch of the Great Sun being carried to a harvest festival.

rank could be conferred on her husband, but aside from that, there was little movement between classes.

The Natchez Great Sun, or chief, was also unusual. He inherited his position through his mother, who belonged to the Sun rank, rather than being selected by a tribal council. Unlike other Indian chiefs, the Great Sun was an autocratic* ruler with considerable power.

* **autocratic** ruling with absolute power and authority

When French explorers entered the lower Mississippi River valley in the mid-1600s, the Natchez population numbered about 4,000. At first relations between the Natchez and the French settlers who followed in the early 1700s were friendly, but friction soon developed. In 1714 Jean-Baptiste Le Moyne de Bienville, the governor of the French colony of LOUISIANA, built Fort Rosalie on the banks of the Mississippi River. French settlers soon arrived, taking over rich farmland in the heart of Natchez country. The Indians tried to force them out, but French troops intervened. In 1729 French expansion crossed into a Natchez village and sacred site.

Outraged, the Natchez attacked, killing about 250 French settlers and destroying Fort Rosalie. Then followed two years of bloody warfare known as the Natchez Revolt. The French and their Choctaw allies systematically drove the Natchez from their villages and killed them. Indians who fled across the Mississippi River were pursued. In 1731 the French rounded up the last group of Natchez, about 400 Indians, and sold them into slavery in the West Indies. Those Natchez who managed to escape during the raids were scattered throughout Oklahoma and South Carolina. Within only a few years, the Natchez ceased to exist as a distinct people.

Native Americans

When Europeans first landed on North American shores in the early 1500s, they discovered that the continent was inhabited. Wherever they went, they found people or signs of people—the embers of a campfire, a canoe pulled up on a beach, or the remains of a settlement. These people, the Native Americans, had lived on the continent for thousands of years. Estimates of their population when the Europeans arrived range from 4 or 5 million to 10 million. The story of colonial North America involves more than the adventures, hardships, and accomplishments of European explorers, traders, missionaries, and settlers. It is also the story of these first Americans.

Christopher COLUMBUS was not surprised to find human beings on the islands he discovered after a long voyage across the Atlantic Ocean. However, the explorer thought he had reached Asia, known then as "the Indies," so he called the people there Indians. Europeans soon realized that the land Columbus had found was not Asia at all, but the name *Indians*—based on a geographic mistake—remained.

From the European point of view, the discovery, exploration, and colonization of the Americas was a heroic enterprise. From the Indian perspective, it was a disaster. With the Europeans came violence, enslavement, and diseases that killed by the thousands. While some Europeans wanted only to trade with the Indians for furs, skins, and other goods, others sought their land—and they killed the Native Americans or drove them away to get it. Still others had more far-reaching goals. They thought the Indians should adopt the Christian religion

NATIVE AMERICANS

Other entries relating to Native Americans:

Abenaki Indians	Iroquois Confederacy	Pontiac, Chief
Aleut Peoples	King Philip's War (1675–1676)	Potawatomi Indians
Apache Indians	Mahican Indians	Powhatan Indians
Brant, Joseph	Metacom	Pueblo Indians
California Indians	Miami Indians	Pueblo Revolt (1680)
Catawba Indians	Micmac Indians	Religions, Native American
Cherokee Indians	Montagnais Indians	Seminole Indians
Chickasaw Indians	Montour, Madame	Shawnee Indians
Choctaw Indians	Narragansett Indians	Squanto
Comanche Indians	Natchez Indians	Susquehannock Indians
Cree Indians	Navajo Indians	Timucua Indians
Creek Indians	Occom, Samson	Tlingit Indians
Delaware Indians	Ojibwa Indians	Tohono O'odham Indians
Eskimo Peoples (Inuit)	Osage Indians	Tuscarora Indians
Fox Indians	Ottawa Indians	Wampanoag Indians
French and Indian War	Pawnee Indians	Wampum
Genizaros	Pequot Indians	Winnebago Indians
Great Basin Indians	Pequot War (1636–1637)	Yamassee Indians
Hopi Indians	Pima Indians	Yuma Indians
Huron Indians	Plains Indians	Zuni Indians
Illinois Indians	Pocahontas	

and European languages, customs, and ways of life. But whether Europeans were cruel or well-meaning, whether they met the Indians in friendship, trade, or battle, the result was usually the same. The Europeans had plans for North America, and they would not let the Indians stand in their way.

From the earliest days of settlement until long after the colonial era ended, Native Americans resisted the European newcomers. In the end, however, the whites emerged victorious. The Indians had to adapt to the changed world as best they could—a process that continues to this day as Native Americans struggle to preserve their traditional values and customs while taking their place in the larger society.

With the exception of some cultures in Mexico, Native Americans did not use writing until they learned the European languages. As a result, they left no written records of life before Columbus's momentous first landing. What is known about these Indian civilizations comes from Native American oral histories and traditions; from journals, letters, and reports written by the Europeans of the time; and from modern archaeology*. Together these sources provide an idea of life in the Americas before European colonization.

archaeology study of past human cultures, usually by digging up ruins

Early Peoples of North America

The story of the first Americans began in northeastern Asia, in the cold land now known as Siberia. The world was locked in the grip of an Ice Age that

* *strait* narrow waterway connecting two larger bodies of water

* *caribou* large deer, similar to reindeer

* *artifact* ornament, tool, weapon, or other object made by humans

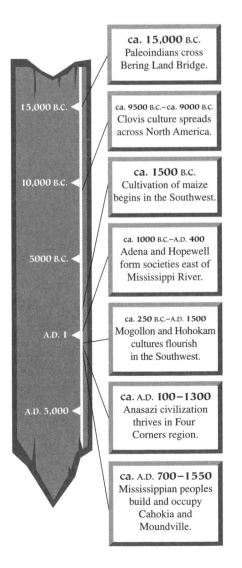

ca. **15,000** B.C.
Paleoindians cross
Bering Land Bridge.

ca. 9500 B.C.–ca. 9000 B.C.
Clovis culture spreads
across North America.

ca. **1500** B.C.
Cultivation of maize
begins in the Southwest.

ca. 1000 B.C.–A.D. **400**
Adena and Hopewell
form societies east of
Mississippi River.

ca. 250 B.C.–A.D. 1500
Mogollon and Hohokam
cultures flourish
in the Southwest.

ca. A.D. **100–1300**
Anasazi civilization
thrives in Four
Corners region.

ca. A.D. **700–1550**
Mississippian peoples
build and occupy
Cahokia and
Moundville.

covered part of the continents with huge glaciers. Despite these harsh conditions, people had been moving north in Europe and Asia for thousands of years, populating the Ice Age world. The nomadic hunters kept pushing northeast, following herds of game. At some point, they moved beyond Asia.

During the Ice Age, an enormous amount of the world's water was frozen in the glaciers, lowering the level of the oceans. At that time, Siberia and Alaska—separated today by an ocean strait*—were connected by a windy plain called the BERING LAND BRIDGE, which animals and people could cross. This is how the first people came to the Americas—pursuing game animals such as the woolly rhinoceros, mammoth, caribou*, and musk oxen. Scientists have found no evidence of human life in the Americas before the arrival of the Siberian migrants in the late Ice Age.

Exactly when the first migrants arrived remains a mystery. However, scientists do know that people were living in Siberia about 18,000 to 20,000 years ago. They also know that the earth began warming up about 15,000 years ago, causing the glaciers to shrink and rising waters to wash over the land bridge. This means that nomads most likely crossed to the Americas between 20,000 and 15,000 years ago—probably in many slow waves of migration. As the ice sheets grew smaller, hunters moved south from Alaska and spread out across the land. Archaeologists call these early people Paleoindians, which means "early Indians." They were the ancestors of most Native American cultures that developed throughout North and South America.

The Clovis People.   About 9500 B.C. a new culture, a way of life with its own tools and customs, arose among the Paleoindians of North America. Archaeologists call it the Clovis culture because they first found its artifacts* at a site near Clovis, New Mexico—though Clovis artifacts have also turned up in many other places across the continent. These sites show that humans had spread throughout North America very rapidly, perhaps in as little as 500 years. The total population was still small, however, numbering no more than a few thousand people.

As the glaciers retreated, the vast grasslands east of the Rocky Mountains supported huge herds of game. Those same grasslands were home to scattered bands of Clovis people, who roamed enormous territories in search of game and wild foods such as berries and roots. Much information about the Clovis people comes from sites on the plains where the hunters killed bison, mammoth, and other animals. Archaeologists have found stone points among the bones of butchered beasts. Clovis hunters attached these points to wooden spears for stabbing or throwing.

The Clovis culture flourished for only about 500 years. Around 9000 B.C. North America started becoming much warmer and drier. Woodlands spread across the eastern part of the continent. A number of the large animals disappeared, probably wiped out by a combination of climate change and overhunting. As the land and the wildlife changed, so did the roving bands of Paleoindian hunters.

Adapting to a New Landscape.   For 11,000 years, right up to modern times, cultures rose and fell as the people of North America developed new ways of life suited to the wide range of climates and natural resources. Groups on the

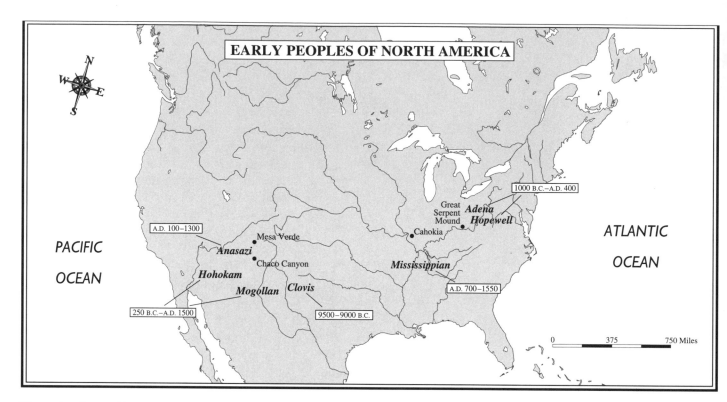

EARLY PEOPLES OF NORTH AMERICA

PACIFIC

OCEAN

ATLANTIC

OCEAN

1000 B.C.–A.D. 400

Great
Serpent
Mound

Adena
Hopewell

Cahokia

A.D. 100–1300

Mesa Verde

Anasazi

Chaco Canyon

Mississippian

Hohokam

Mogollan *Clovis*

A.D. 700–1550

250 B.C.–A.D. 1500

9500–9000 B.C.

0   375   750 Miles

The earliest known Native Americans, the Clovis people, died out more than 10,000 years before Europeans visited the continent. By contrast, remnants of the Mississippian culture that arose around A.D. 700 lasted well into the colonial period.

Great Plains remained big-game hunters, using their hunting techniques to stalk BUFFALO herds. Others adapted to the harsh desert conditions of the dry western interior, living on scarce plant foods and small game such as rabbits. Some camped near marshes, lakes, or rivers or on the ocean coasts, where they could live on fish, waterbirds, and sea mammals such as seals. In the Eastern Woodlands, people hunted deer and smaller game and also ate plants and fish.

At first all the Native Americans were hunter-gatherers who lived by hunting, gathering plants and nuts, and fishing. Gradually, some peoples learned to grow useful plants, but none relied on agriculture to provide a major food source. Then around 1500 B.C., the cultivation of MAIZE and beans spread north from what is now MEXICO. Within a few centuries, these crops had become the basis of Native American life in the southwestern part of the continent, and by about A.D. 1000, they had spread to the midwestern and southeastern regions. Gradually, some northeastern Indians adopted these crops as well.

The people who adopted agriculture became less nomadic. They tended to settle in villages, although some of them left their villages after the crops had been harvested to spend the winter in hunting camps. Nearly all Native American groups remained fairly mobile. A community might move its entire village after a few years or a few generations to give the soil time to recover its fertility.

Because agriculture could support a number of people living together in one place, large settled communities began to appear in the Southwest, where the cultivation of maize began. Early villages consisted of clusters of houses partially dug into the ground. The earth provided insulation to keep the dwellings warm during the cold nights and cool during the hot days. When people needed more room and storage space, they moved above ground and built thick-walled structures of adobe, or sun-dried clay. These structures

developed into pueblos—villages that consisted of large buildings with many small chambers connected to one another.

Mogollon, Hohokam, and Anasazi. The Mogollon and Hohokam cultures flourished in the Southwest between 250 B.C. and A.D. 1500. The Mogollon were pueblo dwellers who lived in the arid and sometimes mountainous region that is now eastern Arizona and southwestern New Mexico. Mogollon women were skilled in making pottery. Painted in black and white or in various colors, their pots and jars showed scenes of people, insects, animals, and mythical beings. The Hohokam of the southern desert did not build pueblos. They lived in pit houses or huts made of poles and brush.

The Anasazi civilization, located in the Four Corners region, where Utah, Colorado, Arizona, and New Mexico meet, lasted from A.D. 100 to about 1300. The Anasazi built major clusters of pueblos in Chaco Canyon in New Mexico and Mesa Verde in Colorado. Pueblo Bonito, the largest structure at Chaco Canyon, had more than 800 rooms. Although Chaco Canyon's pueblos could hold as many as 6,500 people, its water and other resources could support only about 2,000. Archaeologists think that people from outlying communities came to stay in the canyon during festivals and religious ceremonies.

The Anasazi deserted their pueblos in Chaco Canyon around 1200. Historians do not really know why. Most believe that a long drought drove the people into smaller settlements in more fertile areas. The same thing happened about a century later at Mesa Verde, where the Anasazi had built tall pueblos like modern apartment buildings, stacked against cliff walls and under overhangs. Although the cliff dwellers used a system of ditches and reservoirs to collect and store rainwater, a period of dry weather forced them to spread out into smaller communities that could more easily survive on scarce resources.

Mound Builders. A very different tradition developed along the Mississippi and Ohio rivers and in the southern and southeastern part of North America. The Adena and Hopewell people of this Eastern Woodlands region had been hunter-gatherers. After maize and beans reached the area, their successors began to create a culture based on agriculture.

Flourishing from about 1000 B.C. to A.D. 400, the Adena and the Hopewell are known for the large mounds of earth and stone they built over the graves of their dead. With each burial, the mounds grew larger. Important people such as shamans* and leaders were buried in the mounds, along with artifacts such as masks, carved pipes, copper ornaments, and shells. The burial sites sometimes included other people, who may have been sacrificed as part of the funeral ceremony.

These people created entire landscapes of straight, circular, and octagonal mounds, using simple stone tools and baskets to move the dirt. The most spectacular site is the Great Serpent Mound in Ohio, shaped like a huge snake coiled along a ridge with a burial mound between its jaws. It measures 1,400 feet in length.

The Mississippian peoples, who emerged about A.D. 700, created highly organized societies. Their priests and rulers lived in special quarters, received food and other tributes* from their subjects, and were buried with many artifacts. Some of these objects had been obtained through elaborate and far-flung networks of trade and gift giving with Native Americans across the

* **shaman** person with spiritual and healing powers

* **tribute** payment made to a dominant power

North America's First Settlements

One of the most hotly debated questions among scholars is the date of human settlement in North America. Some researchers have claimed that people lived in the Americas as early as 50,000 years ago, but the evidence does not support their claims. The oldest human site that archaeologists can reliably date is Pennsylvania's Meadowcroft Rockshelter. People first lived at this spot about 12,500 B.C. Fort Rock in Oregon and a few other sites date from about 10,000 B.C.

continent. Cahokia, one of the largest Mississippian communities, was located across the river from the modern city of St. Louis. At its height in about A.D. 1000, Cahokia may have had as many as 20,000 inhabitants. The site contained more than 100 large earthen mounds built for religious purposes and burial.

Later Mississippian tribes, such as the NATCHEZ, continued the artistic and landscaping traditions. They also maintained a complex trade network that transported shell beads, copper, and pottery across a wide portion of North America.

Indians of Colonial Times

By the time the Europeans arrived in North America, Native Americans formed hundreds of societies across the continent that lived in very different ways. Societies within a given region were likely to share broad characteristics such as language, arts and crafts, marriage customs and family organization, and religion, but each had its own unique cultural features.

Along the coasts of Alaska, Canada, and Greenland were the ALEUTS and the ESKIMO. They sometimes hunted but lived mainly off fish and sea mammals such as seals. Using new tools such as harpoons and small skin boats,

Native American tribes in colonial times did not settle in fixed locations. Some tribes regularly migrated from place to place, while others were forced from their homelands as European colonists took over.

they took to the sea to hunt whales, and whale hunting assumed an important role in both their economy and their culture. Inland a different culture developed across what is now central Alaska and northern Canada. In this region of marshes, rivers, and lakes, the CREE, the Chipewayan, and other Indians survived by hunting elk, moose, caribou, and waterbirds.

The Native Americans of the Northwest, from Alaska through Oregon, created complex societies along rivers, on islands, and on the coast. Fish and sea mammals provided abundant food, giving people the time and resources to develop crafts. Tribes such as the TLINGIT, Haida, and Tsimshian produced canoes, masks, totem poles, and household objects such as boxes out of carved and painted wood. One of the many ceremonies of these and other northwestern tribes was the potlatch, a feast at which people gave lavish gifts to friends and followers.

Farther south, the Indians of California fished and hunted sea mammals on the coast. The region's mild climate and plentiful food supply supported a population of about 300,000 Native Americans at the beginning of the colonial era. Some CALIFORNIA INDIANS established trade relations with tribes of the Southwest, exchanging seashells and beads for pottery and turquoise. Some southwestern Indians practiced no agriculture but survived largely on wild plant foods, such as mesquite pods. However, the Pueblo and HOPI were skilled farmers who raised corn, beans, and squash. The NAVAJO also settled in the region and borrowed farming techniques from the Pueblo.

The GREAT BASIN INDIANS—the Shoshone and Paiute—were located in present-day Nevada and Utah. They did not build permanent communities but were experts at living off the harsh land, especially at gathering wild plant foods such as pine nuts. North of them, in present-day Idaho and eastern Oregon and Washington, lived the Flathead, Umatilla, Nez Perce, and Yakima Indians. They, too, were hunter-gatherers, but the basis of their diet was the plentiful supply of salmon and other fish in the Columbia and Snake rivers.

The PLAINS INDIANS—the Blackfoot, Cheyenne, Arapaho, and others—inhabited the great belt of grassland that ran through the center of the continent from what is now Canada to northern Texas. The Plains Indians were hunters who built an economy and a way of life around the bison, in the same way that the Arctic people built theirs around the whale. The APACHE lived where the southern part of the Great Plains merges into the mountain and desert landscape of the Southwest.

East of the Mississippi, Native Americans relied on a combination of farming, hunting, fishing, and gathering wild foods. Large tribes of the southeastern region included the CHEROKEE, CHOCTAW, CATAWBA, CREEK, and CHICKASAW. The northeastern region was home to a great variety of tribes, from the MICMAC of Nova Scotia to the WINNEBAGO of present-day Wisconsin.

Along the Atlantic Coast, Algonquian-speaking Indians—including the WAMPANOAG, DELAWARE, and POWHATAN—settled near rivers, seashores, and lakes that provided reliable sources of fish, shellfish, and waterbirds. They lived in semipermanent villages and cultivated corn and other crops. Their canoes turned waterways into routes of travel and communication in this hilly, densely forested part of the continent.

Remember: Words in small capital letters have separate entries, and the index at the end of Volume 4 will guide you to more information on many topics.

Iroquoian-speaking tribes such as the Mohawk and the Seneca lived in the region that is now New York State and along the St. Lawrence River. The HURON INDIANS settled on the north side of Lake Ontario at the very edge of corn-growing territory. They produced enough corn to trade it with tribes farther north for furs and fish, which they then passed on to their neighbors to the south. The Huron operated a trade network that covered much of eastern North America.

Forms of Government

* **anthropologist** person who studies human societies and cultures, especially family and political structures

Native Americans' social and political organizations were as varied as the landscape in which they lived. However, anthropologists* have identified three basic kinds of organization: bands, tribes, and chiefdoms.

Bands. A band consisted of a small number of families, generally related to each other, who often hunted or gathered food together. They had no formal political structure or law. Instead, they maintained order by the strength of custom and by the social pressures placed on individuals by other members of the band. Anyone who no longer wanted to be part of the band could leave and join another group.

Band societies were common in Canada, the Great Basin, California, and central and northern Alaska. The Micmac, who divided themselves into seven bands, provide an example of the way band society was organized. Each band had its own territory and a local leader called the sagamore, who could inherit the office, be appointed by an older sagamore, or be chosen by other band members for his skills and leadership qualities. The sagamore's responsibilities included assigning hunting territories, greeting visitors, leading the band's seasonal movements, settling disputes, and directing the band's men in times of war. The sagamore received advice from the shaman and from the group's elders. Disputes that could not be settled by these counselors were resolved by wrestling matches or, for serious crimes such as murder, by payments or revenge killings. When the bands gathered for feasts each summer, the sagamores discussed matters of common interest to the Micmac.

Tribes. Tribes had larger populations and more complex networks of family relationships than bands. Like a band, a tribe was an association of equals who chose their leaders from the most respected members of the group. In many cases, a tribe was a village led by a headman, assisted by an informal council of elders. Tribes were common throughout North America, especially in places with stable, plentiful food supplies, such as the eastern coast, the Ohio and Mississippi valleys, the Pacific Northwest, and the Plains.

The SHAWNEE INDIANS of the Ohio Valley were organized as a tribe. They lived in a number of villages, each with a civil chief and a war chief. The chiefs, together with elders representing the families, discussed matters of general interest at councils. When serious issues such as war arose, the meetings included all tribal members. Both men and women could address the group and share in the decision making.

status social position

Chiefdoms. Unlike bands and tribes, chiefdoms were not societies in which everyone had equal status* and some degree of independence. In chiefdoms, chiefs held supreme political authority and, with their council, oversaw the activities of the general population. Chiefs controlled the production, distribution, and use of food and other resources. Individuals became chiefs because of their lineage and seniority or their standing within the group, though in some cases ability also played a part.

Chiefdoms were much rarer than bands and tribes. They developed in areas of especially rich resources, such as the Southeast and the Pacific Northwest. In the late 1500s, a collection of 25 or so tribes in the Chesapeake Bay region of Virginia formed a chiefdom under a leader named Powhatan. Having conquered or pressured the tribes into accepting his control, Powhatan created a political structure that included subchiefs in each small settlement and a chief over each tribe. Chiefs could be male or female. Among their duties were greeting visitors, collecting tribute such as corn and hides, and carrying out the orders and plans of the supreme ruler, Powhatan. His word was law on such matters as war, peace, alliances, and the payment of tribute, and he did not hesitate to use force to punish a disobedient tribe.

Not all chiefdoms were held together by force. The Natchez Indians developed a complex social and political structure based on their religion. They believed that their leader, called the Great Sun, was a god-king with total authority over the tribal members. A council of advisers—including war chiefs, priests, and officials in charge of public festivals—helped the Great Sun govern the tribe. A council of elders representing the villages also met with the Great Sun. The society was divided into nobility and commoners.

The Nootka of Vancouver Island were one of many tribes of the Northwest ruled as a chiefdom. The Nootka society was divided into three classes: chiefs and their families, commoners, and slaves. A chief could use slaves to enforce his will on commoners who were unwilling to pay tribute or follow his orders.

confederacy alliance or league of peoples or states

Confederacies. Occasionally, groups of tribes joined together in loose political associations called confederacies*. The tribes within a confederacy did not give up their independence to follow a central ruler, but they did agree to work together for the advantage of all in trade or war. The best-known of these associations was the IROQUOIS CONFEDERACY of the Northeast, sometimes called the Five Nations. It consisted of the Mohawk, Oneida, Onondaga, Seneca, and Cayuga tribes, joined in 1722 by the TUSCARORA of North Carolina. The Iroquois Confederacy was formed at least a century before Europeans arrived in North America.

Native Americans and Europeans

Contact between the Native Americans and the Europeans was not a single event. It consisted of a series of encounters and invasions spanning more than 300 years. The effects of this contact spread across North America like ripples from a stone dropped into a pond. Even tribes that had not yet had direct contact with Europeans were affected by the new diseases, trade goods, and animals introduced to the continent. For tribes that met the Europeans, the

French colonists in Canada engaged in trade with many Native American tribes. This illustration by C. W. Jeffreys shows Indians displaying their wares outside a Canadian trading post, which they were not allowed to enter.

first encounter turned into a long, uncertain—and sometimes violent—process of adapting to the newcomers' presence.

French, Dutch, and English Contact. In the 1500s, Indians living along the Atlantic coast had contact with European explorers such as Jacques CARTIER as well as with the crews of fishing boats that stopped to dry fish, repair their vessels, or take on freshwater or other supplies. The Indians exchanged furs and food for items such as glass beads and iron axes. They used many of these objects as ornaments and buried them with their dead. European manufactured items also entered the wide-ranging Native American trade network and were passed along from person to person.

The Europeans did not bring only trade goods. With them came diseases, including measles and influenza, that had never appeared in the Americas before. Europeans had lived with these illnesses for thousands of years and had developed some resistance to them. Native Americans, however, fell ill in great numbers and died as the diseases swept through their populations. Smallpox was especially destructive, killing thousands of Indians everywhere from the WEST INDIES and Mexico to the coast of Canada.

Some scholars believe that the newly introduced diseases wiped out the entire population in some regions. Early European accounts and archaeological evidence show that a number of societies disappeared suddenly. In 1540s, for example, French visitors met Iroquois Indians along the St. Lawrence River. When the French returned to the area in 1603, the Indians were gone. But it is not always possible to tell whether Indians died or simply moved away, either because of war or in an attempt to flee disease.

From the early 1600s, Native Americans on the Atlantic coast encountered growing numbers of French, Dutch, and English visitors. Traders, missionaries, and settlers began establishing permanent footholds in America. The French, who concentrated their efforts along the St. Lawrence River, maintained the best relations with the Indians, generally treating them with respect. Unlike the Spanish, who sometimes herded Native Americans into mission churches at gunpoint, French Roman Catholic priests ministered

only to those who actively sought religious instruction. In turn, Indians welcomed young French boys into their communities to learn their languages and customs.

The French formed alliances with the Native Americans of what is now Canada. In 1609 Samuel de CHAMPLAIN and his soldiers used their guns to help a group of Algonquin and Huron Indians defeat a Mohawk war party. This incident had long-lasting effects—it earned the French the friendship of the Huron and Algonquin and the hatred of the Iroquois Confederacy.

The Dutch were active along the Hudson, Delaware, and Connecticut rivers. At first they were more interested in trade than in settlement. They formed alliances with the Mohawk, who helped the FUR TRADE by maintaining order. Swedish settlers traded firearms and ammunition to the Indians. Guns soon played a major role in relations among Native American tribes. For example, the SUSQUEHANNOCK INDIANS used muskets obtained from the Swedish to force other, less well armed tribes to pay them tribute.

The English, as the Indians soon discovered, often acted more like raiders than visitors. They made unreasonable demands, entered people's homes to steal food and supplies, looted graves, and kidnapped Native Americans for sale into slavery across the ocean. Occasionally an Indian tribe joined the slave trade, selling captives from other tribes to the English. After the English founded Charleston, South Carolina, in 1670, the Chickasaw attacked the Choctaw and other lower Mississippi tribes in search of slaves to sell in Charleston's market. French officials who arranged a truce in 1702 estimated that the Chickasaw had killed 1,800 Choctaw and carried off 500, losing 800 of their own people.

Not all exchanges between the two peoples were violent. Whites and Native Americans also adopted elements from each other's culture. From the Indians, Europeans learned to grow new crops such as corn, to build and use CANOES for transportation, and to treat diseases with local plants and HERBS. Many colonists adopted Native American hunting, fishing, and farming practices to feed their families. Indian people soon learned to use items introduced by white settlers, including metal tools, firearms, and kettles. The Indians did not abandon their old ways but adapted them to use the new materials, such as substituting cut metal arrowheads for stone ones. Glass beads and woven cloth coats, shirts, and blankets added to but did not replace shell beads and buckskins as Native American clothing.

One new product had an especially destructive effect on Native Americans—liquor. Offered as a gesture of friendship and later widely used in trade, it was eagerly accepted by a population not used to alcohol. Over the years, alcohol destroyed many Indian lives and families. Numerous chiefs begged the whites to ban the traffic in liquor, but its use continued to increase among Native Americans, as did alcoholism.

Spanish Contact. After establishing colonies in the West Indies and Mexico, the Spanish turned their attention to the northern frontier of their American empire. First they searched for gold and other riches. Finding no treasure, they decided to establish a claim to the land—and to its inhabitants. Across the vast region known as the Spanish Borderlands*, whites and Native Americans led one another in a complex dance of war, peace, enslavement,

* *Spanish Borderlands* northern part of New Spain, area now occupied by Florida, Texas, Arizona, New Mexico, and California

Native Americans

* **mestizo** person of mixed Spanish and Indian ancestry
* **mulatto** person of mixed black and white ancestry

* **strategic** key part of a plan; of military importance
* **buffer zone** neutral area between two enemy areas

* **friar** member of a religious brotherhood

See map in Missions and Missionaries (vol. 3).

alliance, trade, and cultural exchange for 300 years. On one side were the Spanish, mestizos*, and mulattoes*. On the other were hundreds of Indian groups, ranging from nomadic Apache and Comanche hunter-warriors to town-dwelling Pueblo farmers in the Rio Grande Valley.

The Spanish wanted to conquer the Native Americans, convert them to Christianity, teach them to live like Europeans, and make them subjects of the Spanish crown. The Indians resisted being forced into these new patterns. Yet they eagerly accepted European cloth, metal tools, and guns. The Spanish also introduced cattle and HORSES. Within a short time, the Plains Indians and some southwestern tribes had become skilled riders who could hunt buffalo—or make war—on horseback. In New Mexico, the Spanish met Indians riding horses, wearing leather armor, and carrying muskets and even a bugle—all stolen in raids.

The Spanish focused first on colonizing FLORIDA because of its strategic* location. Florida guarded the sea route used by treasure ships bound for Spain and would serve as a buffer zone* against English activity on the Atlantic coast. In the 1500s, Roman Catholic missionaries worked at turning the local Indians into Christians, causing unrest and some revolts. The Spanish sent troublemakers and those who refused to become Christians into slavery in the West Indies. Many Native Americans also perished of disease.

Like other Indians, the Florida tribes were caught up in European politics. English colonists gave guns to their allies, the YAMASSEE and Creek Indians, and sent them into Florida to attack the Spanish and the Native Americans controlled by them. To the dismay of the Spanish, some Florida Indians sided with the English, who did not force them to convert to Christianity. After the British won control of Florida in 1763, the Spanish left the region, taking the last of the Christianized Indians to Cuba and Mexico.

In the deserts and mountains of the western Borderlands, Spanish friars* built MISSIONS, churches or chapels that became the centers of missionary villages. Forts called PRESIDIOS protected the missions, and the presidio soldiers often forced the reluctant Indians to obey the friars. The missions not only spread Christianity among the Native Americans but also taught European crafts such as painting, metalworking, weaving, and carpentry. Once the missions and presidios were established, Spanish colonists set up cattle ranches. Occasionally, they hired Indians as vaqueros, or cowboys.

By insisting that the Native Americans give up their nomadic habits and their scattered residences to settle in church-centered communities, the missionaries were calling for radical change. Not only would the Indians have to convert to Christianity, but they would also be forced to reorganize their entire economic, social, family, and community life. When Indians rebelled, the Spanish crushed the revolts.

Whites and Native Americans formed other kinds of relationships in the Borderlands. Marriages between the two peoples sometimes occurred, leading to a growing population with various combinations of white, Indian, and black ancestry. There was also much trade. Even during times of rebellion, the yearly trade fair at Taos, New Mexico, brought the most aggressive tribes of the region into the economic marketplace—often to exchange captured whites or Christianized Indians for ransom payments. In addition, Native Americans who fled missionary communities sometimes joined whites in

partnership, working in mines or serving as the guides, interpreters, and allies of Spanish troops.

There was also a vast and tragic traffic in human beings as the Spanish enslaved Indians who did not bend to their will. Sent to the mines and woolen mills of Mexico or the plantations of the West Indies, these Native Americans met miserable ends. In return the Indians frequently captured whites, especially women and children, either for ransom or to raise the children as Indians.

Conflicts with Colonists

From the start, relations between Europeans and Native Americans were colored by violence on both sides. Despite many friendships, alliances, and periods of peace between the races, conflict was all too common during the colonial period and beyond.

Not all the conflict occurred between whites and Indians. Native Americans also fought each other. Some tribes tried to win the support of the Europeans, hoping to obtain weapons or troops to help them wage war against their enemies. In the same way, the Europeans sought Indian allies in their struggle against rival European powers.

In the East. Thousands of people died in the 1600s in wars that pitted Indians against colonists throughout eastern North America. New Englanders and their Mohegan and NARRAGANSETT allies crushed the PEQUOT INDIANS in the PEQUOT WAR. Farther south, in Virginia, English colonists destroyed the chiefdom of the Powhatan Indians in a series of wars. During the 1640s, the Dutch fought several wars with the Munsee and Esopus tribes. In the north, the tribes of the Iroquois Confederacy, bent on controlling trade between other Indians and Europeans, waged relentless war against the French and their Indian allies, such as the Huron of Canada.

Tension over the land and its uses led to KING PHILIP'S WAR in the 1670s. Indians in southern New England who did not want to move to the "praying

In 1609 French explorer Samuel de Champlain and his soldiers joined a party of Algonquin Indians in a battle against the Iroquois. After a shot from Champlain's gun killed the chief, the Iroquois confederacy became bitter enemies of the French.

Nemattanew, Indian Spiritual Leader

In the early 1600s, Native Americans struggled to make sense of the new elements that had suddenly transformed their world—firearms, deadly new diseases, and Europeans who took their land. In the confusion of the times, some spiritual leaders promised protection against European guns and sicknesses. One was a Powhatan named Nemattanew, who claimed that English musket balls could not harm him. An organizer of a raid on the Virginia colonists in 1622, Nemattanew was killed by musket fire just before the attack was to begin. His companions hid the leader's body so that his followers would not lose faith in his powers.

* **badlands** region with highly eroded soil and little vegetation

towns"—settlements of Christianized Indians—found themselves living on tiny plots of land, surrounded by settlers who were cutting down the forest and driving away the game. They began attacking white settlements, and soon the revolt spread as far north as Maine. With the help of their Mohawk allies, the English hunted down the rebels, forever breaking the power of the New England tribes.

In 1689 the conflict between France and England spread to North America, in what became known as KING WILLIAM'S WAR. Tribes allied with the two powers went to war as well. Thousands of Indians died or were driven from their homes. The same thing happened in the Ohio Valley in the late 1600s. The northwestern frontier became a vast battleground where the English and the French struggled for allies and control. Iroquois warriors attacked Shawnee Indians who supported the French. When French troops marched on Iroquois towns, the Indians burned their homes rather than let them fall to the enemy.

In 1701 the Iroquois, disappointed by the failure of the English to back them up against the French, declared themselves neutral in conflicts between these European powers. For more than 50 years, the Iroquois were able to balance their relationships with the French and the British, focusing on trade and diplomacy rather than war. But during that time, fighting between European colonists and other Native Americans continued. In Maine the Abenaki Indians tried to keep settlers out of their lands. In the south, the Creek, Cherokee, and Yamassee tribes united briefly in a struggle to drive out British traders and settlers. The British managed to turn the Cherokee against the Creek, however, and kept the Indians of the region fighting among themselves.

For years tension had been building between the French and the British, and in the 1750s, the two powers drifted toward a showdown in North America. Most Native Americans, regarding the British as the bigger threat, sided with the French. They were successful at first, but the French could not keep them supplied with guns, ammunition, and food. When it became clear that the British were going to win, the Delaware, Shawnee, and some other tribes deserted the French. The end of the FRENCH AND INDIAN WAR in 1763 did not bring peace between Native Americans and whites, however. Neither did the end of the colonial era. The eastern Indians had been killed, driven away, or absorbed into the fringes of white society. But on the western frontier, fighting continued for many years.

In the Southwest. As they moved into the Borderlands, the Spanish found three general kinds of Native American societies. The first were the hunter-gatherer bands who lived in the rugged badlands* that stretched for hundreds of miles north of central Mexico. The Spanish called these people *chichimecas,* which means "dirty, uncivilized dogs" in the language of the Aztec Indians. The Spanish made ruthless war on the Chichimec Indians, who fought back with ambushes and lightning-fast raids. The CHICHIMEC WAR reached a peak in the 1580s. Disease and Spanish military force helped end it. However, the turning point came when Spanish authorities made it illegal for settlers to enslave the Chichimec people—a practice that had been responsible for much of the fighting. By around 1600, the Chichimec frontier was more or less peaceful.

The Spanish also encountered farming Indians who lived in fixed settlements. Most of these tribes at first accepted the presence of Roman Catholic missionaries, but sooner or later most rebelled against the strict and sometimes cruel Spanish. One such uprising, the PUEBLO REVOLT in 1680, drove the Spanish out of New Mexico for 12 years. In each case, the Spanish eventually reconquered the rebellious region—often at the cost of many lives on both sides.

Finally, in the northern deserts and the vast Texas plains lived nomadic Indians such as the Apache and Comanche. These Native Americans, who acquired horses in the 1600s and became expert riders, posed a serious threat to settlement in the Southwest. They ambushed trade shipments and military columns and raided both white and Pueblo settlements. They stole cattle and horses—and sometimes people. The Spanish eventually negotiated a peace with the Comanche, with both parties agreeing to attack their common enemy, the Apache.

The Borderlands had never been entirely at peace. Indians had often fought each other before the Europeans arrived, especially in areas of scarce water and food. But by introducing firearms and horses and by embarking on a policy of conquest, the Spanish increased the level of conflict. In the 1700s, the French and British became interested in the region, seeking allies among the Borderlands tribes for strikes against the Spanish. For most of the colonial period, Spain used a combination of force, bribes, and threats but barely managed to balance war and peace in the Borderlands. Not until the Native American population was greatly reduced and weakened by disease, enslavement, alcohol, and war could the whites truly claim to have conquered the Borderlands. (*See also* **Agriculture; Economic Systems; Family; Food and Drink; Housing; Land Ownership; Languages; Medical Practice; Music and Dance; Recreation and Sports; Religions, Native American; Technology; Warfare and Diplomacy.**)

Naval Stores

See *Industries; Ships and Shipbuilding.*

Navajo Indians

*T*he Navajo Indians of the Southwest are the largest tribe in the United States today. They have adapted to their environment, borrowing skills from other groups while developing their own culture. During colonial times, the Navajo frequently came into conflict with Spanish settlers. When the United States gained control of the Southwest in the mid-1800s, the Navajo continued to clash with white settlers in the area.

The Navajo, originally a nomadic group from what is now northwestern Canada, probably migrated to the Southwest sometime in the 1300s or 1400s. They were not a unified tribe but lived in small groups of related families, each with its own leaders. Their language is unrelated to other Indian languages of the Southwest except for that of the APACHE INDIANS, who probably also came from the north.

After the Navajo arrived in present-day Arizona, they gradually adopted a way of life centered on agriculture. They borrowed farming techniques from the PUEBLO INDIANS, who had been in the region for thousands of years. However, unlike the Pueblo, who settled in towns, the Navajo preferred to live on small, isolated family plots.

The Navajo made a place for themselves in the region, staging frequent raids on the Pueblo for food and land. Despite the hostility between the two tribes, the Navajo imitated the Pueblo in many ways. They learned Pueblo techniques of pottery, sand painting, and weaving and also borrowed elements of Pueblo ceremonies. But the Navajo modified the Pueblo styles and rituals* to meet their own needs. Their ceremonies, mainly concerned with healing, included chants that were sung to create a balance between humans and nature.

The Navajo first had contact with the Spanish in the early 1600s. Beginning in the 1700s, Spanish Franciscan* missionaries tried unsuccessfully to convert the Indians to Christianity. Although they rejected European religion, the Navajo did adopt the Spanish practice of sheep raising. It soon became one of their major economic activities. Sheep provided the Indians with meat and with wool to make clothes. They also used the wool for blanket making, which developed into an important Navajo craft.

Throughout the late 1700s and early 1800s, the Navajo and Spanish were frequently at war. The Spanish attacked Navajo villages, taking men, women, and children as slaves. The Navajo countered by raiding Spanish settlements for food and livestock.

Hostility between the Navajo and whites continued after the United States gained control of the Southwest in the 1840s. The Navajo signed treaties with the U.S. government in 1846 and 1849. But the Indians continued to fight until 1863, when U.S. troops defeated them and destroyed their homes. Forced to move to New Mexico, the Navajo were allowed to return a few years later to a reservation in Arizona and New Mexico, which grew into the largest reservation in the United States. (*See also* **Native Americans.**)

* **ritual** ceremony that follows a set pattern

* **Franciscan** member of the Order of Friars Minor, a religious brotherhood

Navigation

* **maritime** related to the sea or shipping

*T*he word *navigation* has two meanings, one general and one specific. The specific meaning refers to the art of determining location and setting a course. The general meaning includes every kind of maritime* activity.

The explorers, traders, and sea captains of the colonial era needed to know where they were on the earth's surface in order to reach their destination. They relied on compasses, MAPS AND CHARTS, and a few other simple tools to find their location. Even before the age of European exploration began in the 1400s, seafarers knew how to tell their latitude, or distance north or south of the equator. For centuries they had been using the astrolabe, a tool developed by ancient astronomers to measure the height of the sun above the horizon. To determine latitude, a person calculated the sun's height at a particular location, then consulted tables listing its height at various latitudes on the same day of the year. (The method also worked with the moon and certain bright stars.) In the 1500s, mariners replaced the astrolabe with a device called the cross-staff, which was easier to use.

Navigators of the colonial period also had compasses to indicate in which direction they were sailing. But finding their longitude, the distance

Sailors in the 1400s and early 1500s calculated their latitude with the help of a device called an astrolabe. This engraving by Jan Collaert, based on an original by Stradanus, shows explorer Amerigo Vespucci using an astrolabe.

east or west of a particular line between the North and South poles, was more difficult. Accurate clocks are needed to measure longitude, and such clocks were not available until the mid-1700s. Before that time, navigators used a method called dead reckoning to estimate longitude. They kept records of their speed and the direction in which they sailed during every four- or eight-hour period and used this information, along with observations of latitude, to pinpoint their position on a map. Sometimes they were right—and sometimes they were very wrong. Dead reckoning led many mariners astray, occasionally to watery deaths when their ships hit unexpected reefs.

Many sailors did not rely on formal navigation at all but simply used instinct, experience, and the position of the sun to guide them through familiar waters. This was especially true of coastal trading boats, fishermen, smugglers, and others whose work did not take them on long open-sea voyages. In colonial North America, people often navigated lakes, rivers, and coastal waters in this way.

* **rigging** network of lines or ropes that raises, lowers, and positions a ship's sails

Seafaring was a dangerous business. A sailor's life was filled with hardships, including harsh weather and accidents. Many mariners were crushed by shifting cargo or fell to their deaths from the slippery, wind-tossed rigging*. Their wages were low, and the food provided by shipowners was usually scanty and sometimes rotten. The lack of fruits and vegetables on long voyages led to a disease called scurvy, which caused sailors to suffer frequent bleeding and loose teeth. Sailors had few rights and sometimes suffered rough treatment from cruel captains. Despite these disadvantages, however, men continued to seek the seafaring life. It provided a way to escape the boring, humdrum existence of a landbound apprentice, farm laborer, or servant. (*See also* **Exploration, Age of; Fish and Fishing; Ships and Shipbuilding.**)

Navigation Acts

*T*he Acts of Trade and Navigation, better known as the Navigation Acts, were a series of laws passed in the 1600s that governed England's trade and the trade of its colonies for many years. With these acts, PARLIAMENT tried to protect England's interests in the colonies, to restrict foreign competition in trade, and to encourage English shipping.

The first official Navigation Act, passed in 1651, attempted to prevent foreigners from profiting from trade with England's colonies. In particular, they were meant to keep Dutch merchants—the great rivals of the English—away from the colonies. The act required all goods exported from or imported to the colonies to travel on English-owned vessels. In addition, three-fourths of every ship's crew had to be English.

The act governed trade between other nations and England as well. Goods shipped between England and another country could travel only on English vessels or on vessels from that country. In addition, such goods had to be sent directly from the country where they were produced. Scotland fell under the category of a foreign country until it united with England in 1707 to form Great Britain.

In 1660 a new Navigation Act placed limitations on the export of certain products from the colonies to protect England's supply of valuable resources. Colonial merchants could ship tobacco, sugar, and indigo* only to England or another English colony. Later the list of "enumerated goods"—products placed under trade restrictions—expanded to include rice, molasses, beaver skins, lumber, copper, and iron. Merchants were allowed to ship items that were not on the list directly to foreign ports from the colonies. However, the goods still had to be transported on English vessels, and these vessels had to be built in England or an English colony.

A 1663 law controlled colonial imports as well as exports. Goods from Asia and Europe had to travel to the colonies from England. Any products shipped directly to the English colonies from another country were highly taxed. Exceptions were made for certain items, such as salt and some wines.

Because many colonial merchants attempted to get around the 1660 act by SMUGGLING, England passed a new law in 1673 that required merchants to pay a heavy duty on all enumerated goods leaving colonial ports. The Navigation Act of 1696 further tightened control over colonial shipping. It created courts to enforce trade regulations and established a customs* service to

* **indigo** plant used to make a blue dye

* **customs** tax on imports; agency that checks imported goods and collects such taxes

monitor shipping. Customs officials were sent to 50 ports along the North American coast.

To some extent, the colonies benefited from the acts. The New England shipbuilding industry grew as a result of England's need for vessels, and the tobacco colonies enjoyed a ready market for their crop in England. However, the restrictions did increase prices on some goods in the colonies. (*See also* **Trade and Commerce.**)

Netherlands

*U*ntil the late 1400s, the area that includes the present-day Netherlands was divided into a number of separate provinces ruled by surrounding kingdoms and noble families. Several of these provinces joined together during the colonial period to form an alliance called the United Provinces of the Netherlands. In the 1600s, the Dutch, the people of the United Provinces, created a great commercial empire that extended from Asia to North America.

Road to Unification. In the 1300s and 1400s, the provinces of the Netherlands, known as the Low Countries, began to develop trading ties throughout northern Europe. Many towns and ports became flourishing commercial centers. At the time, the region was ruled by the dukes of Burgundy (now part of France).

In the late 1400s the Low Countries passed, through marriage, to the Hapsburgs, a powerful dynasty* in central Europe and SPAIN. In 1555 the Hapsburg emperor Charles V gave the Low Countries to his son, King Philip II of Spain. Tensions soon arose between the two countries over religion and politics. Spain was a Catholic country, but most of the inhabitants of the Low Countries were Protestant. Attempts by Philip II to stamp out Protestantism and to enact economic and political measures that favored Spain led to discontent and rebellion among the Dutch in the 1560s.

One of the leaders of the rebellion was William I, prince of the House of Orange, the most important Dutch noble family. Under William's leadership, the rebels succeeded in driving the Spanish from the country's northern provinces in 1574. But Spain remained in control of the southern provinces.

In 1579 the northern provinces formed a political alliance called the Union of Utrecht, and two years later they declared independence from Spain. Spain, however, refused to recognize their independence. Fighting between the Dutch and the Spanish broke out again in 1621. The conflict became part of the Thirty Years' War, then raging in Europe between Catholic and Protestant powers. The war ended in 1648 with the signing of the Peace of Westphalia. Under this treaty, Spain and the other nations of Europe recognized the full independence of the United Provinces of the Netherlands, as the northern provinces were now called.

Golden Age. During the late 1500s and early 1600s, the Dutch had created a great commercial empire that controlled most of the trade of northern Europe. This trade not only financed the rebellion that led to independence from Spain, but it also provided the money needed to develop overseas

* *dynasty* succession of rulers from the same family or group

* **charter** written grant from a government conferring certain rights and privileges

colonies. However, the States General—the representative assembly of the United Provinces—did not become directly involved in colonization. Instead, it granted charters* to private companies to develop trade and establish colonies throughout the world.

The two most important trading companies in the Netherlands were the DUTCH EAST INDIA COMPANY, founded in 1602, and the DUTCH WEST INDIA COMPANY, founded in 1621. The East India Company controlled trade with Asia, but it failed to establish any permanent colonies there. The West India Company launched the colony of NEW NETHERLAND in North America.

The 1600s were an era of great prosperity for the Netherlands. Dutch merchants traded in spices from Asia and furs from North America. Dutch ships carried the trade goods of other nations and became involved in the African SLAVE TRADE. Prosperity helped create a golden age of Dutch culture, and the painters and philosophers of the Netherlands became renowned throughout Europe. The Netherlands also became the most tolerant* country in Europe, allowing groups such as Jews and English Puritans to live peacefully and enjoy a high degree of freedom.

* **tolerant** allowing different views and behavior

European Wars.   The commercial power of the Netherlands led to conflicts with other nations. In the mid-1600s, the Dutch fought a series of wars with England after the English Parliament passed the NAVIGATION ACTS, laws that attempted to restrict Dutch trade in North America. In 1664 the Dutch lost New Netherland to the English. Soon after these wars ended, however, the Netherlands formed an alliance with England, and this was reinforced by the marriage of William III of Orange to the English princess Mary. The couple later became rulers of England.

Wars against France, Spain, and other nations weakened the Dutch empire in the late 1600s. This decline continued throughout the 1700s. In 1795 French troops invaded the Netherlands and renamed it the Batavian Republic. The French emperor Napoleon Bonaparte later absorbed the country into his empire. The Netherlands regained its independence in 1814 and became a constitutional monarchy ruled by the House of Orange, the dynasty that had helped unite the provinces of the Low Countries more than 200 years before. (*See also* **European Empires; Exploration, Age of.**)

New Amsterdam

*N*ew Amsterdam was the capital of NEW NETHERLAND. The DUTCH WEST INDIA COMPANY began building the town in 1625 on the southernmost tip of Manhattan Island. In 1664 the English took control of New Amsterdam and renamed it NEW YORK CITY.

Peter Minuit, the first director general of New Netherland, purchased Manhattan from the Indians in 1626 in exchange for trade goods worth 60 guilders, or about $24. At that time, New Amsterdam was already under construction. The detailed plans drawn up by the West India Company called for a five-sided fort with two gates connected by a street. The houses of the director general and members of his council were built around the marketplace in the center of the fort. A wagon road outside the fort led to the company farms.

This illustration shows New Amsterdam, capital of the Dutch colony of New Netherland, in 1659. Under the directorship of Peter Stuyvesant, the residents of New Amsterdam repaired the city's fort (A), finished the church (B), and improved the houses and streets. To maintain law and order, the city also had a prison (E), gallows (G), and pillory (H), where minor criminals were held for public viewing.

* **autocratic** ruling with absolute power and authority

Life was harsh for the early residents of New Amsterdam. Company leaders exercised rigid control, and the director general and council members argued constantly. In 1628 the first ordained minister to arrive in the colony reported that the people had little food and little freedom. Moreover, their housing was primitive, with most of the colony's 270 settlers crowded in bark huts near the walls of the fort.

The next decade saw several improvements in New Amsterdam. The company built a new fort, including barracks for soldiers. Residents gained a bakery and more houses. A new church was begun, but an Indian war in 1637 interrupted construction. Director General Willem Kieft's unwise attempts to tax local Indians and to meet all resistance with violence kept New Amsterdam constantly under attack for several years.

When Peter STUYVESANT took over as director general in 1647, New Amsterdam was once again in poor condition, and the settlers were discouraged. Stuyvesant and his council made peace with the Indians, passed rules to control public drunkenness, and sent out work crews to repair streets, houses, and fences. Money was raised to build a school, finish building the church, and repair the fort. Despite Stuyvesant's accomplishments, his autocratic* rule angered many people and led to public protests. In 1652 the Dutch West India Company instructed Stuyvesant to establish a more democratic city government for New Amsterdam. He did so but continued to fight the new leaders for control of the city.

A truce in 1655 cut short another war with the Indians, and New Amsterdam enjoyed a brief period of peace. In Europe, however, the Dutch and English fought a series of wars, and in 1664 the Dutch were forced to give up New Netherland. New Amsterdam passed into the hands of the English, becoming New York City. The Dutch briefly recaptured New York in 1673 and renamed it New Orange, but the English regained control of the city in 1674 and continued to hold it until the American Revolution. (*See also* **Netherlands.**)

New England Colonies

See *British Colonies; Connecticut; Massachusetts; New Hampshire; Rhode Island.*

New England Confederation

Established in 1643, the New England Confederation—also known as the United Colonies of New England—was a political union of the Massachusetts, Connecticut, Plymouth, and New Haven colonies. Its aim was to provide a common defense and to spread Puritan beliefs. Because of religious and political differences with the member colonies, Rhode Island and Maine were not invited to join the confederation.

Fear of Indian attack was the main reason for the confederation. The PEQUOT WAR had ended only a few years earlier, and the Indian threat remained strong. The colonies also worried about the possibility of Dutch and French expansion into New England. In addition to their military goals, the members hoped that the confederation would be useful in spreading Puritanism and in handling problems such as capturing runaway servants and escaped prisoners.

The government of the confederation consisted of eight commissioners, two from each colony. The commissioners met at least once each year, and six of them had to approve a decision before it could take effect. They had the authority to negotiate with foreign governments and other colonies, to oversee relations with Indians, and to resolve disputes between member colonies.

Most powerful during its early years, the New England Confederation grew weaker in the 1660s, after New Haven merged with Connecticut. The alliance came to an end in 1684, when Massachusetts, the largest member, lost its charter* from the English crown, although the other members continued to meet until 1689.

* **charter** written grant from a ruler conferring certain rights and privileges

New France

The French colony of New France occupied an enormous expanse in North America. Stretching from the Atlantic Ocean to the Great Lakes and beyond in the northern part of the continent, it also included parts of the Mississippi River valley. Colonization of this vast area proceeded very slowly, and New France remained thinly settled throughout its history. Although it never fulfilled France's hopes for a profitable overseas venture, the colony did play a strategic* role in the power struggle between France and Great Britain.

* **strategic** key part of a plan; of military importance

Regions of New France

New France was divided into five administrative zones, with a central government located at QUEBEC. The province of Acadia included present-day NOVA SCOTIA, New Brunswick, Prince Edward Island, and part of the Gaspé Peninsula. Its economy revolved around fishing and farming, and Acadia developed trading relations with neighboring regions, including the English colonies of New England. Acadia had its own governor and provincial government headquartered at the town of PORT ROYAL.

The second region, Labrador and the King's Posts, included all of the territory north of the Gulf of St. Lawrence. This thinly populated area had a seasonal economy based on fishing and whaling. Consisting of scattered trading posts and a few fishing communities, it did not have its own provincial government.

The main province of New France was CANADA, which covered both shores of the ST. LAWRENCE RIVER inland as far as MONTREAL. The heart of France's North American empire, this area contained most of the colonial

* **subsistence farming** raising only enough food to live on

* **charter** written grant from a ruler conferring certain rights and privileges

population and served as the administrative, social, and economic center of New France. During its early years, subsistence farming* and the FUR TRADE dominated the economy of Canada. Agricultural production and trade began to expand in the late 1600s and early 1700s.

The territory beyond Montreal—known as the *pays d'en haut* (upper country)—extended westward along the upper reaches of the St. Lawrence River. Primarily a fur-trading area, the region had few settlers. The fifth section of New France, the *Mer de l'Ouest* (Western Sea), included the area around the Great Lakes and extended westward. French missionaries and traders gradually pushed southward from the Great Lakes into the Mississippi River valley. This region, known as the Illinois country, later became part of the French colony of LOUISIANA.

Early History

The history of New France began with the explorer Jacques CARTIER, who discovered the Gulf of St. Lawrence in 1535 and then sailed up the St. Lawrence River as far as present-day Montreal. He called the area Canada, after an Indian word for village. An attempt by Cartier to start a settlement in Canada failed, but his voyages established France's claim to the region that later became the center of New France.

Early Settlement. For the rest of the 1500s, France did little to colonize North America. It focused its attention on problems at home, including religious wars between Catholics and Protestants. A period of peace in the early 1600s finally allowed France to launch a plan for colonization. Its first efforts consisted of granting royal charters* to groups of private investors who wanted to start colonies.

In 1605 a group of French merchants established a temporary base at Port Royal in Nova Scotia. From there, the explorer Samuel de CHAMPLAIN

In 1535 explorer Jacques Cartier sailed up the St. Lawrence River. His voyage established French claims to the region that became New France.

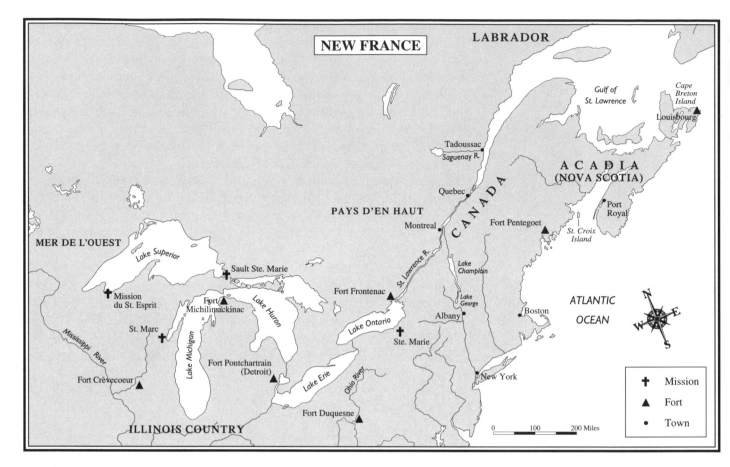

At its height, New France extended well into the Great Lakes region. During a series of wars in the 1700s, however, France lost virtually all its North American territory to Britain.

led expeditions along the Atlantic coast and the St. Lawrence River in search of a good location to start a colony. In 1608 Champlain and Pierre du Gua, Sieur de Monts, founded Quebec—France's first permanent settlement in North America. Quebec later became the administrative center of New France.

Settlement of Quebec proceeded very slowly. Fur traders established trading networks with Native Americans, and JESUITS and other missionaries arrived to work with the Indians and convert them to Christianity. But the colony failed to attract large numbers of colonists, in part because of the harsh climate. Meanwhile, a permanent French settlement was established at Port Royal in 1610, laying the foundations for the region of Acadia. From the beginning, Acadia was plagued by tensions—conflicts between groups within the province and the threat of attack from the English, who also claimed the territory.

The French crown finally stepped in to help. In 1627 Cardinal Richelieu, a high royal official, formed the COMPANY OF ONE HUNDRED ASSOCIATES to speed the colonization of New France and to establish the beginnings of a North American empire. Although granted control over the entire continent north of Florida, this commercial company focused its efforts on Canada and Acadia. It set up an administration to govern New France and began to recruit colonists.

Royal Control. For about 35 years, the Company of One Hundred Associates struggled to expand the fur trade and lure colonists to New France. The

British capture of Port Royal in 1627 and Quebec in 1629 dealt a temporary blow to colonization efforts, but the French recaptured both settlements in 1632.

Despite the colony's slow but steady growth, the company was beset by financial problems. It also had difficulty defending the colony from threats of Indian and English attacks. The French government finally brought an end to the company in 1663 and took direct control of the COLONIAL ADMINISTRATION of New France.

Once under royal control, New France became a part of the centralized government of France. The colony had two main government officials: a governor-general, who served as overall military commander and handled relations with other colonies and with Native Americans, and an intendant, who was "responsible for justice, public order, and finance." Both were appointed and supervised by authorities in France. Canada, the most populated province, developed a sophisticated system of local government. Acadia and the other regions, however, had no organized local government. They were controlled by military governors who answered directly to royal officials in Quebec.

To encourage faster colonization of New France, the French crown created the SEIGNEURIAL SYSTEM, a pattern of landholding in which individuals were granted the rights to large pieces of property in exchange for attempting to bring settlers to work the land. Under this system, settlement in Canada began to expand along both sides of the St. Lawrence River. Subsistence farming was the region's main economic activity.

Growth and Conflict

In the mid-1600s, New France entered a period of expansion that extended its borders far beyond Canada and Acadia into the Great Lakes region and the entire Mississippi Valley. This expansion brought France into increasing conflict with Britain over control of North America.

Expansion of New France.   French explorers, traders, and missionaries continued to push westward throughout the late 1600s and early 1700s. Attracted by furs, land, and other possibilities, these people extended the territory of New France into the region around the Great Lakes. Colonization was discouraged because officials considered fur trading the most important activity. Military and fur-trading posts sprang up at strategic locations throughout the area.

From the Great Lakes, the French moved both westward and southward. In the 1670s, the explorers Louis JOLLIET and Jacques Marquette led expeditions to the upper reaches of the Mississippi River and traveled south on the river as far as present-day Arkansas. Nine years later, René-Robert LA SALLE continued exploring the river to its mouth at the Gulf of Mexico and claimed the entire Mississippi Valley region for France. Most of that territory never became part of New France and later was governed as the colony of Louisiana.

In the early 1700s, French explorers pushed farther and farther west from the Great Lakes, opening an area to trade that extended to the foothills of the Rocky Mountains. Most of this region remained a wilderness during the colonial period, traveled only by explorers and fur traders.

Fort Detroit

In 1701 Antoine de la Mothe Cadillac and 100 colonists and soldiers founded a military base on the Detroit River at the western end of Lake Erie. Serving as a fort, mission, and trading post, Fort Pontchartrain du Détroit occupied a key position in the region. Cadillac persuaded many Indians to settle near the fort, and he encouraged marriage between the Europeans and the Indians. He believed it would help cement relations between the two peoples and strengthen French control of the area. In the early 1700s, Fort Detroit was the only frontier outpost in the "upper country" with a significant number of French colonists.

* **populous** having many inhabitants

Despite this territorial expansion, New France remained very thinly populated, especially compared to the British colonies. By 1755 Canada—the most populous* region of New France—had only about 55,000 people. In comparison, the British colonies claimed more than a million inhabitants. The lack of settlement weakened French control over its North American colonies.

Conflict with Britain. As French territorial claims in North America grew, France came into increasing conflict with Britain, its chief rival in the competition for an overseas empire. Between the late 1600s and mid-1700s, the two nations fought a series of wars in both Europe and North America.

During the second of these wars, known in North America as QUEEN ANNE'S WAR (1702–1713), France lost Acadia to Britain. An exposed border area, Acadia had always been claimed by both countries, and it had suffered numerous attacks from British colonists over the years. France also gave up all rights to NEWFOUNDLAND, a large island off the North Atlantic coast also claimed by the British.

With the loss of Acadia, the French took steps to strengthen their position in other areas of New France. In 1714 they began building a new fortress at the port of LOUISBOURG on Cape Breton Island, located off the northern coast of Nova Scotia. From this fort, the French could guard the approach to the St. Lawrence River, which led to the heart of New France.

In the 1750s, the French started to build a string of forts from the Great Lakes to the Ohio Valley region to defend their claims in this area. However, the British also laid claim to the Ohio Valley. Conflict over the territory led to the outbreak of the FRENCH AND INDIAN WAR, the final struggle between Britain and France in North America.

Lasting from 1754 to 1763, the war resulted in a great victory for Britain. The French lost the capital city of Quebec in the decisive Battle of the Plains of Abraham in September 1759. But they still held Montreal and continued to fight until the following September. Under the TREATY OF PARIS of 1763 that ended the war, France ceded* all its North American possessions east of the Mississippi River to Britain, except for the tiny islands of Miquelon and St. Pierre off the coast of Newfoundland. Spain, which had become involved in the war in 1762, received the territory of Louisiana under a separate agreement.

* **cede** to yield or surrender

With France's defeat, New France ceased to exist. French culture, however, remained firmly rooted in the St. Lawrence Valley and Nova Scotia and continued to play a dominant role in the life of those areas. It still does. (*See also* **Cities and Towns; Economic Systems; European Empires; Exploration, Age of; Government, Provincial; Land Ownership.**)

New Hampshire

*T*he colony of New Hampshire, located between MASSACHUSETTS and MAINE, was settled by the English in the 1620s. The colony had little land along the Atlantic Ocean, but its hilly interior contained valuable pine forests. Most of New Hampshire's towns grew up along the coast.

Before the arrival of the colonists, the ABENAKI and other Indian tribes lived in the region. English explorers Martin Pring and John Smith were among the first European visitors. Smith's description of the area attracted

People

Ætatis suæ 21. Aº. 1616.

Plate 1

In his history of the Jamestown colony, John Smith told of his capture by the Powhatan Indians and his rescue by Pocahontas, the chief's daughter. Pocahontas later married English colonist John Rolfe. This portrait of the Indian princess in European clothing was painted in London, which she visited in 1616.

Plate 2
George Whitefield helped ignite the Great
Awakening, a religious revival in the British
colonies. A powerful preacher, Whitefield
traveled widely, attracting enormous
crowds wherever he spoke.

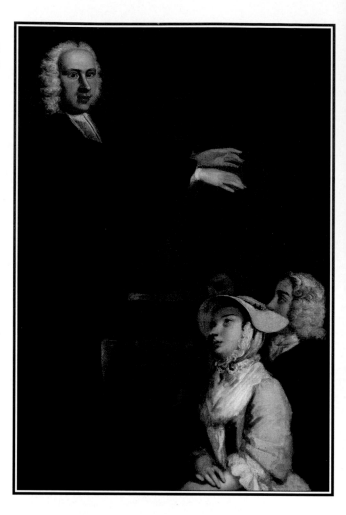

Plate 3
Spanish missionaries and soldiers led the way in colonizing California.
The priests attempted—with mixed results—to bring Christianity and
European ways to the Native Americans. This illustration of Indians
dancing in front of the Spanish mission at San Francisco was made by
Louis Choris in 1813.

Plate 4
During the colonial period, women had few opportunities in the business world. Anne Catherine Green, however, took over her husband's printing shop after his death and gained great respect in Maryland. She served as the colony's official printer and published the weekly *Maryland Gazette*. Charles Willson Peale, one of the leading artists of the day, painted her portrait in 1769.

Plate 5
Well-to-do colonists often commissioned an artist to create a family portrait. Members of this family, dressed in their Sunday best, were painted in the late 1700s by an unknown artist.

Plate 6
A former slave, Olaudah Equiano (also known as Gustavas Vassa) taught himself to read and write. His heart-rending account of his forced voyage from Africa and his life as a slave was published in 1789 and became a best-seller.

Plate 7
This painting by Edward Savage (perhaps started by Robert Edge Pine) recreates a major moment in American history, as members of the Second Continental Congress vote on the Declaration of Independence in 1776. Among those shown are Thomas Jefferson, John Adams, Roger Sherman, John Hancock, and Benjamin Franklin.

considerable attention in 1614, and shortly afterward, England's Council for New England began to issue grants for settlements there. In 1622 Sir Ferdinando Gorges and Captain John Mason received a grant that included most of present-day Maine and New Hampshire. The following year David Thomson established New Hampshire's first settlement at Odiorne's Point, near what is now Portsmouth.

Mason received a new grant in 1629 for the land between the Merrimack and Piscataqua rivers. He named it New Hampshire. Settlers arrived from England and Massachusetts and established the towns of Strawberry Bank (now Portsmouth), Dover, Exeter, and Hampton. Mason died, and Massachusetts laid claim to the four towns in 1641. Almost 40 years later, Mason's grandson protested that Massachusetts had no right to the territory. Authorities in London agreed, declared New Hampshire a separate colony, and appointed a governor in 1679.

New Hampshire's location near the French settlements of the St. Lawrence River valley made it the scene of conflicts between France and England in North America. Because the French had alliances with local Indian tribes, New Hampshire's towns suffered frequent Indian raids during King William's War and Queen Anne's War. The attacks left the colony in turmoil, and in 1699 the English placed Massachusetts and New Hampshire under the authority of one governor. When peace returned, settlers began again to flow into New Hampshire. They staked claims along both sides of the Merrimack River, harvested timber, and established farms in the countryside.

In the 1740s, New Hampshire once again received its own royal governor, and the colony began to expand westward. Between 1749 and 1764, the governor issued a total of 138 grants of land to settlers in an area that is now Vermont. New York, which had been issuing grants in the same territory, disputed the New Hampshire grants. New Hampshire colonists held firm and formed a militia*, the Green Mountain Boys, to defend their claims. About the same time, the colony acquired its first college when Reverend Eleazer Wheelock founded Dartmouth as a school for Indians.

The independence movement spreading through the British colonies gained support in New Hampshire when the colony's governor, John Wentworth, sent aid to the British army in Massachusetts. In December 1774, New Hampshire colonists attacked a British fort on their coast, carrying away powder and guns. The following spring they revolted against Wentworth, who fled for safety, ending royal government in New Hampshire. The colony's militia fought in various conflicts during the American Revolution, including the Battle of Bunker Hill. New Hampshire patriots* also sailed from Portsmouth to raid British ships. New Hampshire was the first colony to adopt a new state constitution in January 1776. When New Hampshire approved the United States Constitution on June 21, 1788, it brought the number of states in the union to nine—the total needed for the Constitution to take effect.

See map in British Colonies (vol. 1).

* **militia** army of citizens who may be called into action in a time of emergency

* **patriot** American colonist who supported independence from Britain

New Haven Colony

See *Connecticut.*

See map in British Colonies (vol. 1).

* **proprietor** person granted land and the right to establish a colony

* **dissenter** person who disagrees with the beliefs and practices of the established church

Settled first by the Dutch and Swedes, New Jersey later became one of the 13 original British colonies. Under the English, the colony was split into East Jersey and West Jersey, and it remained divided for almost 40 years. Though smaller and less powerful than neighboring Pennsylvania and New York, the colony played an important role in the AMERICAN REVOLUTION.

Early Settlement.

When the Europeans began exploring present-day New Jersey, the DELAWARE INDIANS occupied the land. Among the earliest European visitors to the area was Giovanni da Verrazano, who sailed along the New Jersey coast in 1524 in the service of France. In 1609 Henry HUDSON, an Englishman exploring for the Dutch, sailed into Newark Bay in northern New Jersey. Dutch fur traders arrived in the region soon after.

In the 1620s, the DUTCH WEST INDIA COMPANY began to encourage settlement of the region, which became part of NEW NETHERLAND. A patroonship, or large estate, established at the site of what is now Jersey City failed to attract colonists. But small Dutch communities sprang up along the Hudson and Delaware rivers. In the mid-1600s, SWEDISH SETTLEMENTS on the lower part of the Delaware began to spread into the southern part of New Jersey.

English Settlement.

In 1664 the Dutch lost New Netherland to the English. King James gave the territory to his brother, the Duke of York. The duke kept part of the colony, which was renamed New York, and granted the lands between the Hudson and Delaware rivers—now called New Jersey—to his friends Lord John Berkeley and Sir George Carteret. The two divided the area between them.

As proprietors*, Berkeley and Carteret hoped to profit from their colony. In 1665 they appointed Philip Carteret, Sir George's cousin, as governor. He encouraged settlement by granting land in New Jersey to PURITANS, QUAKERS, and religious dissenters* from other English colonies and from Europe. Increasing numbers of English colonists began to settle in the colony alongside the Dutch and Swedish settlers already there. As a result, the colony's population became very diverse, with people from many different religions and backgrounds.

Division of the Colony.

In 1674 Lord Berkeley sold his half of New Jersey to two Quakers, Edward Byllynge and John Fenwick. Two years later the colony was officially split into East Jersey and West Jersey. Byllynge and Fenwick held West Jersey, while East Jersey remained in the hands of Sir George Carteret.

The proprietors of West Jersey hoped to make their colony a haven for persecuted Quakers, who soon began settling there in great numbers. But Byllynge and Fenwick disagreed about many issues. Eventually, the colony was divided into 100 land shares—Fenwick received 10 of the shares and Byllynge kept the rest. Byllynge gradually sold most of his land, often in small amounts, while Fenwick held on to all of his shares. In 1688 the Council of Proprietors of West Jersey was formed to handle conflicts over land, which continued for many years.

East Jersey remained in the hands of the Carteret family until 1682, when the colony was sold to a group of Quaker investors. This group—which included William PENN—divided the land into shares and began selling them to

individuals. The Board of Proprietors of East Jersey was formed in 1685 to help distribute the shares and handle arguments over land rights.

By the early 1700s, settlement in East Jersey had spread to the southwest from the Hudson River and Newark Bay area. Many small towns and farms developed throughout the region. Only about 3,500 people lived in West Jersey, stretched out in a thin band east of the Delaware River. The northwestern edges of East Jersey and the central parts of West Jersey were largely unsettled. The economies of the two Jerseys remained limited to small-scale farming. The colonies did not develop ports or trade to challenge the cities of New York and Philadelphia, and they continued to be primarily agricultural.

Unification of the Colony.

Political problems in East and West Jersey mounted, particularly over the issue of land rights. The proprietors had repeatedly sold their interests in the colonies to other investors, who in turn had sold them again. The colonists began to question whether the proprietors had a legitimate right to govern.

In 1688 the English crown canceled the charters of the Jerseys, New York, and the New England colonies and forced them all to become part of the DOMINION OF NEW ENGLAND. Although this political arrangement lasted only a short while, it further weakened the power of the Jersey proprietors. Riots erupted in the 1690s, and the governments collapsed.

Under pressure from the English crown, the proprietors finally agreed to give up their right to govern. In 1702 Queen Anne united East and West Jersey to create the colony of New Jersey and placed it under royal control. The proprietors continued to manage land rights.

From 1702 to 1738, New Jersey shared a royal governor with New York, though it maintained a separate assembly. Despite royal control, conflicts over land and opposition to the proprietors continued, and riots broke out again in the 1740s.

New Jersey also suffered from religious and political divisions. The western part of the colony, which remained mostly Quaker, consisted of large estates held by wealthy landowners. Eastern New Jersey, by contrast, had many small farms and towns and was inhabited primarily by Puritans and Anglicans*. These differences continued for many years.

The American Revolution and After.

On the eve of the American Revolution, New Jersey had a large number of Loyalists, people who wanted to remain within the British empire. But in the end, the colony voted for independence and supported the war. Several important Revolutionary battles were fought in New Jersey because of its strategic* location between New England and the southern colonies.

In 1787, when representatives from the states were drawing up plans for a new government for the United States, New Jersey struggled to make sure that small states such as itself would be protected and have equal rights under the new Constitution. Its efforts led to the creation of the two houses of Congress—the House of Representatives, which gave the states representation based on their population, and the Senate, which gave equal representation to all states. New Jersey became the third state to approve the Constitution. (*See also* **British Colonies; Colonial Administration; Government, Provincial.**)

* ***Anglican*** member of the Church of England

* ***strategic*** key part of a plan; of military importance

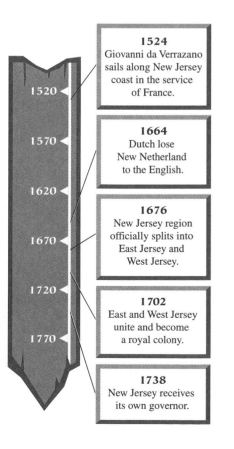

1524
Giovanni da Verrazano sails along New Jersey coast in the service of France.

1664
Dutch lose New Netherland to the English.

1676
New Jersey region officially splits into East Jersey and West Jersey.

1702
East and West Jersey unite and become a royal colony.

1738
New Jersey receives its own governor.

1520
1570
1620
1670
1720
1770

New Mexico

* **Spanish Borderlands** northern part of New Spain, area now occupied by Florida, Texas, New Mexico, Arizona, and California

* **outpost** frontier settlement or military base

* **mestizo** person of mixed Spanish and Indian ancestry

 See first map in Exploration (vol. 2).

* **New Spain** Spanish colonial empire in North America; included Mexico, the area now occupied by Florida, Texas, New Mexico, Arizona, and California, and various Caribbean islands

* **friar** member of a religious brotherhood

* **viceroy** person appointed as a monarch's representative to govern a province or colony

* **pueblo** Indian village; apartment-like dwelling of multiple levels with rooms for many families

Soldier and Peacemaker

Governor Juan Bautista de Anza's daunting task was to make peace with the Comanche and win them as allies against the Apache. A cool and courageous soldier, Anza won the Comanche's respect on the battlefield—by marching into their country and ambushing and killing their chief. Seven years later, after much negotiation, Comanche leaders came to a colorful and impressive ceremony that Anza arranged. With flowery speeches, he gave them gifts. They dug a hole and then refilled it as a sign that their war was over.

New Mexico was the first region in the western part of the Spanish Borderlands* that Spain explored and colonized. The Spanish hoped the area would turn out to be another Mexico—a land filled with riches. Their hopes were not realized, but the province of New Mexico survived as a dusty, hardworking outpost* of Mexico. It became a meeting place of cultures where the PUEBLO INDIANS of the Rio Grande, the fierce, roving APACHE and COMANCHE tribes, and European and mestizo* soldiers, missionaries, and settlers from Mexico met, clashed, and mingled.

The Spanish found New Mexico to be an unforgiving land of rugged mountain ranges, high plateaus, and few water sources. However, early Native American civilizations such as the Mogollon, Hohokam, and Anasazi developed ways of life suited to the region's harsh climate and geography. Their descendants, the Pueblo Indians, were living in villages there and farming when the Spanish arrived in the late 1500s.

Exploration and Early Settlement. The Spanish came to New Mexico in search of treasure. For centuries officials in New Spain* had heard rumors of legendary golden cities somewhere in the western part of North America. The remarkable journey of Alvar Núñez CABEZA DA VACA, who crossed the continent with three companions, gave new life to these tales. His account led Spanish officials in Mexico to believe that the SEVEN CITIES OF CÍBOLA, rich Native American kingdoms, lay to the north. In 1540 they sent Francisco Vásquez de CORONADO to look for the legendary cities. Instead of glittering palaces, the disappointed expedition found adobe villages inhabited by ZUNI INDIANS. They also found the Grand Canyon—which failed to console them for the complete absence of gold, diamonds, and emeralds.

Forty years later Catholic missionaries made their first attempt to convert Native Americans who lived along the Rio Grande. Although the friars* met their deaths at the hands of the Indians, their expedition revived interest in the land Coronado had explored. New stories about silver mines began to circulate.

In 1583 the king of Spain ordered his viceroy* in New Spain to send someone to the frontier lands in the north to bring the Indians living there under Spanish control and to convert them to Christianity. The viceroy awarded a contract for this mission—the colonization of New Mexico—to Juan de OÑATE. In return for an annual salary, the title of governor, and the right to distribute land to his followers, Oñate agreed to pay the expenses of bringing 200 soldiers and their families to the Rio Grande and building a settlement there.

Oñate arrived in New Mexico in 1598, built a church, and founded San Gabriel as his capital. But the new colony did not prosper, and Oñate did not find the deposits of gold and silver that he had expected. He lost men in clashes with the Indians as well as from desertion. In 1607 the Spanish crown removed him from office and made the province of New Mexico a royal colony.

That same year Governor Pedro de Peralta took up his duties. His first act was to establish a new capital high above a stream in an uninhabited valley. He called it SANTA FE. New Mexico's population began to increase, though not as quickly as Spanish officials expected. Colonial authorities and the ROMAN CATHOLIC CHURCH engaged in a long and sometimes violent struggle for control of the province. Consumed by this contest, the Spanish failed to focus on growing trouble in the Indian pueblos*.

Chimayó Sanctuary, north of Santa Fe, was built in 1816, five years before the end of Spanish rule in New Mexico. According to legend, the dirt from the floor of the church has mystical healing powers.

Until the 1670s, Franciscan missionaries had been at the forefront of Spanish activity in New Mexico. They forced Native Americans to build churches, to learn European crafts such as blacksmithing and carpentry, and to follow work schedules. They also attempted to stamp out Pueblo religious practices, which they considered evil. Aided by Spanish soldiers, the missionaries whipped and hanged Native American religious leaders and broke into kivas—chambers that the Indians considered sacred—to destroy religious objects such as masks. In 1680, pushed beyond their limit, the Indians turned against the Spaniards in a bloody uprising. The PUEBLO REVOLT drove the Spanish out of New Mexico for more than ten years.

The Later Colonial Years. In 1692 Diego de Vargas led Spanish troops north into New Mexico. When he reached Santa Fe, he found that the Indians had turned the former governor's palace into a pueblo. At first it seemed that Vargas might reconquer New Mexico without violence, but in the end he had to go to war. He learned from earlier mistakes, though, and left the kivas untouched. By the end of the century, he had restored peace between the Spanish and the Pueblo, and the Spanish government granted the Indians ownership of their lands.

During the next century, Spanish settlers—mostly sheep ranchers—moved into the province and established new towns such as Socorro in the north and Albuquerque in the south. By 1799 New Mexico's population consisted of about 20,000 Spanish and 10,000 peaceful Indians. Other more warlike tribes lived in the border mountains and beyond. Each year bands of nomadic Apache, Comanche, Ute, and sometimes NAVAJO came to trade at a great fair at Taos, where they swapped buffalo hides, buckskins, and horses for Spanish goods and Pueblo food. By universal agreement, the fairs were peaceful—but the rest of the time, these tribes raided white settlements and Indian pueblos throughout New Mexico. White settlers staged attacks on the Indians as well. The toll of deaths, some by torture, mounted. Indians and Europeans seemed locked in an endless cycle of violence.

The turning point came in 1776, when King Charles III separated the Spanish Borderlands from New Spain and made the northern region a new military department of the Spanish empire. He appointed a capable general to organize the frontier defenses and provided him with 2,000 extra soldiers. That general gave the task of bringing the hostile Indians under control to Juan Bautista de Anza, the new governor of New Mexico. Anza carried out the assignment with skill, determination, and imagination. He arranged a series of alliances and treaties that brought peace to the region and encouraged new settlement and economic growth.

The British, and later the Americans, posed a different threat. While exploring North America, they frequently crossed the borders of Spanish territory. In 1807 Spanish authorities arrested an American army officer named Zebulon Pike, who had been on a mission to explore the West. After the Spanish released Pike, he provided Americans with their first description of the New Mexican capital of Santa Fe.

In the following years, the people of Mexico fought a war to end Spanish rule. After Mexico won independence in 1821, the Spanish colonial era in New Mexico came to an end, and Mexico took control of the region. New Mexico became a territory of the United States in 1850, as a result of the Mexican War, and a state in 1912. (*See also* **Exploration, Age of; Mexican Independence; Native Americans.**)

*T*he Dutch had only one North American colony—New Netherland— and they held it for only 50 years. That colony was neither very large nor very prosperous and did not get off to a good start. The Dutch government neglected New Netherland in favor of activities elsewhere, and the directors of the company that ran it argued about its goals. The colony's settlers had to endure Indian wars and invasions by settlers from other colonies. Yet in spite of all these difficulties, New Netherland became a thriving center of trade and agriculture.

The heart of New Netherland lay in the HUDSON RIVER valley in what is now New York State. The colony's population, the most diverse in North America, consisted of black and white people from many countries. But the basic culture of New Netherland was Dutch. Long after the Netherlands had lost its claim to the land, the Dutch heritage of that region lived on to become part of the culture of the United States.

Early Years. The Dutch presence in North America began with Henry Hudson's 1609 voyage of exploration along the Atlantic coast from Delaware Bay to the mouth of the Hudson River. The DUTCH EAST INDIA COMPANY, which imported silks, spices, and other Asian goods to Europe, had sponsored Hudson's expedition in the hope that he would find a northern sea route to China. Although Hudson did not find such a passage, he sparked Dutch interest in trading for furs with the Indians of North America. Traders sailed to the coast he had explored, entering into fierce and sometimes bloody competition. The government of the Netherlands restored order in 1614 by giving another organization, the New Netherland Company, a charter* for all trade rights between Maine and Virginia.

* **charter** written grant from a government giving certain rights and privileges

Thriving Patroonship

Kiliaen Van Rensselaer established Rensselaerswyck, his Hudson River valley estate, on some of the richest farmland in the region. A West India Company fort in the middle of Rensselaerswyck protected the estate and became the principal fur-trading post in New Netherland. Bakers, tailors, shoemakers, blacksmiths, carpenters, and other crafts workers settled in the patroonship to sell goods and services to the traders. Waterpower from the Hudson drove mills that ground grain and sawed logs for the booming construction industry. By the 1650s, the patroonship stretched along both sides of the river and had 1,000 inhabitants.

* **outpost** frontier settlement or military base

The company's first act was to build an outpost* called Fort Nassau on the upper Hudson River, near present-day ALBANY, to serve as a base for its FUR TRADE with the Indians. But the New Netherland Company's charter ended in 1618, and for a few years, the territory once again became the site of cutthroat competition. In 1621 a new charter gave trading rights in the area to the DUTCH WEST INDIA COMPANY, a large organization with worldwide operations. The West India Company dealt in gold from Africa, sugar and wood from Brazil, and salt from the West Indies. New Netherland was just one of the company's many interests—and not, in the eyes of some company directors, a very important one.

Peter Minuit.   The first settlers, about 30 families, arrived in New Netherland in 1624. The company spread them out among three isolated trading posts in the valleys of the upper Hudson River, the Connecticut River, and the Delaware River. The plan was for these and later colonists to create farming communities that would support trading posts along all three rivers. But the outposts ran into trouble with Indians, partly because some Dutch leaders unwisely became involved in conflicts between local tribes. When Peter Minuit, the colony's new director general, arrived in 1626, he quickly took steps to make New Netherland safer and more efficient.

Minuit gave the Indians some inexpensive trade goods in exchange for Manhattan Island at the mouth of the Hudson River. He then pulled all the settlers back from the outposts to Manhattan. NEW AMSTERDAM, a village at the southern tip of the island with a port that remained free of ice all year round, became the colony's capital and main settlement.

By this time, the directors of the West India Company were engaged in a debate over their goals in New Netherland. Some wanted to encourage colonization and build a large Dutch community to keep other powers from taking over the territory. Other directors were more interested in trade and feared that settlers would compete with the company's traders. In 1629 the directors agreed to allow private individuals to colonize New Netherland. People who settled 50 colonists at their own expense would receive a large tract of land and the right to govern those who lived on it. Several of these estates, called patroonships, were established, but only one of them flourished. Located in the upper Hudson River region, it was called Rensselaerswyck after its founder, Kiliaen Van Rensselaer. The other patroonships failed, and the West India Company took back the land.

Minuit had supported colonization and the patroonships, and this made him unpopular with some company directors. His directorship ended in 1631. He left New Netherland struggling for survival, lacking settlers and financial resources. The 1630s and 1640s brought new troubles. The colony's leaders became involved in a series of Indian wars that forced farmers to flee to Manhattan for safety. English settlers from New England began moving into territory in the Connecticut River valley that the company regarded as its own. The English eventually forced the Dutch to give up this region in a 1650 treaty.

Meanwhile, the population of New Netherland was growing steadily. In the late 1630s, the West India Company had decided to encourage settlement by relaxing the rules that had made it difficult for colonists to own land and

New Netherland

The small Dutch colony of New Netherland lasted only 50 years before being taken over by the English in 1664. Most of the Dutch settlers chose to remain in the colony, adding a strong Dutch influence to what became New York.

NEW NETHERLAND

engage in trade. Not all the new settlers came from the Netherlands. European nations from Norway to Croatia were represented in the colony's population, half of which was non-Dutch. Some of these settlers had lost their homes in European wars. Blacks from Africa and the West Indies, most of them slaves but some free, and JEWS from Brazil and Europe also lived in the colony. In 1644 a visitor to New Netherland remarked that he could hear 18 languages spoken in the streets of New Amsterdam.

The Stuyvesant Years.   The colony's last director general, Peter STUYVESANT, took charge in 1647. Stuyvesant was an honest, capable, and energetic official, but he was also stubborn and autocratic*. During his years as director, the company further loosened its once-strict control over New Netherland. The colonists gained some degree of self-government, and New Amsterdam officially became a city with a governing council.

Immigration increased during Stuyvesant's directorship, despite several wars with the Indians. A new settlement at the present site of Schenectady marked the farthest reach of Dutch expansion to the north. Another important event of Stuyvesant's rule was the conflict between the Dutch and the Swedish in the Delaware River valley. Sweden and the Netherlands had long been trading partners in Europe, and many Dutch merchants had business connections in Sweden. In the 1630s, a West India Company director who

* **autocratic** ruling with absolute power and authority

was not satisfied with the slow pace of colonization in New Netherland entered into a secret partnership with the Swedish government to establish an American colony. To lead this venture, they chose Peter Minuit. He founded New Sweden on the Delaware River, near what is now Wilmington.

The West India Company was not pleased to see the Swedish moving into its territory, but it lacked the strength to push them out. At first Dutch and Swedish settlers even joined forces to drive out English intruders, burning their houses and barns. But when Stuyvesant took over as director general of New Netherland, he was determined to reclaim the Delaware Valley for the company. Aided by a large warship from the city of Amsterdam, Stuyvesant forced the soldiers of New Sweden to surrender in 1655. Most of the colonists from Sweden and Finland, however, remained in their own villages as a "Swedish nation" within New Netherland.

After the mid-1650s, New Netherland experienced a burst of growth. But the Dutch colony was under pressure from the English, who had settled New England to the north and the Chesapeake Bay area to the south. England wanted to control the entire Atlantic coast of North America. Disagreements over trade and colonization led to a series of wars between England and the Netherlands in the mid-1600s. These conflicts, called the Anglo-Dutch wars, marked the end of New Netherland. In August 1664, Stuyvesant surrendered the colony to an English fleet, and New Netherland became the English colony of New York.

Nine years later, during the Third Anglo-Dutch War, the Netherlands recaptured the colony and controlled it for 14 months. In the end, however, the Dutch returned New York to the English in exchange for rights to the colony of Surinam on the northern coast of South America. Many of the colonists who had settled in New Netherland remained, even after the colony passed permanently into English hands. Their language, customs, food, clothing, and architecture remained distinctively Dutch for several generations. (*See also* **European Empires; Exploration, Age of; Immigration; Land Ownership; Swedish Settlements; Trade and Commerce.**)

New Orleans

regent person appointed to govern while the rightful monarch is too young or unable to rule

See map in Spanish Borderlands (vol. 4).

*L*ocated on the banks of the MISSISSIPPI RIVER, New Orleans was settled by the French in the early 1700s. The city played a key role in France's plan to gain control of the Mississippi Valley. It served as the capital of LOUISIANA under French and later Spanish rule.

Louisiana's governor, Jean-Baptiste Le Moyne, Sieur de Bienville, founded New Orleans in 1718. The new town included a fort to protect the water route to Biloxi—then the main settlement of Louisiana—and a fur-trading post. It was named to honor the Duc d'Orleans, the regent* of France.

Under French rule, New Orleans remained a primitive town and an unprofitable port. But in 1736 the French did establish a hospital for the poor there, Charité, which is now the oldest hospital in North America. The TREATY OF PARIS of 1763 transferred control of Louisiana—and New Orleans—to Spain.

The new Spanish governor, Antonio de Ulloa, arrived four years later to take charge of the colony. In 1768 French settlers in the colony rebelled

against Ulloa's administration, forcing him out of office. A Spanish expedition led by Alejandro O'Reilly arrived in New Orleans to put the revolt down. After restoring order, O'Reilly executed the rebel leaders and replaced French forms of government with Spanish systems.

* *indigo* plant used to make a blue dye

Under Spanish rule, New Orleans became a bustling shipping center. Products such as indigo*, tobacco, lumber, and furs came down the Mississippi River on flatboats to the city, where they were transferred to ocean-going ships. After fires swept New Orleans in the late 1700s, local officials required that all houses of more than one story be built of brick. Well-constructed houses and public buildings began replacing rickety wooden structures.

New Orleans's reputation for glamour and gaiety began in colonial times. The many soldiers stationed at the fort during French and Spanish rule spurred the development of a lively nightlife, including drinking, gambling, and dancing. At one time, there were so many ballrooms in New Orleans that city officials tried to close some down. Theater and opera productions added to the spirited entertainment scene. The residents of New Orleans enjoyed parades and festivities on MARDI GRAS and other religious holidays.

* *aristocratic* referring to people of the highest social class, often nobility

* *mulatto* person of mixed black and white ancestry

The customs of different ethnic groups also contributed to making New Orleans an exciting, colorful place. The original French and Spanish settlers, known as CREOLES, became the aristocratic*, landowning class. ACADIANS—French refugees from British Nova Scotia—formed another distinct group. Their descendants came to be known as Cajuns. A large percentage of New Orleans's population consisted of blacks and mulattoes*, both free and slave. Immigrants from Ireland and other European countries added to the cultural mix.

Spain controlled New Orleans for nearly 40 years. Then, under the terms of the Treaty of San Ildefonso, Louisiana returned to France in 1803. The city remained in French hands for only 20 days before France sold Louisiana to the United States. New Orleans thus became part of the expanding American nation. (*See also* **Race Relations.**)

See maps in European Empires (vol. 2).

*N*ew Spain was Spain's colonial empire in North America. Centered in MEXICO, it extended from the SPANISH BORDERLANDS—the area now occupied by Florida, Texas, New Mexico, Arizona, and California—south to present-day Panama. Various islands in the WEST INDIES, including Cuba and HISPANIOLA (present-day Haiti and the Dominican Republic), were also part of New Spain. After 1565 the Philippine Islands, located off the coast of Asia, came under the administrative control of New Spain as well.

When Hernando CORTÉS defeated the Aztec Indians in Mexico in 1521, he named the territory he conquered New Spain. The Spanish crown quickly began to establish its authority there and to take over surrounding areas. In 1535 the crown formed an administrative region called the Viceroyalty of New Spain that included all of Spain's possessions in North America and Central America. It was governed by an official known as a VICEROY. Spain later established other viceroyalties in South America.

The Spanish crown divided New Spain into various towns and provinces and established a complex system of administration to govern them. The authority of the viceroy extended throughout all of New Spain, but his control was actually limited. For the most part, provincial governors and other regional officials ruled the territories outside Mexico.

New Spain ceased to exist after 1821, when Mexico gained its independence from Spain. Mexico controlled the Spanish provinces of Central America until they declared their independence in 1823. The Spanish Borderlands remained under Mexican rule until taken over by the United States in the mid-1800s. (*See also* **Colonial Administration; European Empires; Government, Provincial; Mexican Independence.**)

New Sweden

See *Swedish Settlements.*

New York

aken over in 1664, the Dutch colony of NEW NETHERLAND became the English colony of New York. This Dutch-English background as well as the settlers of varied origins who arrived later made the colony a place of considerable diversity. In the conflicts between Britain and France and again in the struggle for independence during the American Revolution, New York played a leading role because of its central location in the British colonies.

Early Exploration and Settlement. The first European to visit the area was Giovanni da Verrazano. Arriving in 1524, the Italian explorer who worked for France took a brief sail into the mouth of the HUDSON RIVER. In 1609 the English navigator Henry HUDSON guided his ship the *Half Moon* up the Hudson River while exploring for the Dutch. That same year, French explorer Samuel de CHAMPLAIN entered northern New York from the St. Lawrence Valley and explored the lake that now bears his name.

Soon after Hudson's voyage, Dutch merchants began sending trading ships to the Hudson River valley. In 1614 the Dutch established a temporary fort and trading post called Fort Nassau near present-day ALBANY. Several years later, the government of the Netherlands granted the DUTCH WEST INDIA COMPANY a charter to establish a colony in the region.

Dutch colonists began settling the colony of New Netherland in 1624. Their two earliest and most important settlements were Fort Orange (on the site of Albany) and NEW AMSTERDAM, which became the colony's capital.

The Dutch controlled New Netherland for only 40 years. England also claimed the region and resented the Dutch settlements that were wedged between its colonies of Virginia and Massachusetts. In 1664 an English fleet sailed into the Hudson River and forced the Dutch to surrender New Netherland.

See map in British Colonies (vol. 1).

The king of England gave the conquered territory to his brother James, the Duke of York. The duke granted the lower part of the territory to two nobles, who established the colony of NEW JERSEY. He kept the rest for himself, renaming it New York. New Amsterdam soon became known as NEW YORK

When the English took over the Dutch city of New Amsterdam in 1624, they allowed the Dutch colonists to continue to attend their own churches. William Burgis made this engraving of the New Dutch Church on Nassau Street in 1731.

CITY. The Dutch recaptured New York in 1673, but the English took it back the following year.

Early Years of English Rule.

After gaining control of the colony, the Duke of York quickly began the task of making it more English. Working through royal governors, he changed the laws of the colony to follow the English system of law. The new legal code granted personal freedoms and provided for local governments in Albany and New York City. The duke also encouraged English settlers to move into the area. In 1683 he established a representative assembly for the colony.

Although the English put their governmental system into effect with no problem, establishing their culture in the colony was more difficult. Many Dutch settlers had stayed on under English rule, but they remained faithful to the Dutch Reformed Church and Dutch traditions and customs. Immigrants from Germany, Scotland, France, and other countries added to the mix of ethnic, social, and religious groups. As a result, New York became one of the most diverse colonies in North America.

In 1685 the Duke of York inherited the throne of England, becoming James II. As king, he tried to gain more control over the colony by canceling its charter and dissolving its representative assembly. He then made New York part of the DOMINION OF NEW ENGLAND, which was governed by Sir Edmund ANDROS. These actions led to a period of unrest and violence in New York.

During this time in England, religious conflict broke out between Protestants and Catholics. In 1688 Protestant forces removed James, a Catholic, from the throne and replaced him with the Protestant monarchs William and

Mary. News of these changes reached New York the following year. The Dominion of New England came to an end, leaving New York with no strong governing institutions.

Acting on a rumor that Catholics were going to invade the colony, Jacob Leisler, a local merchant and a fierce opponent of Catholicism, led an uprising in 1689. With the support of the colony's militia*, he seized New York City's fort and declared himself lieutenant governor of New York. LEISLER'S REBELLION increased the political turmoil in New York, and his heavy-handed policies angered many colonists.

In 1691 William and Mary appointed a new governor for New York and sent a small army to restore order. Leisler was arrested and hanged for treason. To help smooth things over with the colonists, the English crown granted New York an elected assembly. For many years, the assembly was the scene of bitter debates between people who had supported Leisler and those who had opposed him. Throughout the rest of the colonial period, the governors of New York had to balance their relationships with these groups carefully to keep peace in the colony.

militia army of citizens who may be called into action in a time of emergency

Growth and Development.

New York grew and developed slowly at first. During the late 1600s and early 1700s, the colonial government's policies restricting land ownership discouraged new settlement. To raise revenue and gain support, several of New York's royal governors continued the Dutch practice of granting huge tracts* of land in the Hudson River valley to wealthy families. One of the largest was the Livingston Manor, given to Robert LIVINGSTON. As a result, only a limited amount of land suitable for farming remained for other settlers.

tract area of land

Good land was still available in the western part of the colony during this period, but life on that frontier proved to be extremely dangerous because of conflicts with the French and their Indian allies. These conflicts disrupted the FUR TRADE, a very important economic activity in New York during its early years. War and political clashes also interfered with the colony's economic development. After 1713, however, the situation started to improve. New York's economy shifted away from furs, and grains, meat, and other foods became major export products. The colony also developed a thriving shipping industry and began to compete with the prosperous ports of Boston and Philadelphia.

Growing trade with Britain and the West Indies helped improve the colony's economy and attract increasing numbers of immigrants. Between 1720 and 1770, the population of the colony soared from about 36,000 to about 168,000—including about 19,000 African Americans, the largest number of any northern colony—and began spreading throughout the Hudson and Mohawk river valleys. During that time, Albany became an important center for upper Hudson Valley agriculture, and New York City became a leading colonial port. More and more of the colony's settlements were linked by roads, rivers, and networks of trade.

A Battleground Between Britain and France.

Because of its location—bordered by New England, New France*, and the western frontier—New York played a strategic* role in the conflict between Britain and France. The Hudson River, Lake George, and Lake Champlain formed a chain of

New France French colony centered in the St. Lawrence River valley, an area known as Canada; included the Great Lakes region and, until 1713, Acadia (present-day Nova Scotia)

strategic key part of a plan; of military importance

131

interconnecting waterways that served as an invasion route between New France and the British colonies. The ST. LAWRENCE RIVER and Great Lakes provided access to the western parts of the colonial frontier.

In the late 1600s, Britain attempted to counter the French by maintaining an alliance with the tribes of the IROQUOIS CONFEDERACY, which controlled the Mohawk River valley and western regions of New York. After 1700, however, the Iroquois decided to remain neutral. But some of them did become involved in the struggles between the two European powers.

During the first colonial wars between Britain and France—KING WILLIAM'S WAR (1689–1697), QUEEN ANNE'S WAR (1702–1713), and KING GEORGE'S WAR (1744–1748)—the French and their Indian allies launched devastating raids on frontier settlements in New York. New Yorkers responded by joining British expeditions against New France. The colony played an even greater role in the FRENCH AND INDIAN WAR (1754–1763). Albany became the center of British operations in that war, and the area north of Albany remained a battleground for much of the war.

One of the key figures of the French and Indian War was Sir William JOHNSON, a wealthy merchant and landowner and New York's superintendent of Indian affairs. In 1754 Johnson took part in the ALBANY CONGRESS, a meeting of colonial representatives that was called to discuss defensive measures against the French. Johnson helped plan Indian policy at the congress and was involved in persuading the Iroquois to end their neutrality and renew their alliance with the British. During the French and Indian War, Johnson led several successful expeditions against the French.

In the years following the French and Indian War, British actions such as passage of the Stamp Act in 1765—which placed a tax on paper goods and documents—caused widespread resentment in the colonies. New Yorkers joined other Americans in challenging British authority with protests and boycotts* of British goods. In October 1765, New York City hosted the Stamp Act Congress, a meeting in which representatives of nine colonies gathered to discuss ways to resist British policies.

Despite such activities, New York was not a leader in rebellion against the British. As the movement for independence grew, New Yorkers were divided over the issue. The colony included thousands of Loyalists, people who did not want to break away from Britain. In addition, many of the wealthy people who controlled New York's assembly feared the changes a revolution might bring. As a result, New York was the last colony to sign the Declaration of Independence, delaying approval until July 9, 1776. But the following day, the colony's assembly declared New York a free state.

Once war broke out, New York became a major battleground of the Revolution. About a third of all battles were fought there, and Britain's Indian allies regularly raided the state's frontier region, causing widespread destruction. A key part of British military strategy was to gain control of New York, driving a wedge between New England and the southern states and ending American unity. In September 1776, the British captured New York City and held it for the remainder of the war. But they failed to take the rest of the state. Britain's defeat at Saratoga, New York, in October 1777 is considered the turning point of the American Revolution. In November 1783, two years after the end of the war, the British finally withdrew from New York City.

* **boycott** refusal to buy goods as a means of protest

New York's Blacks

African Americans were part of New York City's diverse population from the time the English took over in 1664. By 1698 about 14 percent of the people living in the city were black. Most of them were slaves in the homes of merchants and artisans. Although free blacks also lived in New York, their small community shrank during the 1700s as the English grew more reluctant to grant freedom to slaves. Two major slave revolts occurred during this period, but slavery continued to be part of New York's economy.

New York played an important role in the early years of the newly independent United States. New York City served as the nation's capital from 1785 to 1790, and George WASHINGTON took the oath of office as the first President at Federal Hall in Manhattan. The state grew rapidly in the late 1700s and early 1800s. By 1820 New York had become the most populous* state in the United States. (*See also* **British Colonies; Colonial Administration; Government, Provincial.**)

* *populous* having many inhabitants

New York City

Originally founded by the Dutch as NEW AMSTERDAM in 1626, New York became one of the most important cities in the British colonies. Its central location at the mouth of the Hudson River helped it develop into a prosperous port and a thriving commercial center. The city also served as the capital of the colony of NEW YORK and later, for a short time, as the capital of the United States.

The English took possession of New Amsterdam in 1664, when they seized NEW NETHERLAND from the Dutch. They named both the colony and the city New York in honor of the Duke of York, the brother of the English king. The Dutch recaptured the city in 1673, but England succeeded in taking it back the following year.

In the early years of English rule, colonial authorities allowed city residents considerable political and religious liberty. They hoped that this freedom would promote economic growth and ensure the loyalty of the Dutch settlers who remained in New York. The city's first charter*, granted in 1686, gave citizens various rights, including that of owning and selling land. The charter established a government patterned after city governments in England. It divided New York into districts, or wards, and allowed each of them to elect two representatives called aldermen. The city's highest official, the mayor, was appointed by the colonial governor upon the aldermen's suggestion. Together the mayor and aldermen acted as both a city council and a court.

New York grew steadily throughout the next century, and by 1770 its population had reached about 20,000. The people came from many different cultural, religious, and social backgrounds. There were Dutch, French, German, Portuguese, and Spanish settlers, as well as those from Great Britain. The population also included a significant number of African slaves and a small community of FREE BLACKS, as well as a small Jewish community.

As New York City grew, it became more prosperous and cosmopolitan*. Civic improvements included streetlights in 1697 and fire-fighting equipment in 1731. The *New York Gazette,* the city's first newspaper, began publication in 1725, and King's College—now Columbia University—was founded in 1754.

New York's growth and prosperity did not occur without problems. In 1689, after Protestants reclaimed the English throne, a colonist named Jacob Leisler seized power in the city. He claimed he was protecting it from a feared Catholic invasion, but English authorities hanged him for treason, and LEISLER'S REBELLION left deep divisions in New York. In 1712 and again in 1741, the city experienced some of the largest slave rebellions in the colonial era.

In the 1760s, New York City suffered a serious economic crisis. High unemployment, inflation*, and taxes all contributed to New York's opposition

* *charter* written grant from a government conferring certain rights and privileges

See color plate 5, vol. 1.

* *cosmopolitan* worldly, not provincial and narrow; having wide interests and knowledge

* *inflation* increase in prices

to British colonial policies in the period leading up to the American Revolution. In October 1765, the city hosted a congress to protest the STAMP ACT, which required colonists to pay taxes on paper goods and documents. New York's SONS OF LIBERTY, formed about this time, encouraged colonists to disobey the Stamp Act. New Yorkers organized a COMMITTEE OF CORRESPONDENCE in 1774, and the city held its own "tea party" the same year. But many leading citizens of New York hesitated to support the movement for independence. While opposing British policies, they wished to remain loyal to the crown.

In the early months of the Revolutionary War, the British captured New York and remained in control of the city until November 1783. Many Loyalists* found refuge there. After the war, New York gradually began to recover. It served as the capital of the United States from 1785 to 1790, and by the early 1800s, it had become the largest city in the nation. (*See also* **Cities and Towns; Slave Resistance.**)

* **Loyalist** American colonist who remained faithful to Britain during the American Revolution

Newfoundland

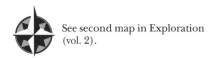

See color plate 4, vol. 1.

See second map in Exploration (vol. 2).

* **cede** to yield or surrender

*T*he island of Newfoundland lies off the coast of Canada between the Gulf of St. Lawrence and the Atlantic Ocean. During the colonial period, the French and the English competed for control of the island because of the rich fishing grounds in the surrounding waters.

The first Europeans to set foot in Newfoundland were probably Norse explorers, who called it Vinland. The Norse built a settlement on its north shore around 1000, but they did not remain there long. In 1497 the explorer John Cabot landed on the east coast of the island, which the English king Henry VII called "the new founde lande." Cabot's glowing reports of the region's well-stocked waters brought fishing ships from England, France, Portugal, Spain, and the Netherlands. The sailors who came to Newfoundland to fish needed to preserve their catch for the long journey home. Some packed the fish in salt, but others went ashore to dry it in the sun. As a result, small fishing communities grew up along the shore during the 1500s.

The English explorer Sir Humphrey GILBERT landed on the eastern coast of Newfoundland in 1583 and claimed the island for England. In 1621 George CALVERT founded an English settlement on the island but abandoned it after several years. About 40 years later, the French established a colony on the south shore at present-day Placentia. In the early 1700s, Newfoundland was the scene of land and sea battles between England and France during QUEEN ANNE'S WAR. Defeated, France ceded* the island to Britain in the TREATY OF UTRECHT (1713) but was granted the right to land its ships along part of the coast. Newfoundland became a British colony and received a royal governor.

During the FRENCH AND INDIAN WAR, the French attacked the island. However, the TREATY OF PARIS, signed in 1763 after the war, confirmed Britain's right to Newfoundland and left France only the small, nearby islands of St. Pierre and Miquelon. The British later added Labrador, on the Canadian mainland, to the territory governed by Newfoundland. Newfoundland became a province of Canada in 1949. (*See also* **Canada; Fish and Fishing; Norse Settlements.**)

Newport

See map in British Colonies (vol. 1).

*L*ocated on an island off southeastern RHODE ISLAND, the town of Newport developed into one of the most important seaports in the British colonies. It was founded in 1639 by a group of people from the Massachusetts Bay colony who disagreed with the religious policies imposed by the PURITANS of Massachusetts. Like Roger WILLIAMS, the founder of nearby Providence, these dissenters* wanted to be able to worship in their own way.

The colonists from Massachusetts settled first on the northern end of Aquidneck Island, creating the community of Portsmouth. But after disputes among the settlers, two of them—William Coddington and John Clarke—led a group to the southern end of the island and founded Newport.

The leaders of Newport established a policy of religious toleration*, which encouraged QUAKERS, JEWS, and members of other religious groups to settle there. The town's location and fine harbor attracted many merchants, who set up trading connections with other British colonies and with the West Indies and Africa. Their international trade, which involved the buying and selling of rum, molasses, and slaves, brought great wealth to local merchants. It also led to the opening of sugar refineries and rum distilleries and to the development of a shipbuilding industry to supply trading vessels.

By the mid-1700s, Newport was flourishing. In 1758 James Franklin, a nephew of Benjamin Franklin, founded the community's first newspaper—the *Newport Mercury*. Public and church-run schools provided instruction for the children of Newport. The town's large and prosperous Jewish community finished construction of Touro Synagogue in 1763. A fine example of colonial architecture, it is the oldest synagogue in the United States today.

Like other New England towns, Newport became involved in the turmoil leading to the American Revolution. In 1765 many of its citizens demonstrated against the STAMP ACT, participating in several days of rioting. During the Revolution, British troops took over Newport from 1776 to 1779. The British occupation took a heavy toll on the town. Many of its wealthy residents fled, moving inland to avoid the British. In addition, the British destroyed many of the town's buildings.

In July 1780, a French army of 6,000 soldiers arrived at Newport to support the American patriots* in the war. The French made the town their military headquarters until the following June, when they advanced to Virginia to assist the Americans in the final campaigns of the war.

Many wealthy merchants and other citizens did not return to Newport after the Revolution ended. As a result, the town entered a period of economic decline. Although Newport never regained its former economic importance, it became a fashionable seaside resort for well-to-do Americans beginning in the mid-1800s. (*See also* **Rum Trade; Slave Trade.**)

Newspapers, Magazines, and Pamphlets

*N*ewspapers flourished in the British colonies of North America. Widely read, they promoted the easy exchange of news and ideas and helped create a sense of unity and shared culture throughout the colonies. Magazines did not appear until late in the colonial period, but pamphlets on a variety of topics were published as early as the mid-1600s. In the years leading up to the American Revolution, political pamphlets and

Most colonial newspapers supported the patriot cause during the Revolutionary period. This masthead from the *Massachusetts Spy* urges the colonies to "join or die" and begs "Great Liberty" to lead them on.

* **Spanish Borderlands** northern part of New Spain, area now occupied by Florida, Texas, New Mexico, Arizona, and California

* **broadside** large sheet of paper, printed on one side, that was handed around or posted on buildings and walls

newspapers played a leading role in shaping political thought in the British colonies. Neither the French colonies nor the Spanish Borderlands* had newspapers.

Development of Newspapers. In the early 1600s, printers in the English colonies issued broadsides*, which reprinted items from newspapers in England and occasionally included news about colonial events. These broadsides did not appear on a regular basis, however, and were not real newspapers.

The first attempt to create a colonial newspaper was *Publick Occurrences Both Forreign and Domestick.* Published in Boston on September 25, 1690, it lasted for only one issue. Government officials quickly put an end to the paper because the publisher had failed to obtain permission to print it. An article criticizing the government's conduct of King William's War might have contributed to the paper's extremely short run.

The *Boston News-Letter* was the first successful newspaper in the British colonies. Founded in 1704, it continued to appear until 1776. Two more newspapers began publication in 1719—the competing *Boston Gazette* and the *American Weekly Mercury* of Philadelphia. The number of newspapers in the colonies rose steadily thereafter. By 1776 there were 39 papers, published in 23 different colonial cities, including a German-language paper in Pennsylvania. Only Delaware lacked a newspaper.

The most famous colonial newspaper was the *Pennsylvania Gazette.* First published in 1728, the paper was purchased by Benjamin FRANKLIN the following year. He quickly turned it into a great success. Besides printing his own witty writing, Franklin introduced a number of new features in his paper, such as the first weather report, the first political cartoon, and humorous articles.

Newspaper Content and Circulation. Colonial newspapers came out weekly. Daily publication did not begin until after the American Revolution. Most papers of the early 1700s consisted of only two pages, occasionally expanded to four. By the mid-1700s, four-page newspapers were becoming common, and the size of the pages increased.

European news dominated the content of colonial newspapers. Printers freely copied articles from London newspapers. But because these papers arrived by boat, the foreign news might be three or four months old. Most local news was related to business. In port cities, for example, papers included

information about the arrival and departure times of ships. Many newspapers provided information about local markets.

Colonial newspapers generally contained at least one page of advertisements, which helped cover the costs of printing. The majority of ads concerned the sale of goods, animals, and other property. Some offered a reward for the return of runaway slaves.

While the content of most colonial newspapers was basically the same, there were exceptions. A number of literary newspapers flourished in the 1720s and 1730s. Papers such as the *New England Courant* and *New England Weekly Journal* published stories, essays, and poems in addition to the news.

Although newspapers generally had no editorials, many began to print letters from readers commenting on colonial events and issues. In 1735 John Peter ZENGER, the publisher of the *New York Weekly Journal,* was arrested and tried for libel* after his paper printed letters criticizing the royal governor of New York. A jury found Zenger not guilty, and his case helped establish the principle of freedom of the press.

Colonial newspapers generally were not sold in shops or on the street. Available through subscription, they were delivered or mailed to readers' homes or businesses, and the development of newspapers was closely linked to the expanding postal system. The cost of a yearly subscription was high, often equal to the weekly wages of a worker. Although the popular *Pennsylvania Gazette* boasted a weekly circulation of more than 2,000, most papers had circulations of between 300 and 600 copies per week. The number of people who read the newspapers was much higher, however. Family members and neighbors shared papers, and taverns and coffeehouses had copies for their customers.

*** libel** making a false statement that damages a person's reputation

Importance of Newspapers.
Newspapers played an important role in colonial life. At a time when most news and information was spread by word of mouth, newspapers helped keep the public informed about events. Because publishers often reprinted articles from other colonial papers, people knew what was happening throughout the colonies. This sharing of experiences contributed to the development of a common colonial identity.

Beginning in the 1760s, the tone and content of newspapers changed drastically. Before then, publishers generally tried to present information in a fairly neutral way. As tensions between Great Britain and the colonies grew, however, publishers began to take sides. Some supported Britain, but most criticized British authority. Newspapers became a place for colonists to air their feelings on these vital issues, which helped rouse opposition to British colonial policies.

Magazines and Pamphlets.
Magazines did not appear in the colonies until 1741. *The American Magazine,* published by Boston printer Andrew Bradford, reported on the proceedings of colonial legislatures. The same year Benjamin Franklin brought out *General Magazine,* which covered a wider range of subjects. Neither publication lasted more than a few months.

Over the next 35 years, 18 magazines were launched in the colonies. Few remained in business for more than a year because there were not enough readers to support both weekly newspapers and monthly magazines. The most successful, *American Magazine and Historical Chronicle,* was published in Boston from 1743 to 1746. It included information on debates in the British Parliament, the proceedings of colonial legislatures, and stories on colonial developments.

Pamphlets on various topics appeared throughout the colonial period. During the Revolutionary era, however, pamphlets increased dramatically in number and importance. Political pamphlets had a central role in developing and debating the crucial issues facing the colonies. Of the hundreds of pamphlets published during that time, *Common Sense* by Thomas PAINE was by far the most popular and most reprinted. (*See also* **Press in Colonial America.**)

Norse Settlements

The Norse—also known as Vikings—landed in North America nearly 500 years before Christopher Columbus's famous voyage to the continent. Around the year 790, these people set sail from the northernmost lands of Europe to raid and trade as far south as the Mediterranean Sea and as far east as Russia. The Norse also sailed west across the Atlantic to the coast of what is now Canada.

In the 800s, the Norse were Europe's finest ocean navigators. Their shipbuilders had learned to make sturdy vessels that could weather the stormy North Atlantic Ocean and could land on any beach. With these ships, Viking chieftains and warriors from Norway and Jutland (Denmark) spread terror, raiding coastal communities in Ireland, England, and France. They also looked around for new lands to settle.

Moving Westward. Increased travel and trade had introduced the Norse to the treasures of other kingdoms, giving chieftains an appetite for the riches they could obtain on foreign shores. At the same time, a long period of unusually warm weather lengthened the growing seasons in northern Europe. As agriculture flourished, the population increased. Soon all of the good farmland was occupied, especially in Norway, and men who had no property sought new territory across the sea.

Already skilled at maneuvering their ships up and down the rocky coasts of their homeland, Norse voyagers colonized several groups of small rocky islands in the northern Atlantic. From these bases, they reached an island they called Iceland in the 870s. Norse chieftains and their followers soon settled the habitable* parts of Iceland.

The Viking practice of island-hopping helped them travel farther westward. Their ships, although sturdy enough to withstand long voyages, could not carry enough supplies to get a crew across the ocean. To extend their reach across the North Atlantic, the Vikings needed a chain of settlements where they could obtain water and food.

Greenland Settlements. Vikings blown off course on their way to Iceland had caught glimpses of land to the west. When an outlaw named Erik the Red was banished from Iceland, he decided to search for this land. He skirted the coast of a place he called Greenland—a huge island off the coast of arctic Canada. Greenland's east coast was a forbidding mass of ice, but the west

* *habitable* able to be lived in

The first Europeans to set foot on North America were the Norse, or Vikings. These skilled seafarers established a settlement in Newfoundland around 1000—nearly 500 years before Columbus made his famous voyage.

coast had grassy fields above the steep coast. Although no trees existed on the island, Erik believed that livestock and people could live there. Around 985 he brought hundreds of colonists from Iceland to Greenland, and they founded settlements on the west coast. Within two or three generations, the Norse had filled all possible farm sites, and the population had grown to nearly 6,000.

For a few centuries, the Greenland settlements flourished and had fairly regular contact with Norway and, through Norway, with the rest of Europe. After the Norse became Christians, Greenland even boasted a bishop and a cathedral, with imported bells and stained-glass windows. The Greenlanders sent seal furs and walrus ivory to Europe in exchange for goods they could not produce at home, such as grain, wood, iron, and cloth.

After about 1300, the weather turned colder, producing long, bitter winters in Greenland and making North Atlantic voyages more hazardous. Then a plague struck Europe, bringing economic decline. European contact with the Greenland settlements declined, then ended. In Greenland, the ESKIMO moved into Norse territory, but the Norse did not adopt the skills and customs of these people who had learned to live off the cold and harsh land. Without aid from Europe, the Greenlanders were doomed. They no longer possessed oceangoing vessels, and by the end of the 1400s, the last of them had died. But before the Greenland colony disappeared, it produced the first European contact with America.

Vinland.   That contact occurred in the early days of Norse settlement, around 1000. Leif Eriksson, son of Erik the Red, sailed west from Greenland and landed at three places. He called them Helluland (Flat Stone Land), Markland (Forest Land), and Vinland (Grape Land). Helluland was what is now known as Baffin Island in northern Canada, and Markland was the peninsula that juts off Canada's east coast—present-day Labrador. The likeliest location of Vinland is the island of NEWFOUNDLAND. There, at a place called L'Anse aux Meadows, archaeologists* have discovered the only

* *archaeologist* scientist who studies past human cultures, usually by digging up ruins

known traces of a Viking settlement in North America. The Norse probably visited it occasionally to gather wood and repair their ships.

Norse literary works called sagas—written several hundred years after the events they describe—tell of several attempts to establish permanent settlements in Vinland. Conflicts with the local Indians and fights among themselves led the Norse to abandon the area. The Vikings were the true European discoverers of America, but by Columbus's time, Europeans had all but forgotten the Norse adventure in America. (*See also* **Exploration, Age of.**)

North Carolina

See map in British Colonies (vol. 1).

*N*orth Carolina was originally part of an enormous land grant known as the Carolinas, named in honor of the English king Charles II. Ruled as a single province for many years, the Carolinas eventually split into two separate colonies—North Carolina and SOUTH CAROLINA. At first the northern part of the province developed more slowly than the southern part. But by the mid-1700s, North Carolina had become one of the fastest-growing colonies in North America.

Early Exploration and Settlement.   The coast of North Carolina was first explored in 1524 by Giovanni da Verrazano, an Italian navigator sailing for France. Spanish explorers and missionaries followed soon after and tried, unsuccessfully, to start a colony.

In the 1580s, Queen ELIZABETH I of England granted Sir Walter RALEIGH the right to establish a colony in the region. The first attempt to found a community on ROANOKE ISLAND off the coast of North Carolina failed, and the settlers returned to England. In 1587 John WHITE brought more than 100 colonists to the island to try again. The settlement they built became known as the Lost Colony because its inhabitants mysteriously disappeared sometime between 1587 and 1590.

The first permanent settlements in North Carolina were not established until the 1630s, when colonists from Virginia moved to the area in search of good land. In the following years, several English settlements sprang up around Albemarle Sound, a large bay south of Virginia's JAMESTOWN COLONY.

In the meantime, King Charles I of England had granted the territory south of Virginia to Sir Robert Heath in 1629. Heath failed to establish any settlements in the region, however, and his grant was taken back by King Charles II in 1663. That same year, the king granted eight men a charter* to colonize the Carolinas. As proprietors* of the Carolinas, they took the first steps to set up an organized colony.

* *charter* written grant from a ruler conferring certain rights and privileges
* *proprietor* person granted land and the right to establish a colony

* *exemption* excused from an obligation

Development and Growth of the Colony.   In 1664 the proprietors divided the Carolinas into two regions: Albemarle to the north and Clarendon to the south. They offered various benefits to encourage settlement, including generous land grants and tax exemptions*. When colonists began to arrive in 1669, the proprietors proposed a plan of government called the Fundamental Constitutions of Carolina, drafted by English political thinker John Locke. The document gave political power to individuals on the basis of the amount of land they owned.

See color plate 3, vol. 1.

Albemarle grew slowly at first, with colonists migrating south from Virginia. The flow of people increased dramatically after 1676, when social unrest and problems with the Indians in Virginia led to BACON'S REBELLION. But the Cape Fear region of Carolina, part of Clarendon County, attracted few settlers because it seemed to have little good land. Albemarle and Clarendon, centered on Charles Town (present-day CHARLESTON), drifted apart. In 1712 Albemarle received its own governor and became a separate colony known as North Carolina. Colonization of the Cape Fear region began the following year.

Settlers continued to migrate to North Carolina during the early 1700s. Most raised TOBACCO, corn, and livestock on small, isolated farms with the help of indentured servants* and slaves. Another important product was tar, made from the sap of pine trees. North Carolina produced so much tar for the naval stores* industry that after independence it came to be known as the Tarheel State.

North Carolina faced several obstacles to growth and development. Long, narrow islands off the coast prevented large ships from reaching coastal settlements. Large swamps and dense forests made communication over land difficult. In 1711 a destructive war erupted with the TUSCARORA INDIANS, who were eventually defeated and forced to leave the area. Only five towns were established during this time: Bath, New Bern, Edentown, Beaufort, and Brunswick.

In 1729 the British crown bought the rights to North Carolina from seven of the eight proprietors and took control of the colony. Once it became a royal colony, North Carolina began to grow more rapidly. As agriculture and industry developed, increasing numbers of settlers poured into the colony, making it one of the fastest growing in British America. Many of these settlers were German and Scotch-Irish immigrants who arrived from the middle colonies by way of the Great Wagon Road.

Many of the newcomers began to settle in the backcountry regions of North Carolina's western FRONTIER. As the number of white settlers in those areas increased, conflicts erupted with the CHEROKEE INDIANS and other tribes. Unable to stop the flow of colonists, the Indians gradually had to move farther west over the Appalachian Mountains.

In the late 1760s, settlers on the frontier became increasingly resentful of high taxes and various policies of the colonial assembly, which was controlled by wealthy landowners from the eastern part of North Carolina. In 1768 the frontier colonists organized a movement to "regulate" their own affairs. Known as REGULATORS, they threatened local officials, seized control of local governments, and occasionally committed acts of violence. A colonial militia* sent by the governor crushed the movement in 1771.

The American Revolution. While frontier settlers were showing their displeasure with their colonial government, colonists throughout North Carolina were expressing their anger against the British government. Many North Carolinians protested the STAMP ACT and other laws passed by PARLIAMENT, organizing boycotts* of British goods and other forms of resistance.

In May 1775, the citizens of Mecklenburg, North Carolina, adopted anti-British resolutions* that suspended the royal colonial government—in effect declaring independence from British rule. A year later, in April 1776, North

* ***indentured servant*** person who agreed to work a certain length of time in return for passage on a ship to the colonies

* ***naval stores*** tar and other products from pine trees that were used on ships

* ***militia*** army of citizens who may be called into action in a time of emergency

* ***boycott*** refusal to buy goods as a means of protest

* ***resolution*** formal statement adopted by a legislature or other organization

Carolinians adopted the Halifax Resolves, which authorized their delegates to the Second Constitutional Convention to support independence from Britain.

Several battles of the AMERICAN REVOLUTION took place in or near North Carolina. In October 1780, North Carolina frontiersmen defeated British troops at the Battle of King's Mountain, South Carolina, helping to slow the enemy's advance. The Battle at Guilford Courthouse in March 1781, the most important Revolutionary battle in North Carolina, inflicted heavy losses on the British.

cede to yield or surrender

After the Revolution, North Carolina continued to grow, particularly the western parts of the state. In 1784 the state ceded* its western territory to the United States government. Residents of that region established a short-lived state called Franklin, an area that later became the state of Tennessee.

In the late 1780s, North Carolinians debated the new United States Constitution. Many small farmers opposed it because it created a strong central government. The state rejected the Constitution in 1788 but voted to approve it the following year. (*See also* **British Colonies; Colonial Administration; Government, Provincial.**)

North, Lord Frederick

1732–1792
British prime minister

repeal to undo a law

*F*rederick North served as prime minister of Great Britain from 1770 to 1782. Determined to hold on to the nation's American colonies, North took steps to strengthen British control. But his policies only increased the colonists' resentment, contributing to the AMERICAN REVOLUTION and the eventual loss of the 13 colonies.

Educated at Oxford University, North belonged to a noble English family. In 1754 he was elected to PARLIAMENT, and in the course of his long career, he held many government posts. When he became prime minister in 1770, Lord North was faced with the difficult task of trying to please King GEORGE III, Parliament, and the American colonists.

By the time North came to office, the British government had already started to tighten its hold over the colonies. The first steps had included enforcing trade regulations and introducing new taxes on imported goods sold in the colonies. In addition, Parliament insisted that the Americans contribute to the costs of protecting and governing the colonies. Having enjoyed a high degree of self-government for many years, the colonists bristled at these changes.

Hoping to calm the angry colonists, the new prime minister had Parliament repeal* all the new import duties—except the tax on tea. But this one remaining tax still troubled the Americans, and in December 1773, they rebelled against British authority by destroying a shipload of tea at the BOSTON TEA PARTY. Parliament, under North's leadership, responded with the INTOLERABLE ACTS of 1774—a series of measures punishing the Massachusetts colonists for their actions. Instead of strengthening British rule, however, these acts brought increased defiance from the colonists. Although at this point neither side expected a war, tensions between the Americans and the British continued to rise. In April 1775, they erupted at the Battles of LEXINGTON AND CONCORD.

Meanwhile Lord North proposed a new plan: Britain would not tax any colony willing to pay its own costs for defense and administration. He sent his representatives to New York in 1776 to discuss the plan, but before they arrived, the SECOND CONTINENTAL CONGRESS issued the DECLARATION OF INDEPENDENCE. No longer focused simply on taxation, the Americans were determined to be free of British rule.

North remained in office through the Revolutionary War but resigned in March 1782, after Britain's defeat. He continued to serve in Parliament and, upon his father's death in 1790, inherited the title of Earl of Guilford. (*See also* **Colonial Administration.**)

Northwest Passage

For hundreds of years, Europeans sought a direct sea route to Asia. After the "discovery" of North America, European explorers began looking for a waterway that linked the Atlantic and Pacific oceans. They probed the eastern and western coastlines and traveled down rivers in search of the fabled waterway known as the Northwest Passage. The dream of finding the passage drove much of the exploration of North America.

The Quest for a Passage to Asia. In 1493 Christopher COLUMBUS returned to Europe with word that he had reached land by sailing west across the Atlantic. He believed that he had arrived in Asia, though not in the wealthy kingdoms of China and India. However, by the time of his death in 1506, many European navigators, mapmakers, and geographers realized that Columbus had found an unknown continent.

Columbus's voyage of discovery did not bring the princes and merchants of Europe closer to the silks, spices, and gems of the East. These luxury goods were in high demand in European markets, but their overland journey from Asia was time-consuming and expensive. As the goods traveled slowly through such places as Turkestan, Persia, Arabia, and Egypt, each trader or agent along the way added a fee. European merchants knew that finding a direct route to China and India by sea would allow them to make huge profits.

As early as 1499, the Portuguese navigator Vasco da Gama had shown that ships could travel around the southern tip of Africa to the Asian ports that lay beyond. Some years later, in 1521, Ferdinand Magellan and his crew sailed around the southern tip of South America and across the vast Pacific Ocean. Both routes, however, were long and dangerous.

England, France, and the Netherlands kept looking for another way to reach Asia. Because Spain and Portugal controlled South America, the northern European nations directed their attention to North America. They hoped to find a route around or through the continent by sailing north and west from Europe. Explorers searching for the Northwest Passage risked the treacherous storms, fog, and ice of the North Atlantic Ocean.

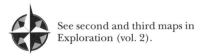
See second and third maps in Exploration (vol. 2).

High Hopes and Disappointments. France launched the first explorations for a Northwest Passage. In 1524 French silk merchants persuaded King Francis I to sponsor a voyage by an Italian navigator named Giovanni da Verrazano. Although the explorer scoured the Atlantic coast from what is now North Carolina north to NEWFOUNDLAND, he failed to find a passage through the land mass. The French tried again in 1535 with Jacques CARTIER,

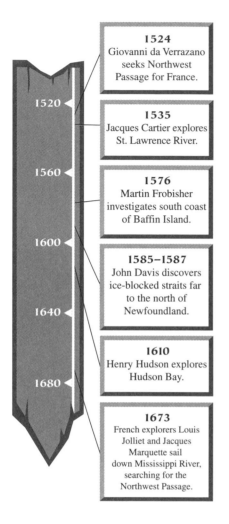

1524
Giovanni da Verrazano seeks Northwest Passage for France.

1535
Jacques Cartier explores St. Lawrence River.

1576
Martin Frobisher investigates south coast of Baffin Island.

1585–1587
John Davis discovers ice-blocked straits far to the north of Newfoundland.

1610
Henry Hudson explores Hudson Bay.

1673
French explorers Louis Jolliet and Jacques Marquette sail down Mississippi River, searching for the Northwest Passage.

* *strait* narrow waterway connecting two larger bodies of water

who explored the ST. LAWRENCE RIVER. Cartier discovered that rapids blocked the river, but he heard stories from Indians of a water route through North America somewhere to the west.

The English joined the search for the passage in the 1570s, when Martin Frobisher made several voyages far north of Newfoundland. He explored the southern coast of Baffin Island, a large island that lies between Greenland and the mainland of arctic Canada, but became sidetracked by an unsuccessful quest for gold. John Davis, looking for the passage in the 1580s, went farther north and west than Frobisher had gone. Davis found several straits* that he thought might be entrances to a Northwest Passage, but ice filled these northern waterways, forcing him to turn back.

English interest in finding the passage grew in the early 1600s, especially after Henry HUDSON sailed into the large bay in northeastern Canada now known as Hudson Bay. The explorer's sailors mutinied and abandoned Hudson to die. Then they returned to England to tell of the bay that seemed to lead westward. But in later years, mariners who explored the Hudson Bay thoroughly found no passage leading out of it. Although Frobisher and those who came after him failed to find a passage to Asia, they did map much of the North American coastline.

The search for the Northwest Passage shifted to the continent's interior, fed by vague Indian accounts of rivers and inland seas somewhere to the west. French and English explorers hoped that the Great Lakes or the Mississippi River would lead to a passage, but they did not. Meanwhile, navigators of several nations searched the continent's Pacific coast for the western end of the passage—also without success. Still, until well after the colonial period, explorers of the American West continued to seek the inland sea and the great westward-flowing river. Not until the mapping of North America was nearly complete did geographers finally admit that the Northwest Passage they had hoped to discover did not exist.

There *is* a Northwest Passage—in fact, there are several. They wind through the maze of desolate islands and ice-choked waterways that stretch northward from arctic Canada toward the North Pole. During the 1800s, explorers pieced together these hazardous routes—at the cost of many lives. The first person who actually sailed through the Northwest Passage was the Norwegian explorer Roald Amundsen in 1903 through 1906. But his accomplishment did not launch a new route for international shipping. Although a few submarines and ships with special icebreaking equipment have traveled this northern path, cargo ships do not use it. The real Northwest Passage bears little resemblance to the route that inspired the expeditions of so many explorers. (*See also* **Exploration, Age of.**)

Nova Scotia

The province of Nova Scotia occupies a peninsula jutting into the Atlantic Ocean from the eastern coast of CANADA. Attracted by its harbors and the rich fishing grounds nearby, both France and England established settlements there in colonial times. The two countries struggled over Nova Scotia for many years before Britain finally gained control of it.

Early Settlement. In 1497 the explorer John Cabot investigated Nova Scotia's coastline and claimed the area for England. During the 1500s, Spanish and Portuguese ships also visited the shores of Nova Scotia. However, many years passed before the appearance of the first lasting European settlement. In 1605 a French expedition that included Samuel de CHAMPLAIN established a colony at PORT ROYAL on the peninsula's north coast. Colonists from France began to settle in the area, which they called Acadia.

When Europeans arrived in Acadia, the region was inhabited by the MICMAC INDIANS. In addition to farming and fishing, French settlers traded with the Micmac for furs. By the 1620s, the area had begun to attract settlers from Scotland, who formed their own communities. The Micmac lost much of their land to the European settlers and many of their lives to diseases brought by the Europeans.

The boundaries of French Acadia were never clearly defined. Although France considered all the land occupied by the modern provinces of Nova Scotia, New Brunswick, and Prince Edward Island to be part of Acadia, the English claimed that New England included much of the same territory. Consequently, when France and England went to war in the 1700s, Acadia was one of the areas they fought over.

Wars Between France and Britain. In 1702 England joined other European powers in attempting to prevent France from gaining control of Spain's empire. The conflict, which followed the death of the Spanish king Charles II, was known as the War of the Spanish Succession (also called QUEEN ANNE'S WAR.) With the renewal of hostilities between France and England, the French and their Indian allies staged a series of raids on New England frontier settlements. In response, New Englanders planned an attack on nearby Acadia. Aided by British naval forces, the colonists captured Port Royal in 1710, renaming it Annapolis Royal.

The TREATY OF UTRECHT, which brought the war to an end in 1713, gave Acadia to the British. They called it Nova Scotia. The only areas in the region

See map in New France (vol. 3).

This 1781 print shows the harbor of Halifax. Founded in 1749, Halifax became the capital of Nova Scotia and attracted settlers from Europe and New England.

that France kept were Cape Breton Island on the northeast, which became Ile Royale, and Ile St-Jean (now Prince Edward Island). Despite the change in colonial government, Acadia continued to be more French than British. The ACADIANS, French settlers who stayed in Nova Scotia, did not give up their French language or their Catholic faith. They also refused to take an oath of loyalty to Britain. As tensions between France and Britain mounted again in the following years, the Acadians remained neutral.

In 1720 the French began constructing a massive fortress at LOUISBOURG on Ile Royale. Its location made the British colonists in New England and Nova Scotia uneasy. When French and British colonists in North America became involved in KING GEORGE'S WAR in 1744, the British quickly moved to attack the still incomplete fort. William Shirley, the royal governor of Massachusetts, organized a volunteer army from New England to join the British Royal Navy's attack on Louisbourg. The fortress fell within two months. But much to the disgust of the New Englanders, it was returned to France a few years later under the Treaty of Aix-la-Chapelle.

To protect Nova Scotia from the French, the British founded the town of Halifax on its south shore in 1749. They stationed both troops and naval vessels in the city. Halifax became the colony's capital, with several thousand settlers from Scotland, Ireland, England, the European continent, and New England.

As the conflict with France continued to simmer, British authorities became more concerned about the Acadians' giving aid to the French. In 1755 all Acadians were required to swear allegiance to the British crown. Those who refused were deported. Some of the exiled French settlers moved to British colonies to the south. Others traveled as far as Spanish LOUISIANA, where a substantial Acadian community developed. As new British settlers arrived in Nova Scotia, they took over the land of the exiled Acadians, strengthening the British position on the peninsula.

By this time, British and French colonists were fighting once more in the FRENCH AND INDIAN WAR. In 1758 the British again attacked and defeated the French forces at Louisbourg. When the war ended, the French had lost all their Canadian territory, including Ile Royale, to Britain. Their only remaining possessions in the region were the tiny islands of St. Pierre and Miquelon. With the expulsion of the Acadians and the French military defeat, Nova Scotia became entirely British. Many colonists from New England migrated north, making up a large part of the region's population by the time of the American Revolution. Some of the exiled Acadians later returned to Nova Scotia and became British subjects.

See map in French and Indian War (vol. 2).

The Revolutionary Period. Most of the New Englanders who had settled in Nova Scotia remained neutral as revolution swept through the American colonies. After the Revolutionary War, many American Loyalists* fled to Nova Scotia and the surrounding area, swelling the population. Cape Breton Island became a separate British colony, made up largely of Loyalists, but it proved too small to govern effectively. In 1820 the island rejoined the colony of Nova Scotia.

In the 1860s, Nova Scotia united with the provinces of Ontario, Quebec, and New Brunswick to form the Dominion of Canada. Today it is part of the independent nation of Canada. The traditions of the earliest Acadian and Scottish settlers continue to play a role in Nova Scotia's culture.

* *Loyalist* American colonist who remained faithful to Britain during the American Revolution

Occom, Samson

1723–1792
Mohegan missionary

Samson Occom, a Mohegan Indian, became a Presbyterian minister and devoted his life to spreading Christianity among Native Americans in New England. Although he accepted the religion of the British colonists, he protested against their seizure of Indian lands.

Born near New London, Connecticut, Occom converted to Christianity at the age of 16. He attended a school run by Reverend Eleazar WHEELOCK in Lebanon, Connecticut, and studied Greek, Latin, Hebrew, and the Scriptures. When Occom's poor eyesight prevented him from going to college, he began preaching in nearby Indian communities.

In 1749 Occom took a teaching position in Long Island with the Montauk Indians, who were impressed with his skills as a teacher. Occom also learned from his students. After studying their culture, he wrote a book entitled *An Account of the Montauk Indians on Long Island.* He married a Montauk woman and in 1759 was ordained as a Presbyterian minister.

In the early 1760s, Occom made three visits to the Oneida Indians of New York to recruit students for Reverend Wheelock's school. He also traveled to Great Britain to raise funds for a new college Wheelock planned to build to educate Native Americans. Occom gave about 300 sermons in Britain and collected a substantial sum of money, which was used to found Dartmouth College. But when Dartmouth began to focus on educating white students rather than Indians, Occom, in disgust, quit working for Wheelock.

After the American Revolution, Occom founded a Christian Indian community named Brothertown in central New York, where he carried on his missionary work. In addition to his volume on the Montauks, he also wrote an autobiography, a collection of hymns, and various sermons. In his best known work, *A Sermon at the Execution of Moses Paul,* he urged his fellow Indians to avoid the sin of drunkenness. (*See also* **Missions and Missionaries; Protestant Churches; Schools and Schooling**.)

Occupations

See *Labor.*

Oglethorpe, James

1696–1785
Founder of Georgia

James Oglethorpe founded the colony of GEORGIA in 1733 as a refuge for debtors and poor people. He served as the colony's first governor and did much to defend British interests in the region against the Spanish in FLORIDA.

Born in London to a well-to-do family, Oglethorpe joined the British army when he was still in his teens. He left the army in 1722, was elected to Parliament, and became involved in various charitable causes, including the founding of a hospital for orphans.

In the early 1700s, England's jails were overflowing with people who had failed to pay their debts. While heading a parliamentary committee on prison reform, Oglethorpe had the idea of starting a colony for debtors in North America. Such a colony would relieve prison overcrowding in England and give debtors a chance to start over in a new land. The colony would also be a haven for religious dissenters*.

* *dissenter* person who disagrees with the beliefs and practices of the established church

James Oglethorpe, the founder of Georgia, wanted his colony to be a haven for debtors, with plenty of available land, no slavery, and religious liberty for Protestants. But after 20 years, Oglethorpe lost his charter and the British crown took over the colony.

* **proprietor** person granted land and the right to establish a colony
* **charter** written grant from a ruler conferring certain rights and privileges
* **buffer** protective barrier between two rivals

Oglethorpe and a group of supporters asked Parliament for permission to establish a debtor colony in America. Parliament hesitated, concerned that helping prisoners would set a bad example for others. Oglethorpe broadened his plan. He proposed that the colony should also include hardworking poor people who would produce silk, wine, and other products for Britain.

King George II approved the plan, and in 1732 he granted Oglethorpe and 20 other proprietors* a charter* to establish a colony in the region between the Carolinas and Spanish Florida. The new colony was to serve as a buffer* between the British and Spanish territories.

Accompanied by about 120 settlers, few of whom were debtors, Oglethorpe arrived in America in February 1733. He founded the settlement of SAVANNAH and quickly began organizing the colony, named Georgia in honor of the king. He established friendly relations with local Indians and negotiated land and trade agreements with them. To protect the colony from the Spanish, Oglethorpe ordered the construction of forts and began a system of military training for the colonists.

Oglethorpe served as Georgia's governor for nine years. During that time, he issued laws that outlawed slavery and banned the sale of rum. He believed that slaves might become a source of rebellion and that rum would weaken the colonists' will to work and their ability to defend the colony. Another law limited the size of landholdings, ensuring that land would be available to poorer colonists. These restrictions on the settlers aroused some opposition in the colony.

When war broke out between England and Spain in 1739, Oglethorpe and his forces drove invading Spanish troops back into Florida. Attempts to capture the Spanish fort at ST. AUGUSTINE in the early 1740s were unsuccessful. But a victory over the Spanish in 1742 ensured the safety of Georgia.

In debt from loans made to colonists, Oglethorpe returned to England in 1743 and resumed his career in Parliament. He never returned to Georgia. Faced with increasing economic problems in the colony, Oglethorpe and the other proprietors turned Georgia over to the British crown in 1752.

Ohio Company of Virginia

British colonists in Virginia created the Ohio Company to establish settlements and develop trade routes in the upper OHIO RIVER VALLEY. In the 1750s, the company was involved in one of the first major attempts to expand the British colonies west of the APPALACHIAN MOUNTAINS.

In 1747 Thomas Lee and a group of investors from Virginia, Maryland, and Great Britain organized the Ohio Company. By 1749 the investors had obtained a grant from the British government for 200,000 acres of land near Forks of the Ohio (present-day Pittsburgh). If the company brought a certain number of settlers to the area and built a fort to protect the settlements, it would receive an additional 300,000 acres. The company sent an explorer named Christopher Gist to survey the land. It then began to build roads into the region, set up trading posts, and establish communities in what is now western Pennsylvania.

However, the Ohio Company soon met opposition. The land included in its grant was also claimed by the French—who were competing with the

British for territory throughout North America—and by various Native American tribes. Colonists from NEW FRANCE visited the area, insisting on their right to the land in meetings with Indian leaders. Soon French and Indian forces combined to drive back the British settlers. In 1752 they destroyed a village belonging to Miami Indians who had been trading with the British. The French then built a series of forts in the region, between Lake Erie and the Allegheny River.

In 1754 the Ohio Company began construction of its own military base, Fort Prince George, at Forks of the Ohio. However, before the fort was completed, the French captured it, finished building it, and renamed it FORT DUQUESNE. This act brought the rivalry between Britain and France to new heights. Soon the FRENCH AND INDIAN WAR broke out, interrupting the Ohio Company's activities.

In the treaty that settled the war, the British government gained the territory included in the Ohio Company's grant. However, in the PROCLAMATION OF 1763, Britain halted settlement beyond the Appalachian Mountains to appease the Indian tribes living there. Although the Ohio Company had helped establish a British presence in the region at a critical time, it was forced to abandon its efforts. (*See also* **Forts.**)

Ohio River Valley

* **Seven Years' War** series of conflicts in Europe, North America, Africa, and Asia that involved two struggles—one between Austria and Prussia and the other between Britain and France; the American part of the conflict, the French and Indian War, ended in 1763 with Britain defeating France and its ally Spain

* **strategic** key part of a plan; of military importance

* **tributary** stream or river that empties into a larger river

*I*n the early 1700s, the French and British began an intense competition for control of the Ohio River valley. By the mid-1700s, sparks from the rivalry helped ignite the global conflict known as the Seven Years' War*. When the war ended in 1763, control of the valley—and control of the North American continent—passed into the hands of the British.

The Ohio River provides a strategic* link between the Appalachian Mountains and the Mississippi River valley. Formed at the junction of the Allegheny and Monongahela rivers in western Pennsylvania (the site of present-day Pittsburgh), the Ohio flows 981 miles westward. It empties into the Mississippi at what is now the southern tip of Illinois. The name *Ohio* comes from the Iroquois word for "great river."

The early history of European exploration in the region is unclear. A Virginia fur trader named Abraham Wood may have crossed the Appalachian Mountains and claimed the river for the British in the 1650s. French explorer René-Robert Cavelier, Sieur de LA SALLE, probably navigated the upper Ohio River in 1669.

The valley was completely mapped by the 1680s. French explorers, including Louis JOLLIET, traveled the river and its chief tributaries* from the north. Explorers from Virginia, including Governor Alexander Spotswood, discovered mountain passes into the valley and marked rivers flowing into the Ohio from the Appalachians.

Trappers and traders from Virginia, Pennsylvania, and South Carolina began trickling into the valley in the 1740s. Logstown, near the headwaters of the Ohio River, was the site of a flourishing trade with the Indians. In 1749 the British government granted 200,000 acres of fertile land in the valley to the OHIO COMPANY OF VIRGINIA, a group of planters interested in developing western territories.

See map in French and Indian War (vol. 2).

Alarmed by the Ohio Company's settlement plans, the French sent an expedition of more than 200 men to proclaim France's sovereignty* over the Ohio River valley. At each tributary, the leader of the expedition planted a lead marker stating France's claims. In 1752 the French governor Ange Duquesne sent a raiding party to capture and destroy a settlement of MIAMI INDIANS who were friendly to British colonial traders. Duquesne also built a series of FORTS in the upper Ohio River valley to maintain France's hold on the region.

The British government then authorized Virginia's governor to use force to expel the French from the valley. In 1754 Lieutenant Colonel George WASHINGTON and a group of Virginia militia* were sent to protect workers building a fort at the headwaters of the Ohio River. On their way, they ambushed a small group of French soldiers, killing 10 and taking 21 prisoner. The main French force then attacked Washington's troops, driving them from the valley. These events greatly heightened tensions between Britain and France and contributed to the FRENCH AND INDIAN WAR. (*See also* **Fort Duquesne.**)

Ojibwa Indians

See second map in Native Americans (vol. 3).

The Ojibwa Indians (also known as the Chippewa) were one of the largest and most far ranging Indian tribes of North America. From their original homeland along the shores of Lake Superior and Lake Huron in present-day Ontario, Canada, the tribe spread east, south, and west to hunt and to trade furs with the French and other Native Americans.

An Algonquian-speaking people, the Ojibwa grew corn and squash, hunted and fished, and gathered wild rice. They also made maple sugar and smoked a tobacco made of dried leaves and bark. Widely scattered in small, self-governing groups called bands, the Ojibwa lived in cone-shaped wigwams that were covered in bark or animal hides. They used birch-bark canoes to travel on the vast network of rivers and lakes in their territory.

Ojibwa bands consisted of people related by family and membership in various clans* named after animals and birds. Their religion centered on the spirits that they believed inhabited all living things. A notable feature of Ojibwa culture was the Grand Medicine Lodge, a society whose members performed various healing rituals*.

The first contact between the Ojibwa and Europeans occurred in 1640. Meeting the Indians at waterfalls on the St. Marys River between Lakes Superior and Huron, some French trappers and missionaries referred to them as *Saulteurs,* or "People of the Falls." The name *Saulteaux* is still used in parts of Canada to refer to Ojibwa people.

During the colonial period, the Ojibwa became heavily involved in the FUR TRADE. As they sought to protect and expand their hunting grounds and trade connections, they competed and clashed with other tribes. In the 1640s, they moved onto lands abandoned by the HURON INDIANS after their defeat by the IROQUOIS. In the 1660s, the Ojibwa ousted Iroquois war parties that had entered their territory. Then they began advancing southward, driving the Iroquois from the region south of the Great Lakes and establishing communities there. By the mid-1700s, the Ojibwa had moved into the southeastern part of what is now Michigan, pushing out the OTTAWA INDIANS.

The Ojibwa also began advancing to the west, where they met two tribes that became their long-term enemies—the FOX and the Dakota Indians (also known as the Sioux). After receiving firearms from the French, the Ojibwa drove the Fox from the northern part of present-day Wisconsin. Conflict with the Sioux continued throughout the 1700s, resulting in an expansion of Ojibwa territory into the area now occupied by Minnesota.

After losing many tribal members in a smallpox epidemic in the 1780s, the CREE INDIANS invited the Ojibwa to move into their territory northwest of Lake Superior. In the early 1800s, aided by the horse, the Ojibwa continued their drive to the west into the present-day Dakotas, Montana, and parts of western Canada. The groups that settled in these areas became known as the Plains Ojibwa.

The Ojibwa became involved in colonial conflicts too. During the French and Indian War, they sided with the French and helped defeat British general Edward BRADDOCK near Pittsburgh in 1755. They also participated in battles in upstate New York. The Ojibwa supported the Indian uprising led by Chief PONTIAC in 1763 and joined with the SHAWNEE INDIANS to oppose the advance of white settlers into the Ohio River valley after the 1760s. In the early 1800s, the Ojibwa signed a treaty with the United States, which created reservations within Ojibwa territory. Many members of the tribe continue to live there today. (*See also* **Native Americans.**)

Old Age

Old age was not clearly defined in colonial America. People in their 40s and 50s—middle aged by today's standards—might feel old because they had worked hard for decades and outlived many of their generation. Yet people who reached their 60s and beyond often continued to work and to take an active role in the community, as long as their health and strength allowed. Colonists generally valued the experience, wisdom, and skills of older individuals.

Reaching Old Age. Few people in colonial America lived past their 50s. As late as 1790, less than 2 percent of the population of the BRITISH COLONIES reached age 65 or older. Immigration provided one explanation. Not many older Europeans undertook the long, hazardous journey to America and the struggle to build a new life in a strange land.

High death rates also contributed to the low percentage of older people in the colonies. Diseases such as malaria, dysentery, influenza, and tuberculosis struck down many colonists of all ages, especially the eldest and the youngest members of the community. In the Chesapeake region and the Carolinas, where the hot, humid climate provided a breeding ground for certain diseases, few people managed to reach old age.

Health and Fitness. As in many societies, older colonists often struggled with physical and mental decline and suffered loneliness. The level of comfort in which they lived depended on their economic and family circumstances. People with property and wealth were usually able to maintain their style of living as they grew older. Many arranged for their children to care for them or

Old Age

Elderly widows often spent their last years in the home of one of their children, helping with child care and doing mending and other odd jobs.

Old Age and Witchcraft

Age may have played a role in the accusations of witchcraft that arose in the colonies during the 1600s. Of the 28 women brought to trial for witchcraft in Salem, Massachusetts, 13 were over 60. Those most likely to be accused were elderly widows, poor women with no families, and women who assumed roles not typical of females. Such women either lacked power and people to defend them or had wealth or property, which others envied or saw as a threat. Many of those accused were bold, outspoken women who challenged accepted ideas.

paid for the services of a caregiver. For poor people, on the other hand, old age often brought great hardship. Sometimes town officials made arrangements for a member of the community, perhaps a widow, to look after them. Otherwise, they might be forced to enter a poorhouse—a facility maintained by the community to house needy people. By the 1750s, about one-third of the people living in colonial poorhouses were elderly.

Old age was particularly difficult for women because they often outlived their husbands and had little financial security as widows. A man's children generally received the bulk of his estate, leaving the widow dependent on them. Although adult children were legally responsible for the care of aging parents, the care provided varied greatly from family to family. Many elderly women found themselves confined to a single room in households they had formerly managed but that now belonged to one of their children. Elderly widows with no family or income were among the poorest people in the colonies. Many of them had to depend on public charity for survival.

Attitudes Toward the Aged.   Because so few people lived to old age, colonial Americans generally considered those who reached an advanced age to be particularly fortunate. Older people were respected for their knowledge and experience, which were needed to help colonial towns and villages survive. Older women taught the young about raising children, caring for the sick, managing a household, and useful skills such as weaving. Older men gave advice about crops, livestock, and care of the land or provided information and advice about particular jobs or crafts.

Religion affected colonial attitudes toward the aged. Both Protestants and Roman Catholics viewed old age as a blessing bestowed by God, and elderly people thus were considered worthy of great respect. The PURITANS of

152

* **Spanish Borderlands** northern part of New Spain, area now occupied by Florida, Texas, New Mexico, Arizona, and California

New England, for example, reserved the best seats in meetinghouses for the elderly and listened to their advice on community matters. In the Spanish Borderlands*, Catholic colonists often honored elderly priests and made sure they were well cared for. Among the Native Americans, the aged were respected for their wisdom and their ability to teach the young about the history and beliefs of their people.

While old age in colonial America did not guarantee special consideration or financial security, most elderly people were treated with respect. Some older citizens assumed roles of leadership in communities because of their contributions to society, and colonists looked to them for guidance and inspiration. (*See also* **Death and Burial; Life Expectancy.**)

Olive Branch Petition (1775)

* **petition** formal statement asking a person in authority to address an issue or problem

*T*he Olive Branch Petition was a document that the SECOND CONTINENTAL CONGRESS sent to King GEORGE III in the summer of 1775. It represented a final attempt by the congress to resolve the conflicts between Britain and the colonies and to avoid war.

By the early 1770s, British policies had produced an atmosphere of unrest in the colonies. Among other issues, the Americans resented the taxes and restrictions on trade imposed by PARLIAMENT. In 1775, with tensions high, fighting began. The Americans met the British in battle at LEXINGTON AND CONCORD in April and again at BUNKER HILL in June. Although a full-scale war seemed likely, many colonists still hoped to settle their differences with the British. Expressing this view, John ADAMS wrote that the colonies ought to "prepare for . . . War, but at the same time keep open the Door of Reconciliation—to hold the Sword in one Hand and the Olive Branch in the other."

The members of the Continental Congress followed Adams's advice. In June they created the CONTINENTAL ARMY and appointed George WASHINGTON as commander. A few weeks later, they issued the Declaration of the Causes and Necessity for Taking Up Arms to justify their action. The new army, the document explained, would help defend the colonists' liberties against unjust British policies.

At the same time, the congress made a last attempt to preserve the peace. On July 8—just two days after announcing the military plan—the delegates prepared the Olive Branch Petition. They addressed their petition* to the king rather than to Parliament because they did not recognize Parliament's authority over the colonies. They offered assurances that the colonies remained loyal to the king "with all devotion that principle and affection can inspire." However, they also made clear that, in their view, some of Britain's colonial laws were unreasonable. The petition went on to suggest that the king's ministers might have enacted these laws without his approval and asked the king to intervene on behalf of the colonies.

The Continental Congress sent the petition to Britain with Richard Penn, a grandson of William PENN who was known to be loyal to the king. But George III, who fully endorsed his government's policies, refused to see Penn or to accept the petition. The fighting continued, and the colonies began to move toward independence. (*See also* **American Revolution; Colonial Administration; Independence Movements.**)

Oñate, Juan de

ca. 1551–ca. 1626
Founder of New Mexico

* *viceroy* person appointed as a monarch's representative to govern a province or colony
* *friar* member of a religious brotherhood

Juan de Oñate held the positions of governor, captain general, and *adelantado*—literally, "the one who goes forth"—in New Mexico. The inscription on his coat of arms, a symbol showing his rank and background, makes mention of all three titles.

Setting out from NEW SPAIN in 1598, Juan de Oñate led an expedition to the vast, uncharted borderlands to the north. There he established the first Spanish settlement in the region and founded NEW MEXICO. Oñate had been instructed to pacify the local Indians and to convert them to Christianity.

The son of a wealthy Mexican silver mine owner, Oñate joined the Spanish army as a teenager to fight the Indians in the northern part of New Spain. During his 20 years as a soldier, he won a reputation as a tough, capable fighter.

In the late 1500s, Spain decided to extend its control northward from New Spain. Oñate made a deal with the viceroy* of New Spain in 1595 to colonize the region—which would be called New Mexico—and to search for gold and silver mines rumored to exist there. Oñate would provide the military equipment, livestock, men, and supplies to establish a colony. In return he would become governor of the new province. After three years of preparations, Oñate and his party of colonists—which included soldiers, their families, and Franciscan friars*—set out on their journey.

After months of hard traveling across deserts and mountains, the exhausted expedition arrived at the banks of the Rio Grande in New Mexico. Under Oñate's leadership, the Spaniards built a church and founded the colony's capital of San Gabriel. Relations with the local PUEBLO INDIANS began well, but tensions quickly developed between the two groups.

After restoring order to his colony, Oñate explored widely in search of gold and silver. He sent scouting parties as far east as present-day Kansas and west to the Gulf of California, but they found no riches—only a harsh and difficult land.

The colony experienced many difficulties in its first years, including repeated clashes with Indians. Oñate's strict policies also angered some colonists, who abandoned the settlement during one of the governor's absences. Disappointed by Oñate's lack of success in New Mexico, the colonial government sent a new governor to replace him in 1608.

Oñate moved to Spain, where he served as a royal inspector of mines until his death. He regarded his venture in New Mexico as a failure, but it laid the foundations for a long-lasting Spanish presence in the Southwest. (*See also* **Spanish Borderlands.**)

Oneida Indians

See *Iroquois Confederacy.*

Onondaga Indians

See *Iroquois Confederacy.*

Osage Indians

The Osage Indians lived along the Missouri and Osage rivers of what is now Missouri. They formed early ties with French explorers and traders, who arrived in their territory by traveling along the great river system formed by the Missouri and the Mississippi.

The Osage tribe consisted of two branches: the Great Osage and the Little Osage. Both spoke a Siouan language and lived in villages, growing corn

See second map in Native Americans (vol. 3).

and squash. Twice a year they traveled west across the plains to hunt BUFFALO, which they used for food and clothing. Osage men traditionally shaved their heads, including the eyebrows, except for a long strip of hair about three inches wide on top of their heads. Both men and women wore earrings, bracelets, and tattoos on their arms and chests.

After the Osage met explorers from NEW FRANCE in the 1670s, they began to trade with the French. They exchanged furs for guns and HORSES, which gave them an advantage over their rivals in the region for more than 100 years. In 1755 the Osage joined forces with the French to attack British general Edward BRADDOCK as he attempted to capture FORT DUQUESNE, at the site of what is now Pittsburgh, Pennsylvania.

After the American Revolution, the Osage remained on their land as large numbers of white settlers arrived in the region. However, in 1802 the tribe split. Nearly half of the Great Osage moved south to the Arkansas River, while the rest remained on the Osage River. During the 1800s, the Osage sold most of their land to the United States, then lived for many years in Kansas, and finally settled on reservation land in Oklahoma. (*See also* **French and Indian War.**)

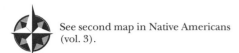

Otis, James

1725–1783
Politician and lawyer

* ***Enlightenment*** European intellectual movement of the 1600s and 1700s, based on faith in the power of reason and the idea that individuals have certain fundamental rights

* ***customs*** tax on imports; agency that checks imported goods and collects taxes

*J*ames Otis was a MASSACHUSETTS political leader during the 1760s. In his speeches and writing, Otis used ideas from the Enlightenment* to defend the rights of the colonists and to protest the policies of the British government.

Born in West Barnstable, Massachusetts, Otis studied law at Harvard College. He served as a lawyer for the British admiralty court in Boston—a position that required him to help enforce British customs* laws. In 1760 Otis resigned rather than defend the use of general search warrants, called writs of assistance, that allowed customs agents to search merchants' warehouses for illegal goods. He then worked on behalf of the merchants to fight the writs. Though he lost his case, his arguments were used by other American leaders in challenging British actions.

Otis quickly became one of the most important political figures in Massachusetts. Many of his speeches criticized acts of PARLIAMENT that dealt with trade and taxation in the colonies. Elected to the Massachusetts legislature in 1761, Otis later headed the Massachusetts COMMITTEE OF CORRESPONDENCE. He also began writing political pamphlets such as *The Rights of the British Colonies Asserted and Proved* (1764). One of his main themes was that the colonists should have the same rights as other British subjects.

In 1765 Otis served as a delegate to the STAMP ACT Congress, where colonists organized their opposition to the British tax on paper products and documents. Otis argued that the British government did not have the right to tax the colonies without giving them representation in Parliament. Nevertheless, he always hoped for a peaceful solution to the conflict between Great Britain and the colonies.

Otis's career ended suddenly in 1769, when a blow to the head during a political dispute left him mentally unstable. Years later he died after being struck by lightning. (*See also* **Enlightenment; Independence Movements.**)

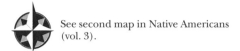

Ottawa Indians

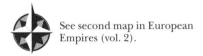

See second map in Native Americans (vol. 3).

During the colonial period, the Ottawa Indians lived in the Great Lakes region, originally on territory around the northern shores of Lake Huron. After the French arrived in the region, the tribe became heavily involved in the FUR TRADE.

Like other Great Lakes tribes, the Ottawa hunted and fished, gathered wild rice and other foods, and grew crops such as corn, beans, and squash. They gained a reputation as great traders, supplying furs to the HURON INDIANS, who in turn traded them to the French. But the Ottawa's alliance with the Huron brought them into conflict with the IROQUOIS—the Huron's traditional enemy. In the 1650s and 1660s, Iroquois attacks forced the Ottawa to flee westward to areas south and west of Lake Superior. However, in 1670 many returned to the eastern and southern parts of the Great Lakes region after the French promised to protect them.

The Ottawa's friendship with the French drew them into the conflict between France and Great Britain. Ottawa warriors often fought alongside the French in battles and in raids on British frontier settlements. After France's defeat in the FRENCH AND INDIAN WAR in 1763, the British took control of the Great Lakes region. That same year an Ottawa leader, Chief PONTIAC, led an unsuccessful uprising against the British in hopes of driving them from the area.

In the early 1800s, the Ottawa surrendered most of their territory to the U.S. government. Some of the Indians remained in the Great Lakes region, but many fled to Canada or moved westward and eventually settled in Kansas and Oklahoma. (*See also* **Native Americans.**)

Pacific Northwest

See second map in European Empires (vol. 2).

pelt skin and fur of an animal

The Pacific Northwest region of North America covers the present-day states of Oregon, Washington, and Alaska, as well as the Canadian province of British Columbia. During the colonial period, the area was home to many native peoples, including the ESKIMO and the ALEUTS in the far north and the Nootka, TLINGIT, Tsimshian, Haida, and Kwakiutl farther south. The Spanish, who explored the Pacific coast from their base in Mexico, were the first Europeans to enter the region. They charted the coast of Oregon in the early 1600s but did not try to establish colonies north of California. The first colonizers of the Pacific Northwest came from Russia.

In the late 1500s, the rulers of western Russia launched an eastward movement to explore Siberia. This forest-covered region stretching across northern Asia was well supplied with fur-bearing animals whose pelts* brought top prices in Russian markets. By 1639 the fur rush had carried the Russians to the Pacific coast. After exploring Siberia's far northeast—and nearly wiping out the valuable fur-bearing animals there—Russians looked eastward to North America.

The first explorer to reach Alaska was a Dane named Vitus Bering, working for Russian king Peter the Great. In the mid-1700s, Bering crossed the part of the North Pacific Ocean that is now called the Bering Sea. In the decades that followed, Russian hunters and traders took hundreds of thousands of seal and otter pelts from Alaskan waters. Small private trading companies organized hunting expeditions to America. Soon RUSSIAN SETTLEMENTS dotted

Alaska's coast and offshore islands. Their effect on the local Eskimo and Aleut peoples was terrible—the Russians enslaved them, made war on them, and infected them with deadly diseases. By the 1800s, two-thirds of the Aleuts had been wiped out.

In 1799 the companies involved in the American FUR TRADE united to form the Russian-American Company. The Russian crown gave the company a 20-year charter* to govern the settlers in Alaska and to control the fur harvest. With its capital in Sitka, Russian America had a population of about 550. Russian holdings in the Pacific Northwest extended as far south as what is now San Francisco. Eventually, Russia's North American colony became unprofitable as furs grew scarce. In 1867 Russia sold Alaska to the United States.

British naval officers such as James Cook and George Vancouver played an important role in exploring and mapping coastal Oregon and Washington in the late 1700s. But the British made no attempt to establish colonies in the region. British explorer Alexander Mackenzie reached the Pacific by traveling across Canada in 1793. Twelve years later, Americans Meriwether Lewis and William Clark arrived on the Pacific coast after an overland journey through the Louisiana Territory. From that time, Britain and the United States competed for control of the Northwest.

In 1821 the British in Canada established Fort George, at the mouth of the Columbia River, as a base for fur-hunting and gold-mining activities. Shortly afterward, American pioneers began pushing westward into the fertile valleys of Washington and Oregon. In 1846 a treaty set the borderline between American territory and British Columbia, which eventually joined Canada in 1871. (*See also* **Canada.**)

* *charter* written grant from a ruler conferring certain rights and privileges

Paine, Thomas

1737–1809
Political author

* *propagandist* person who attempts to influence the thinking of others

* *excise* tax on goods produced and sold within a country

An English writer who moved to the colonies, Thomas Paine championed the cause of political liberty and equality. His most famous work, a 1776 pamphlet entitled *Common Sense,* helped persuade Americans to seek independence from Great Britain. Paine was the first propagandist* to suggest that Americans had a mission to establish a new nation.

Born in Thetford, England, Paine was the son of a poor corset maker. He quit school at the age of 13 to help support his family, but he managed to educate himself by reading widely, attending lectures, and experimenting with various mechanical devices. Through his studies, he came to value scientific reasoning.

Paine's writing talents lay hidden until he was almost 40 years old. He spent years working at a variety of low-paying jobs in England—excise* inspector, schoolteacher, tobacconist, and grocer. During his time as a tax inspector, Paine represented his fellow workers in their efforts to get Parliament to raise their wages. His career as a political writer began when he drafted a pamphlet urging fair treatment of excise employees.

Arguing for higher wages and better working conditions was unheard of at that time, and Paine was fired from his job. Finding himself bankrupt, he decided to do what many others in desperate situations had done—move to

Thomas Paine wrote the most famous piece of colonial political propaganda. His pamphlet *Common Sense*, published in January 1776, attacked the monarchy and called on American colonists to create a free nation.

* *oppression* unjust or cruel exercise of authority

* *anonymously* not named or identified

* *patriot* American colonist who supported independence from Britain

North America. Fortunately, while attending a meeting in London on behalf of the excise employees, Paine had met and impressed Benjamin FRANKLIN. Armed with letters of introduction from the famous American, Paine set sail for Philadelphia in 1774.

In the colonies, Paine supported himself by writing essays for the *Pennsylvania Magazine*. Soon after his arrival, he became involved in the American movement for independence. Paine believed strongly in the right of every individual to equality, liberty, property, security, and freedom from oppression*. In January 1776, he published anonymously* a pamphlet called *Common Sense*. It was an amazing success, selling more than 100,000 copies within its first three months. In the 47-page pamphlet, Paine urged the immediate declaration of independence. He believed that the British system of government—particularly the monarchy—was evil and corrupt. He argued that Americans had a moral obligation to become a model of freedom for the rest of the world by forming a new nation.

When Paine's identity as the author of *Common Sense* was discovered, he became something of a celebrity. He accepted a position as secretary to a congressional committee on foreign affairs and later as clerk of the Pennsylvania assembly. Throughout the AMERICAN REVOLUTION, he continued to inspire and encourage the patriots* in a series of pamphlets called *The American Crisis*. He began the first pamphlet with the stirring words: "These are the times that try men's souls." Paine also served in the Continental Army and raised funds for the military.

On returning to Europe in 1787, Paine attempted to spread the revolutionary movement in England and France. In *The Rights of Man*, he defended the French Revolution and tried to inspire British citizens to overthrow the monarchy. In 1792 the British government branded him a traitor and outlawed him. Visiting France at the time, Paine became a French citizen and was elected to the National Convention. However, a wave of public feeling against foreigners resulted in Paine's being stripped of his French citizenship and imprisoned as a British citizen. While in prison, he began another major work, *The Age of Reason* (1794).

James Monroe, the American minister to France, secured Paine's release by claiming him as an American citizen. In 1802 Paine returned to the United States, where he spent the last seven years of his life in poverty and declining health. Paine had been a hero during his earlier stay in America, but now he was treated as a social outcast. His criticism of George Washington in *Letter to Washington* (1796) and the anti-Christian views he expressed in *The Age of Reason* had turned him into a controversial and unpopular figure. (*See also* **Political Thought; Revolutionary Thought.**)

Painting and Sculpture   See *Art.*

Papago Indians   See *Tohono O'odham Indians.*

Parliament, British

privy council group of officials who advise the king or queen

The role of Parliament, the legislative body of GREAT BRITAIN, is to make laws and establish national policies. For much of the colonial period, Parliament had little responsibility for managing Britain's North American possessions. The colonies basically remained under the control of the English crown and its privy council*. However, the power of Parliament increased dramatically in the mid-1700s, both at home and in the colonies. Taking over responsibilities once held by the monarchy, Parliament began shaping colonial policy.

English Law and the Colonies.   The first English colonists in North America assumed that they still lived under English law. They believed that they were entitled to all "the rights, privileges, and liberties" that people in England enjoyed. They considered themselves subjects of the king and recognized that the final power to make political decisions rested with the English crown. But in their view, the day-to-day governing of the colonies should be handled by colonial ASSEMBLIES—not by officials in England.

Authorities in England did not share the colonists' views about their role. They believed that the North American colonies were completely under the control of the English monarch and Parliament and had no legal rights to

During the 1700s, lawmakers in Parliament gained greater and greater control over the management of the colonies. This picture shows the House of Commons—the part of Parliament made up of elected representatives—in 1747.

An Undeclared Independence

A series of laws passed by Parliament convinced the colonies to break with Britain. Yet the Declaration of Independence, which contains a long list of complaints against the king, never mentions Parliament by name. Instead, it refers to "a jurisdiction foreign to our constitution, and unacknowledged by our laws." In other words, it claims that Parliament never had any right to make laws for the colonies. By this argument, the only tie the colonists had to break was their tie to the king.

* **charter** written grant from a ruler conferring certain rights and privileges

self-government. In practice, though, political troubles at home—and the great distance separating the English government from North America—left the colonies considerable freedom to manage their own affairs for the first 100 years or so of their existence. This tradition of self-government in many areas made it much harder for the colonists to accept the expanded role that Parliament began to play in their lives in the mid-1700s.

Colonial Administration to 1696. During the early colonial period, the English crown had responsibility for managing the colonies—granting charters*, appointing royal governors, and controlling trade. In 1642 civil war broke out between Parliament and King Charles I. After defeating the king, Parliament took control of the government, including the administration of the colonies. In 1650 it passed the first of the NAVIGATION ACTS regulating trade between England and the colonies.

The royal family returned to power in 1660. The new king, Charles II, formed a number of committees to oversee colonial affairs. In practice, however, control of colonial administration was now divided. Parliament continued to make laws governing trade, including several more Navigation Acts between 1660 and 1696 and the Wool Act and the Iron Act. Meanwhile, the king issued charters for new colonies and changed the terms of old ones. The colonies themselves did whatever they could to avoid cooperating with any laws that limited their freedom.

In 1696 King William III created the Board of Trade to govern the colonies and appointed the members of the board himself. The board was to report to his privy council and his minister for colonial affairs, not to Parliament. The Board of Trade and the privy council handled most details of colonial administration. But Parliament remained in charge of policy on matters that involved all or most of the colonies, such as trade and manufacturing. Gradually, Parliament took over many functions of the Board of Trade as well.

Parliament Assumes Control. Parliament took a greater role in colonial policy after the 22-year-old GEORGE III became king in 1763. At the time, Britain was in the final year of the FRENCH AND INDIAN WAR. Britain's defeat of the French gave it control over the eastern half of North America, but the war left the country with enormous debts. The British government had sent its armed forces to defend the colonies and had paid the costs of the conflict. Parliament decided that American colonists should pay some of the military expenses themselves.

To raise money from the colonies, Parliament passed several unpopular laws that imposed new taxes and added new regulations on American shipping. These included the SUGAR ACT OF 1764, the STAMP ACT (1765), and the TOWNSHEND ACTS (1767). Even more troubling to some colonists was the DECLARATORY ACT OF 1766, in which Parliament affirmed that it had "full power and authority" to make laws for the colonies and to overturn laws passed by colonial assemblies.

Having run their own affairs for so long, the colonists were outraged at this flood of new laws. Because they had no representation in Parliament, they felt that they should not be subject to its laws. The cry of "taxation without representation is tyranny" became a slogan for those opposed to Parliament's

interference in colonial affairs. Parliament responded that all British subjects were "virtually" represented in Parliament because Parliament acted on behalf of all citizens. So the taxes were not unfair at all. The colonists, however, rejected this argument.

This conflict over Parliament's rightful powers was one of the main causes of the AMERICAN REVOLUTION. In July 1775, the colonists sent King George the OLIVE BRANCH PETITION, which declared their loyalty to the British crown and asked the king to remove the burdensome laws passed by Parliament. But George refused to accept the petition, and Americans abandoned efforts to resolve their differences with Britain. By issuing the DECLARATION OF INDEPENDENCE in 1776, they rejected Parliament's authority altogether. (*See also* **Colonial Administration; Government, Provincial; Intolerable Acts; Political Thought; Quartering Acts; Trade and Commerce.**)

See *Independence Movements: British Colonies.*

See *Land Ownership: Dutch Settlements.*

*__band__ group of families that lived and hunted together

See second map in Native Americans (vol. 3).

I n colonial times, the Pawnee Indians lived on the Platte River in what is now Nebraska, far from most of the early European settlements. But as European explorers, traders, and settlers pushed farther into the interior of the continent, they had a significant impact on the lives of the Pawnee.

The Pawnee lived in villages made up of large, earth-covered houses. They planted corn, beans, squash, and pumpkins and also hunted for food. Once or twice each year they traveled across the plains in pursuit of BUFFALO. The tribe was divided into four separate bands*, each with its own chief and council. These leaders made decisions regarding hunting, farmland, warfare, ceremonies, and relations with outsiders.

The Spanish explorer Francisco Vásquez de CORONADO met one of the Pawnee in 1541. In later years, members of the tribe had contact with other Spaniards as well as with French and English colonists who ventured into their territory in search of land and furs. Each Pawnee band formed independent trading relationships and alliances with the Europeans. The Indians were deeply impressed by the newcomers' HORSES and soon managed to acquire some for their own use. The Pawnee suffered frequent attacks from enemy tribes in the region, most notably some of the Sioux, who had been forced onto the plains by the Ojibwa. Sometimes the Pawnee turned to Europeans for assistance. For example, in 1720 Pawnee warriors allied with the French fought off an attack by Spaniards and Indians on the South Platte River.

The Pawnee remained in Nebraska well into the 1800s. However, as more Americans moved into their territory, diseases such as cholera and smallpox swept through the tribe, greatly reducing the population. During the 1800s, the Pawnee gave up most of their land to the United States in a series of treaties.

Penn, William

1644–1718
Founder of Pennsylvania

* **dissenter** person who disagrees with the beliefs and practices of the established church

* **toleration** acceptance of the right of individuals to follow their own religious beliefs

* **charter** document stating the principles of an organization

* **proprietor** person granted land and the right to establish a colony

William Penn, the founder of Pennsylvania, became a Quaker as a young man. He saw his colony as a "holy experiment" that would bring together Christians of all kinds to live in peace. This portrait of Penn is the only one drawn during his lifetime.

A member of the Society of Friends, also known as the QUAKERS, William Penn was firmly devoted to the idea of religious liberty. His beliefs shaped not only his own life but also the early history of PENNSYLVANIA, the colony he founded in North America.

Pennsylvania turned out to be something of a disappointment to its founder, who spent only four years there. Today Penn is remembered for his contributions to English legal and religious thought as well as to the development of the American colonies.

Religious Rebel. Born in London to a prosperous, well-connected family, William Penn grew up in the Church of England. His father, an admiral in the Royal Navy, expected William to follow family traditions. He was furious when his son was expelled from Oxford University in 1662 because of involvement with the PURITANS and other religious dissenters*.

Admiral Penn sent his son on a tour of Europe, hoping to take his mind off religion. Instead, the young man spent two years studying religion in France. Upon returning to England in 1665, he tried military service and then studied law. But William Penn was drawn back to religion after witnessing the horrors of the Great Plague, a terrible epidemic that killed thousands of people as it swept through England and Europe in the 1660s.

In 1666 Penn went to Ireland to manage some of his father's property. While there, he came under the influence of a Quaker named Thomas Loe. Greatly moved by Loe's powerful preaching, Penn declared himself a Quaker—becoming a member of an illegal religion. His outraged father threatened to disown him.

Penn spent time in prison for expressing ideas that differed from those of the Church of England, the country's official religion. Yet he continued to speak and write about Quaker beliefs. He believed strongly that people should be free to worship as they please, and he argued forcefully for religious toleration*. After one arrest, Penn used his legal training to argue successfully that the judge's conduct of the case was illegal.

Despite disagreements over religion, Admiral Penn made peace with his son before his death in 1670. William Penn continued his religious activities. He made several missionary trips to Europe, spreading the Quaker faith and forging ties between English Quakers and various European religious groups. Some of these Europeans would later settle in Pennsylvania. In 1672 Penn married a young Quaker woman, Gulielma Maria Springett. In the following years, he was involved in religious activities and in English politics.

Colonial Proprietor. Penn took an active interest in the colonization of North America. When some Quakers gained possession of the colonies that later became NEW JERSEY, Penn helped write a charter* of government that guaranteed various rights, including freedom of speech and religion.

A few years later, in 1681, Penn got the chance to establish a colony of his own in North America. King Charles II had owed Penn's father a large sum of money, and William inherited that financial commitment. He canceled the king's debt in exchange for a royal grant to establish a colony in a large territory west of the Delaware River. Charles named Penn proprietor* of this colony and declared that Penn, or someone appointed by him, would be its governor.

Penn named his colony Pennsylvania, which means "Penn's woods." He hoped it would become a place where all Christians, no matter what their beliefs, could live together in harmony, free of the persecution and conflicts that troubled religious life in Europe. He wrote to a friend, "There may be room there, though not here, for such a holy experiment."

Penn's most important contributions to Pennsylvania were the principle of religious liberty and his insistence on treating the Indians fairly. His Frame of Government (1682) for the colony provided for both an elected council and an elected assembly and guaranteed the basic liberties of the individual. In the introduction to the document, he wrote: "Any Government is free to the People under it . . . Where the Laws rule, and the People are a party to those Laws."

Penn built a handsome house on the river north of the capital of PHILADELPHIA, but because of legal and financial problems in London he spent only about four years in the colony. Besides, being the proprietor of Pennsylvania turned out to be more troublesome than Penn had expected. For one thing, he thought he would make a profit from rents paid by colonists, but the rents proved difficult to collect. Furthermore, the colonists were very independent minded and did not want to follow the laws laid down by Penn and his council. The assembly kept demanding more powers.

Penn's later life was darkened by family tragedies and money troubles. By 1712 he had become so discouraged with his "holy experiment" that he decided to sell his colony to the British crown. Before he could do so, he suffered a stroke that left him helpless and bedridden until his death. His wife and children took over the management of Pennsylvania, which remained the property of the Penn family—at least in name—until the American Revolution.

Pennsylvania

** **toleration*** acceptance of the right of individuals to follow their own religious beliefs

** **patriot*** American colonist who supported independence from Britain

See map in British Colonies (vol. 1).

*T*he founders of Pennsylvania established a tradition of religious freedom and toleration* that was as important in attracting new settlers as the colony's rich farmland. Although one of the last British colonies to be founded, Pennsylvania grew rapidly, and PHILADELPHIA, its capital, emerged as an important center of colonial trade and culture.

Located midway between New England and the southern colonies, Pennsylvania became a meeting place for patriots* in the years leading up to the American Revolution. In 1776 representatives from the colonies gathered in Philadelphia to discuss their problems with British rule. Failing to receive a satisfactory response to their complaints, they voted to declare their independence from Britain.

Early Exploration and Settlement. When Europeans first arrived in North America, about 15,000 DELAWARE, SUSQUEHANNOCK, and SHAWNEE INDIANS lived in the area that later became Pennsylvania. European exploration of the region began with the English navigator Henry HUDSON, who sailed into the mouth of the Delaware River in 1609 while employed by the Dutch. His voyage was the basis for a Dutch claim to this fertile, forested region.

The first people to colonize the area, however, were Swedes. In the 1630s, Sweden opened up a FUR TRADE with local Indians. The Swedes built trading posts and a fort, and in 1643 they founded the area's first permanent

Pennsylvania

When William Penn and his colonists arrived in Pennsylvania in 1682, they agreed to treat the local Indians fairly. This painting by Benjamin West shows the Indians and the English settlers working out the terms of a treaty.

settlement at Tinicum Island in the Delaware River. But their control of the area they called New Sweden was short-lived. In 1655 the Dutch swept down from their colony of NEW NETHERLAND and seized the SWEDISH SETTLEMENTS.

The Dutch had little time to profit from their conquest. In 1664 England seized all Dutch territory in North America. The Delaware River area passed into the hands of the Duke of York, the brother of King Charles II of England.

proprietor person granted land and the right to establish a colony

Penn's "Holy Experiment."
The next stage of Pennsylvania's history began in 1681, when King Charles II named William PENN the proprietor* of the region in order to cancel a debt that the king owed Penn's father. Penn named his colony Pennsylvania, which means "Penn's woods" in Latin.

Penn, who was a QUAKER, looked upon the new colony as a "holy experiment." He did not want to create a state religion, as the Puritans had done in Massachusetts, though he expected that all the settlers would be Christians. He sought to make Pennsylvania a place where Quakers and other Christians could live together peacefully and respectfully.

Penn sent pamphlets throughout Europe, advertising the new colony. From London he planned the organization of Pennsylvania and designed a layout for a settlement to be named Philadelphia. His representatives in America carried out his ideas. Penn insisted that the colonists deal fairly with the region's original inhabitants. He would not allow them to settle on land until they had bought it from the Indians.

Politics and Population.
Pennsylvania's combination of religious freedom and plentiful land drew settlers from various parts of Europe. Most of the first wave of immigrants were Quakers from England, but some came

from Wales and Ireland. They settled mainly in and around Philadelphia, which lay in the southeastern corner of the colony, where the Schuylkill River flows into the Delaware River. The colonists cleared forests, built homes and meetinghouses for worship, and began constructing roads and a harbor to link them with the other British colonies.

Many of the early colonists were educated, middle-class crafts workers. But the settlements also included indentured servants* and slaves. Although opposed by Quakers, slavery remained legal in Pennsylvania throughout the colonial period.

The colony's political organization changed several times during its first years. Penn's original plan of government called for the proprietor or his representative to serve as governor. It also established an elected assembly of representatives that could approve or reject the governor's laws but could not make its own laws. The colonists, however, insisted on this right. By 1701 the assembly had gained the power to tax and to make laws. For the rest of the colonial era, the proprietors and elected representatives competed for political control of the colony. In the decades that followed, the proprietors—Penn's widow and descendants—steadily lost power, though the government remained largely in Quaker hands.

Pennsylvania's population changed and grew more varied over time. A second wave of colonists arrived between 1700 and 1750. These newcomers were German (although they came to be known as the Pennsylvania Dutch, from the German word *Deutsch,* meaning "German"). Like the Quakers, many of them had come to the colony in search of religious freedom. Most belonged to Protestant groups, such as the Amish and Mennonites, that were persecuted in Germany. The Pennsylvania Dutch were primarily farmers. They settled in fertile valleys west and north of Philadelphia. Their culture continues to play a role in some areas of southeastern Pennsylvania.

Starting around 1730, a third wave of settlers arrived in Pennsylvania. Most were Scotch-Irish Presbyterians from northern Ireland. These hardy and independent people tended to migrate to the western frontier, where they took part in the fur trade, hunted, and cleared the forest for pioneer settlements. The mix of these pioneers with those from other waves of colonization created a very diverse society, with people of many cultures, religions, and ethnic backgrounds.

The French and Indian War. During the 1700s, the movement of British settlers toward the western frontier led to increasing conflict with two groups: the Indians and the French. The Indians became angry as white people took more and more of their territory. Over the years, Pennsylvania colonists had drifted away from William Penn's policy of fair treatment for the Indians. The French were alarmed to see British colonists moving across the Appalachian Mountains into the Ohio River country—a region that France claimed and wanted to control.

The French began building forts in western Pennsylvania in the 1750s. The largest was FORT DUQUESNE, on the site of present-day Pittsburgh. In 1754 a group of Virginians, including George WASHINGTON, came to drive the French out of the area. French troops and their Indian allies defeated the Virginians, and the FRENCH AND INDIAN WAR began soon after. The British conquered Fort Duquesne later in the war and renamed it Fort Pitt.

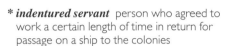

* *indentured servant* person who agreed to work a certain length of time in return for passage on a ship to the colonies

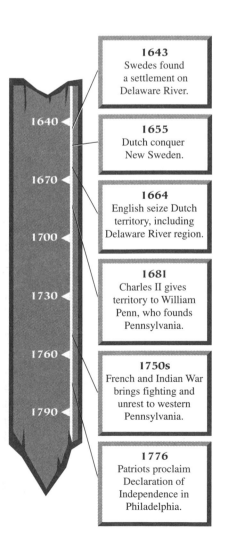

1643
Swedes found a settlement on Delaware River.

1655
Dutch conquer New Sweden.

1664
English seize Dutch territory, including Delaware River region.

1681
Charles II gives territory to William Penn, who founds Pennsylvania.

1750s
French and Indian War brings fighting and unrest to western Pennsylvania.

1776
Patriots proclaim Declaration of Independence in Philadelphia.

1640
1670
1700
1730
1760
1790

165

Pennsylvania

The Mason-Dixon Line

The charters of many British colonies said that their territory ran "from sea to sea"—from the Atlantic Ocean to the Pacific. Such terms were generous but not practical. As settlers pushed westward, many border conflicts arose. Pennsylvania and Maryland quarreled about their border for years before hiring professional surveyors to mark the boundary line. Charles Mason and Jeremiah Dixon worked from 1763 to 1767, hacking and measuring their way along the border between the two colonies. A hundred years later this line—called the Mason-Dixon Line—served as the dividing line between North and South in the Civil War.

Much of the fighting in the French and Indian War occurred in western Pennsylvania. Its frontier settlements suffered many French and Indian raids. The colonial assembly discussed forming a militia* to support British troops, but the Quakers who dominated the assembly opposed war, leaving the British the task of defending the colony.

The war ended in 1763 with victory for Britain. Soon after, the British issued the PROCLAMATION OF 1763, prohibiting colonists from living west of the Appalachians. Despite this ban, colonists continued to settle the lands across the mountains, and pioneer Pennsylvanians helped lead the way.

Commerce and Culture. While colonists pushed Pennsylvania's frontier farther west, the eastern part of the colony was thriving. Philadelphia had become a busy port and a very cosmopolitan* city. By the 1770s, it had a population of about 28,000—making it the largest city in colonial America and the second-largest city in the British empire after London.

Philadelphia's merchants traded with New England, the southern colonies, the WEST INDIES, and ports in Britain and mainland Europe. In addition to a thriving agriculture, Pennsylvania became noted for such industries as shipbuilding, glassmaking, lumbering, papermaking, and cloth production. The colony's rocky hills contained rich deposits of iron ore, and its forests yielded plenty of wood for making charcoal. Together the iron ore and charcoal supported a growing iron industry.

The cultural life of Pennsylvania was as varied and lively as its economy. In 1749 Benjamin FRANKLIN, a leading colonial thinker, helped found the Academy for the Education of Youth in Philadelphia, which later became the University of Pennsylvania. A printer and inventor as well, Franklin also encouraged Philadelphia's development as a major literary and scientific center. Among others who contributed to the cultural life of the colony were botanist John BARTRAM, physician Benjamin Rush, and artists Charles Willson Peale and Benjamin WEST.

Birthplace of Independence. In the 1760s, American colonists grew increasingly impatient with Britain's rule. Massachusetts was first and loudest in opposing British policies, but Philadelphia's location and its leading role in colonial life made it a logical place to hold the Continental Congress.

Like the other colonists, Pennsylvanians had mixed feelings about breaking away from Great Britain. Quakers were pacifists who opposed violence and war, no matter what the cause. Many German settlers were also pacifists or simply did not care about the issue. Some Pennsylvanians remained loyal to the British crown, but the majority believed that Britain, by passing such laws as the TOWNSHEND ACTS and the INTOLERABLE ACTS, was trampling on their rights. The Scotch-Irish, in particular, supported colonial independence.

Pennsylvanians organized protests against British policies and formed COMMITTEES OF CORRESPONDENCE to coordinate anti-British activities. Pennsylvania lawyer and landowner John DICKINSON wrote a forceful document in support of American rights. The most famous statement of those rights, the DECLARATION OF INDEPENDENCE, was presented in 1776 in a Philadelphia building now known as Independence Hall.

Pennsylvania played a leading role in the AMERICAN REVOLUTION. Several battles took place there, and it provided many soldiers and large quantities of supplies for the CONTINENTAL ARMY. With Philadelphia serving as the capital of the newly independent nation, Pennsylvania remained at the center of things after the colonial era came to an end. (*See also* **British Colonies; First Continental Congress; Independence Movements; Protestant Churches; Second Continental Congress.**)

Penobscot Indians

See *Abenaki Indians.*

Pequot Indians

When Europeans began to settle North America, the Pequot Indians were living in southern New England. Their territory included about 2,000 square miles in what is now Connecticut and eastern Long Island. By the 1630s, the Pequot had become involved in trade with both the English and the Dutch.

The Algonquian-speaking Pequot lived in small villages, hunting and gathering, growing MAIZE, and catching shellfish. They also developed a thriving industry creating WAMPUM—strings of beads made from the purple and white shells found on the shores of Long Island Sound. They traded these beads to other Indians of the region, who used them in sacred rituals*. Wampum gained new value when the Europeans began using it to pay for furs, and the Pequot exchanged wampum for goods from the Dutch.

In the early 1630s, diseases brought by European settlers wiped out nearly half of the Pequot's 4,000 members. When the weakened Indians clashed with the English over the murder of a Pequot chief in 1636, they had no allies in the region. Resentful of the Pequot's domination of the wampum trade, the Mohegan and NARRAGANSETT tribes sided with the English. In the short but bitter PEQUOT WAR of 1637, most of the tribe was destroyed—killed, sold into slavery, or forced to join the Mohegan and Narragansett.

The few remaining Pequot Indians split into two groups that never regained their former political or economic power. During the late 1600s, the colonists granted both groups reservations inside what had once been their territory. Both groups survive to this day, and one of them, the Mashantucket, is the wealthiest Indian tribe in the United States.

* **ritual** ceremony that follows a set pattern

See second map in Native Americans (vol. 3).

Pequot War (1636–1637)

The Pequot War was one of the major clashes between Indians and English colonists in New England in the 1600s. It pitted the PEQUOT INDIANS against people from the Massachusetts Bay colony who had settled in the Connecticut River valley.

The struggle between the two groups began in 1636, when the Pequot attacked and murdered a group of English traders who had killed a Pequot chief. The English then demanded that the Pequot hand over the attackers to face justice. When the Indians refused, the colonists made an unsuccessful assault on the Pequot village. The Indians responded by raiding the town of Wethersfield on the Connecticut River. In May 1637, the colonists declared war on the Pequot and sought the help of other Native Americans in the region. They found allies in the NARRAGANSETT and Mohegan tribes, who resented the Pequot's attempt to control trade with the Dutch.

On May 26, the English and their Indian allies launched a surprise attack on the main Pequot settlement on the Mystic River. They killed most of the sleeping Pequot, burned the fort, and went on to attack another village two miles away. The remaining Pequot fled, pursued by the colonists, who eventually caught most of them. The English kept some of the surviving Pequot as slaves, sold others into slavery in the West Indies, and gave the rest to their Indian allies to become part of their tribes.

A few Pequot, including a sachem*, managed to escape. They fled to the territory of the Mohawk Indians to ask for assistance. However, the Mohawk had already made a deal with the Narragansett. They not only refused to help the Pequot but killed their sachem and sent his scalp to the Connecticut colonists.

By the time the Pequot War ended, just a few small groups of Pequot Indians remained. These few survivors soon regrouped and obtained some land in portions of their original territory.

* **sachem** Indian chief

Philadelphia

Settled by people of diverse religious backgrounds and nationalities, Philadelphia became an important center of learning, commerce, and revolutionary activity. Though it was founded later than Boston or New York, Philadelphia grew quickly and by the late 1700s emerged as North America's largest city.

Early Days. The first Europeans to settle in the area that later became Philadelphia were from Sweden. During the 1640s, these early colonists built a fort, a trading post, and a group of houses on the banks of the Delaware River about 90 miles upstream from the Atlantic Ocean. Dutch soldiers from NEW NETHERLAND seized control of the SWEDISH SETTLEMENTS in 1655. But less than ten years later, the Dutch lost all their North American territory to the English.

In 1681 William PENN, an English QUAKER, received a charter* from King Charles II to establish the colony of PENNSYLVANIA. Penn, who wanted to create an ideal colony, carefully planned many of its details. He sent surveyors to choose a site for a colonial capital, one that offered a good harbor. The surveyors decided on a large peninsula where a river called the Schuylkill flowed into the Delaware. Although difficult to navigate, the Delaware River was broad and deep enough to allow large ships to reach the town from the ocean.

Penn called his capital Philadelphia, which means "city of brotherly love." The name reflected Penn's hope that the colony would be a haven of peace and toleration* not only for Quakers but for members of other Christian faiths as well. People from England, Ireland, and Wales began settling in the city. They joined colonists from the early Swedish and Dutch settlements who had remained in the area. Over the next several decades, immigrants

* **charter** written grant from a ruler conferring certain rights and privileges

* **toleration** acceptance of the right of individuals to follow their own religious beliefs

This illustration by W. Birch shows Philadelphia's Arch Street in the late 1700s.

from Germany, Switzerland, and other countries, as well as African slaves, added to the city's growing mix.

Penn was a pioneer in city planning. He decided that he wanted to create a "greene countrie towne." Each building in Philadelphia would stand in the middle of a plot of ground, so that everyone would have fresh air and fires could not spread easily. Trees and gardens in yards would create a rural atmosphere even in the heart of the city. Streets would be broad and straight. The result was a city like a giant checkerboard, with square blocks separated by regularly spaced streets. This checkerboard or grid pattern became the model for many other American cities.

By the mid-1700s, Philadelphia was growing so fast that building lots were divided and subdivided, and streets became lined with narrow brick houses crowded next to one another. Penn's plans for gardens and yards were largely abandoned, though some broad, tree-lined avenues survived from his original design for the city.

Growth and Development. Philadelphia's growth in the 1700s was based largely on its thriving trade. Ships brought manufactured goods to the city from Britain and Europe. They carried away timber and fur from surrounding forests and wheat, corn, pork, beef, and other agricultural products from the rich farmlands north and west of the city. Some of these cargoes

*** artisan** skilled crafts worker

went to the WEST INDIES in exchange for rum, molasses, and sugar. In addition to its success in international commerce, Philadelphia also became an important center of colonial trade.

The development of important industries—especially shipbuilding, papermaking, leather working, glassworking, and metalworking—also boosted Philadelphia's growth. In the mid-1700s, Philadelphia's flourishing commercial and industrial enterprises attracted large numbers of laborers, merchants, and artisans*. The city's population increased steadily, reaching nearly 30,000 by the time of the American Revolution.

Philadelphia became a cultural leader as well as a commercial center. Paved streets, gas street lamps, and three-story, red-brick buildings lent style to the city. Institutions such as the AMERICAN PHILOSOPHICAL SOCIETY, the University of Pennsylvania, and Library Company of Philadelphia promoted learning and the arts. Philadelphian Benjamin FRANKLIN was responsible for much of the city's lively cultural activity. Other notable residents included botanist John BARTRAM, astronomer David RITTENHOUSE, and painter Benjamin WEST.

*** patriot** American colonist who supported independence from Britain

Centrally located between New England and the southern colonies, Philadelphia played an important role in the affairs of the British colonies. It served as a meeting place and crossroads of colonial communication. Although opposition to Britain's policies and the movement for independence developed first in Massachusetts and Virginia, American patriots* selected Philadelphia as the site of the FIRST CONTINENTAL CONGRESS and the SECOND CONTINENTAL CONGRESS.

*** Loyalist** American colonist who remained faithful to Britain during the American Revolution

Like all colonists, the people of Philadelphia were deeply divided on the question of loyalty to Britain. Many of the city's working-class citizens supported the patriot cause and favored independence, but a number of its wealthy upper-class families were Loyalists*. After American patriots proclaimed the DECLARATION OF INDEPENDENCE in 1776 in the Philadelphia State House (now Independence Hall), the city became the headquarters of the Revolutionary government. After independence was won, Philadelphia served as the seat of government under the Articles of Confederation*. In 1787 representatives from the American states assembled in the State House to write a Constitution that created a new government for the UNITED STATES. (*See also* **Cities and Towns.**)

*** Articles of Confederation** plan approved in 1781 to establish a national legislature with limited powers

Pilgrims

*I*n September 1620, 35 Pilgrims and 66 other passengers set sail for North America aboard the *Mayflower*. A few months later they founded PLYMOUTH COLONY, the first European settlement in what became Massachusetts. The Pilgrims were SEPARATISTS, a group of English Protestants who broke away from the Church of England. Although outnumbered by the other colonists, the Pilgrims were the driving force behind the settlement and remained so throughout its history.

Origin of the Pilgrims. The Pilgrims began at Scrooby, a small village in the English county of Yorkshire. Their leader, William Brewster, had become a member of the Puritan sect* while attending Cambridge University.

*** sect** religious group

In July 1620, the Pilgrims set sail from the Netherlands on the *Speedwell*. The ship was supposed to carry them across the Atlantic, but it developed leaks and had to return to port for repairs. As a result, the *Mayflower* made the historic voyage alone.

* *Anglican* of the Church of England

The PURITANS wanted to remain within the Church of England but reform it. They disliked its elaborate ceremonies and disagreed with many of its policies. Brewster and his followers, however, believed that true Christians needed to remove themselves from all contact with "sinners," which meant separating completely from the Anglican* Church. For this reason, they were called Separatists.

Between 1590 and 1607, Brewster attracted about 100 newcomers to his group, now known as the Pilgrims. These included William BRADFORD, son of a wealthy farmer, and John Robinson, a graduate of Cambridge University who became their minister in 1607. Persecuted by their Anglican neighbors and by church authorities, the Pilgrims decided to immigrate to the Netherlands. Other English religious sects had already moved there to practice their faith freely.

In 1609 the Pilgrims obtained permission from the Dutch government to settle in the town of Leiden. After nine years in the Netherlands, their congregation had tripled in size, but many of the Pilgrims were dissatisfied with their situation. They worked hard for little money, their future seemed uncertain, and their children had begun adopting Dutch customs and speaking Dutch.

Leaving for America.   The Pilgrims decided to leave the Netherlands, but they disagreed on their destination. Some wanted to move to Guiana, on the northern coast of South America. But the hot climate, tropical diseases, and its closeness to the hostile Spanish made it an unattractive choice. The group then discovered that the VIRGINIA COMPANY OF LONDON was looking for settlers for its struggling colonies in North America. The company offered a patent* to English people who agreed to pay their own way to the "New World."

* *patent* permission to found a colony

171

To obtain the money needed for their voyage, the Pilgrims contacted Thomas Weston, an English Puritan merchant. Weston proposed that the Pilgrims form a company with several London merchants. The merchants would cover the costs of the trip, and the Pilgrims would repay them with profits made from fishing and trapping furs in America. Brewster and a number of followers agreed to the terms.

On July 22, 1620, the Pilgrims left the Netherlands aboard the *Speedwell,* a 60-ton ship outfitted for the voyage to North America. They sailed to the English port of Southampton to join the *Mayflower,* a second ship hired by the London investors. There they quarreled with Weston over business terms. Though no agreement was reached, the two ships set sail on August 15. The *Speedwell* soon developed leaks, however, and was forced to return to England for repairs in the town of Plymouth. The Pilgrims decided to make the voyage on the *Mayflower.* On September 16, the ship left Plymouth carrying 87 passengers, 14 servants and workmen, and a crew of 48. Only 35 of the passengers were Pilgrims, and only two of them—Brewster and Bradford—remained from the original congregation in Scrooby, England.

The Founding of New Plymouth.

After a crossing of 66 days, during which four passengers died, the crew of the *Mayflower* sighted land on November 19, 1620. However, it soon became clear that the ship had not reached the region mentioned in their patent but had landed about 200 miles to the north. This presented two problems. First, the Pilgrims' patent applied only to the particular area described in it and gave them no legal right to establish a colony in another place. Second, the patent outlined how the colony should be governed. But because the patent was not valid outside the Virginia Company's territory, the plans drawn up for the new colony's government no longer applied.

To keep the group of colonists together and establish a system for maintaining order, Pilgrim leaders drew up a document known as the MAYFLOWER COMPACT. All 41 free adult males on board signed this historic compact. In doing so, they agreed to work together to organize the colony and set up a government, to obey the laws passed by the will of the majority, and to accept the authority of the colony's governor. The colonists chose John Carver as their first governor.

By mid-December the Pilgrims had decided on a location for their colony, which they named New Plymouth. Weakened from their long voyage, many settlers died from disease, and the Pilgrims barely survived the first winter in North America. The next spring, however, they received assistance from a local Indian named SQUANTO, who had learned English while being held captive by an English sea captain. Squanto showed the settlers how to plant squash and fertilize their crops. He also helped them negotiate a peace treaty with Massasoit, chief of the WAMPANOAG tribe that lived nearby. That fall the Pilgrims held a harvest festival to celebrate God's favor in allowing them to survive in their new land. They invited the Wampanoag to this first THANKSGIVING CELEBRATION.

Led by William Bradford, who served as governor of the colony from 1621 until his death in 1657, the Pilgrims struggled to keep their settlement alive. They eventually received a patent for the land where they had settled, but they faced poor farming conditions and many economic problems. The FUR TRADE, which the London merchants had counted on to repay their investment, soon

Remember: *Words in small capital letters have separate entries, and the index at the end of Volume 4 will guide you to more information on many topics.*

died out. The Pilgrims also proved to be more interested in growing crops to feed themselves than in catching fish to repay their investors. With no good harbors, no products to export, and no contacts with other colonies or merchants, the colony proved unprofitable.

In 1691 the much larger Massachusetts Bay colony absorbed New Plymouth. Despite the Pilgrims' failure to maintain the independence of their colony, they were, in the words of William Bradford, the "instruments to break the ice for others who come after with less difficulty." (*See also* **Church and State; Freedom of Religion; Massachusetts.**)

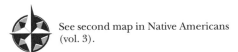

*T*he Pima Indians—also known as the Akimel O'odhams (River People)—lived along several rivers in what is now southern Arizona and northern Mexico. Although they frequently fought with neighboring APACHE INDIANS, the Pima generally lived peacefully with the Spanish settlers in the area and later with the Americans.

Developing a culture based on agriculture, the Pima raised corn, beans, squash, and other crops in irrigated fields. They also hunted for small game and gathered a variety of wild foods. Skilled basket weavers and pottery makers, the Indians lived in small permanent villages made up of round, flat-topped houses covered with grass and mud.

The Spanish explorer Marcos de Niza, the first European to encounter the Pima, traveled through their territory in 1589. In the late 1600s, a missionary named Eusebio KINO went to live with the Indians, and he established nine MISSIONS on their lands. He also introduced livestock and wheat.

The Pima and the European newcomers generally maintained friendly relations. But in 1695 some of the Pima revolted because the Spanish had begun forcing them to pay taxes and work for the Europeans. Spanish soldiers quickly put down the rebellion but not before the Indians had looted and burned Spanish property.

In 1751 a small group of Pima rebelled against the Spanish. Once again Spanish soldiers quickly crushed the uprising—later known as the Pima Revolt. Thereafter, relations between the Pima and the settlers remained peaceful. Americans began settling in the area in the 1850s, after the United States gained control of the Southwest from Mexico. A few years later, the U.S. government began to resettle the Pima on reservations in the region. (*See also* **Native Americans; Tohono O'odham Indians.**)

See second map in Native Americans (vol. 3).

Pinckney, Eliza

ca. 1722–1793
Plantation manager

*E*lizabeth Lucas Pinckney, known as Eliza, managed a plantation in SOUTH CAROLINA. The daughter of an officer in the British army, she was the first planter in the colony to cultivate indigo* successfully. As a result of her work, indigo became an important new crop in the region.

Eliza Lucas was born in the West Indies, where her father served as the lieutenant governor of the island of Antigua. The oldest of four children, Eliza received her education in Britain. She enjoyed reading Greek and Latin classics and legal works.

* *indigo* plant used to make a blue dye

In 1738 Eliza, her parents, and her sister Polly went to live on a plantation on Wappoo Creek in South Carolina. A year later, when the War of JENKINS'S EAR forced Colonel Lucas to return to Antigua, he left 17-year-old Eliza in charge of the plantation. She quickly took over management of the estate.

At the time, South Carolina faced economic difficulties because the war had reduced the market for RICE, the colony's main export. Eliza Lucas decided to grow indigo in place of rice, even though earlier attempts at producing the dye in the area had failed. After several years of experimenting with temperature, soil, and other growing conditions, the young woman—with the help of an experienced indigo maker—produced her first successful crop in 1744. She distributed indigo seeds to other planters, and within a few years, indigo became one of South Carolina's leading exports. By the 1770s, it was the sixth most valuable North American export.

At the age of 22, Eliza Lucas married Charles Pinckney, a lawyer. The couple had four children, three of whom survived to adulthood. In 1758 Charles died of malaria. Eliza once again became a plantation manager, overseeing her husband's numerous properties. After the British colonies gained their independence, her two sons became leaders in the young United States. Charles Cotesworth Pinckney represented South Carolina at the Constitutional Convention and twice ran for President of the United States. Thomas Pinckney served as governor of South Carolina and ambassador to Great Britain. (*See also* **Agriculture; Plantations; Women, Roles of.**)

Pirates

*P*iracy had a long history in Europe. When European nations began exploring and settling the Americas, they brought the practice with them. Pirates differed from PRIVATEERS, who had the authority of their governments to attack vessels from other nations in times of war. Pirates sought wealth and had loyalty to no country.

Piracy in the "New World" flourished first in the Caribbean region, where a new form called buccaneering emerged. Unlike earlier pirates, who had been tied to a home community, buccaneers sailed from any island port that suited them and often camped in deserted spots. Their crews usually consisted of men from many countries, bound together in a society of their own. Those drawn to piracy included runaway slaves and servants, former soldiers and sailors, escaped prisoners, and others dissatisfied with their lives.

Sailing in crowded ships, buccaneers might go hungry or even starve if they failed to capture a ship or attack a town. They also risked hanging if they were caught. But the buccaneering life offered certain advantages. It was a rough democracy in which men elected their leaders and, for the most part, divided their loot fairly. It also held the hope of winning a fortune, although few pirates achieved great wealth—and fewer still lived to enjoy it.

By the late 1600s, buccaneers began seeking new territory outside the Caribbean. In the early days, their favorite target had been Spanish ships carrying gold and silver. But the Spanish had improved their defenses, and Caribbean merchants were trading directly with Spanish ships instead of the pirates. Many buccaneers moved on to the mainland British colonies to seek their fortunes.

One of the most feared pirates of the colonial period was Edward Teach, the English sea captain commonly known as Blackbeard. After sailing for the British, he turned to piracy in 1713 and robbed ships along the coasts of Virginia and the Carolinas.

British colonial governments had passed laws against piracy. In Massachusetts the punishment for this crime was death, and its governors sent out armed ships to attack pirates lurking off the coast. But by the late 1600s, after Great Britain issued the NAVIGATION ACTS forbidding the colonies to trade with foreign countries, the colonies welcomed pirates' contributions to the local economy. Merchants in New York, Charleston, and other towns purchased stolen goods from pirates and in turn sold the buccaneers goods and services while they were in port.

In the 1700s, the British government began a campaign to rid its waters of pirates. It reformed laws, making piracy easier to prosecute, and sent out the Royal Navy to attack pirates and destroy their bases. By the 1730s, large-scale buccaneering in the Atlantic had been crushed. The Caribbean islands, however, remained a favorite haunt for pirates and privateers for many years.

Pitt, William

1708–1778
British political leader

During the mid-1700s, William Pitt became a prominent figure in the British government and led his country's war effort during several crises, including the FRENCH AND INDIAN WAR. His policies helped Britain gain control of the eastern part of North America.

Pitt belonged to a distinguished British family. He studied for one year at Oxford University but left without completing his degree because he suffered from gout—a painful illness that troubled him all his life. In 1735 he became a member of PARLIAMENT. Through his political activities, he met Richard and George GRENVILLE, whose sister, Lady Hester Grenville, he later married.

In Parliament Pitt caused a stir by making speeches against powerful groups in the government and defending people such as the colonists of North America. In 1746 he became paymaster general of the armed forces, with responsibility for distributing large sums of money. He earned a reputation for honesty and gained popularity with the people by making useful reforms in the system of military payments.

In the mid-1750s, the British became involved in wars against other European powers in both Europe and North America. By 1756 they had suffered major losses in battle. Because Pitt had considerable public support, King George II asked him to develop a military strategy and to help organize a new group of government ministers. Pitt held the position of secretary of state, but he had as much influence as a prime minister. He expanded the army and prepared a new foreign policy. Instead of concentrating on winning the war in Europe, Pitt focused on maintaining the North American colonies and taking control of French territory in present-day Canada. He also took steps to improve relations between Britain and its colonies by paying for the colonists' military expenses.

Thanks to these policies, the British won a decisive series of victories over the French, enabling them to add Canada to their empire. However, in 1760 King George II died, and his son, GEORGE III, came to power. The new king and his cabinet were eager to end the war. Because they objected to Pitt's strategy, which involved declaring war on Spain, Pitt resigned from the cabinet in October 1761.

Despite this reversal, Pitt remained active in politics. In January 1766, he gave a speech supporting the American colonists in their opposition to the STAMP ACT. He called for the act—which imposed taxes on legal documents and other paper goods used in the colonies—to be repealed*. Several months later, with the British government in a state of confusion, the king asked Pitt to step in again as leader. Pitt appointed a group of ministers, naming himself lord privy seal, a minor official. He received the title Earl of Chatham and became a member of the House of Lords*. But Pitt fell ill and resigned from the leadership in 1768. In his last years, he continued to deliver moving speeches in Parliament, strongly defending the American colonists' rights. His son, William, followed his father's path into government and served as prime minister. (*See also* **Colonial Administration; Warfare and Diplomacy.**)

* *repeal* to undo a law

* *House of Lords* one of the two houses that make up Parliament

Plains Indians

The term *Plains Indians* refers to many distinct Native American tribes that lived on the Great Plains—the vast region of broad, rolling grasslands between the Mississippi River and the Rocky Mountains. Although they spoke numerous languages and had different ways of living, the Plains tribes shared certain basic characteristics that set them apart from other Indians of North America.

The "Plains culture" came into existence only after the arrival of Europeans on the continent. Based primarily on HORSES and BUFFALO, the culture developed over a period of about 300 years as different tribes migrated and

The Plains Indians built a way of life around the buffalo. They followed the buffalo for great distances, setting up tepees in camps like the one shown in this print based on a Karl Bodmer painting.

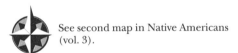
See second map in Native Americans (vol. 3).

* *assimilate* to adopt the customs of a society

mingled throughout the Great Plains region. Plains Indians held on to their way of life longer than most Native American groups. Isolated through much of the colonial period, they did not feel the full impact of white settlement until the 1800s, when pioneers began migrating across the continent. During this period, the tribes fought many wars with settlers in an attempt to keep their land and their traditions.

History of the Plains Indians.   Before the arrival of Europeans in North America, various Indian tribes lived in the Great Plains region. Some— including the PAWNEE, Arikara, and Mandan Indians—depended on agriculture for food; others—such as the Blackfoot Indians—relied primarily on hunting.

During the 1600s and 1700s, other Indian tribes began migrating to the Great Plains region. Many had been forced out of their traditional homelands in the East by European colonists. Others were pushed into the region by Indian tribes moving westward. Among the tribes that relocated to the Great Plains during this period were the Arapaho, Cheyenne, COMANCHE, CREE, Kiowa, Crow, and Lakota—better known as Sioux.

Conflicts arose as tribes competed for territory and hunting areas on the Plains. At the same time, contact among the tribes led to cultural "borrowing." Tribes observed each other and started to assimilate* new ideas and ways of living.

During the 1600s, a common culture began to emerge among the non-farming Indians based on the geography of the Great Plains and the basic needs for survival there. This culture was nomadic, with tribes traveling from place to place to hunt and gather food. Tribes consisted of bands of related families, each with a few hundred members. Going their separate ways most of the year, the bands gathered at certain times for hunting and religious ceremonies. The Plains Indians' way of life depended heavily on both the horse and the buffalo.

Importance of the Horse.

Introduced in North America by the Spanish in the 1500s, horses gradually spread from the Southwest to the Great Plains area. Most Plains Indians began using the animals in the early to mid-1700s.

Horses played a central role in the development of the Plains culture. They enabled the Indians to travel far from fertile river valleys—the only place in the region where crops could be grown easily—and to roam over large areas in search of buffalo and other food. Not all Plains Indian tribes adopted a completely nomadic way of life. Some settled in villages and raised crops, but they left their homes periodically for long hunting expeditions.

Before the Plains Indians acquired horses, they carried their possessions on their own backs or used dogs to pull small loads. Horses could transport heavy loads over long distances, allowing the Indians to move all their belongings from place to place.

The Plains Indians became highly skilled riders, and tribes maintained large herds of horses. Sometimes they enlarged these herds by taming wild horses or stealing horses from other tribes and white settlers. Some Plains tribes, such as the Blackfoot, specialized in breeding the animals. Others, such as the Comanche, developed a profitable trade in horses with white settlers.

> **Remember:** Consult the index at the end of Volume 4 to find more information on many topics.

Importance of the Buffalo.

Before the introduction of horses, buffalo hunting was slow and difficult. The early Plains Indians hunted buffalo on foot and tried to drive the animals over cliffs or into narrow canyons where they could be killed easily. On horseback the Indians could chase buffalo long distances and kill large numbers of them. The Indians became expert at riding through galloping buffalo herds and picking off the animals with lances or bows and arrows.

For the Plains Indians, buffalo meat was a basic food. They ate it both raw and cooked. They also dried the meat so that it would keep for long periods. The buffalo provided the Plains peoples with many other important items. They used buffalo hides to make clothing, tepee coverings, and blankets. From buffalo hair, they made thread and rope, and from buffalo bones, they created various tools.

The greater efficiency of hunting buffalo on horseback enabled the Plains Indians to pursue other activities. As a result, they developed a flourishing trade with tribes in other regions and later with white settlers. They exchanged surplus buffalo hides and dried buffalo meat for agricultural products, such as corn and other vegetables, and various other items they could not produce themselves.

Plains Indian Culture.

Aside from a reliance on the horse and buffalo, the Plains Indians had a number of special traditions. In combat the warriors proved their bravery not by killing or wounding the enemy but by "counting coup"—touching an enemy in battle with the hand, a stick, or other object. Most Plains tribes also had special warrior societies, each with its own distinctive symbols, costumes, songs, and codes of behavior.

Magic held an important place in the spiritual life of the Plains Indians. Among their special possessions were sacred pipes used in peace councils and religious ceremonies and medicine bundles containing plants, parts of animals, and other objects that were thought to have magical powers.

The Indians' spiritual life also included visions experienced in dreams or in trances brought on by fasting, thirst, exposure to the forces of nature, and self-induced pain. The quest for visions played a major role in the Sun Dance, the most important and complex of all Plains Indian ceremonies. The Sun Dance had different names and numerous variations. But its basic purpose was always the same: to renew nature and make contact with the spirit world. (*See also* **Economic Systems; Family; Food and Drink; Languages; Music and Dance; Native Americans; Recreation and Sports; Religions, Native American.**)

Plantations

*C*olonial plantations were agricultural estates that usually produced a single crop and were worked mainly by slave labor. The plantation system was introduced to the Americas by the Spanish and Portuguese, who raised sugar on huge estates in the WEST INDIES and South America in the 1500s.

During the early 1600s, English colonists began to grow TOBACCO on small plantations in Virginia and Maryland. The creation of large-scale plantations, however, did not occur until the late 1600s, when English planters from the Caribbean island of BARBADOS arrived in South Carolina. From there, a plantation system based on large landholdings gradually spread throughout much of the South.

The plantation system was best suited for growing crops that required a great deal of labor but very little skill. Tobacco remained the most profitable plantation crop in the Chesapeake region. Farther south, sugar, RICE, indigo*, and later COTTON were raised on plantations. Rice, introduced in South Carolina in about 1685, soon replaced sugar as the region's most important plantation crop.

The earliest plantations relied mainly on indentured servants* for labor. By the 1680s, however, planters could no longer find enough indentured servants to fill their enormous need for workers. They looked to another source of labor—African slaves. They obtained hundreds and thousands of cheap and dependable workers through the SLAVE TRADE, and SLAVERY became the basis of the plantation system.

Most plantations were highly profitable, making Southern planters among the richest people in the English colonies. Plantations varied greatly in size. Tobacco plantations tended to be small because a farmer could make money from the crop grown on a few hundred acres with no more than a few dozen slaves. Raising sugar and rice, however, required large landholdings and many slaves. Some planters owned up to 50,000 acres and more than 1,000 slaves. British colonists tried to establish plantations in other regions of North America, but the system never took root outside the South.

Plantations were self-sufficient communities, consisting of slave quarters, barns, storehouses, livestock, gardens, orchards, and fields. The slaves not only produced the main crop but also made many other goods—such as food, clothing, and tools—that were needed for everyday life. The plantation system came to dominate the political, social, and cultural life of the South, even though most southern landowners had only small farms and few or no slaves. Planters held most public offices, controlling the politics of the

* *indigo* plant used to make a blue dye

* *indentured servant* person who agreed to work a certain length of time in return for passage on a ship to the colonies

colonies, and plantation families established the customs that came to characterize southern society.

Although plantations brought great wealth to individual southern families, the large-scale production of one or two crops did not lead to a balanced economy. Southern colonists failed to develop manufacturing, trade, banking, and other important economic activities, depending on northern cities and English merchants to finance, market, and export their crops. For all the profits created by the plantation system, in the long run, it weakened the South. However, the problems created by the system did not become clear until after the colonial period. (*See also* **African American Culture; Agriculture; Class Structure in European Colonies; Indentured Servants; Labor; Land Ownership.**)

Plymouth Colony

*P*lymouth colony, established on the southeast coast of present-day MASSACHUSETTS in 1620, was the first permanent English settlement in New England. The colony's founders, a group known as the PILGRIMS, came to North America so they could practice their religious beliefs without persecution.

*** patent** permission to found a colony

*** Anglican** of the Church of England

The Roots of Plymouth Colony.
In the early 1600s, the English government gave large grants of land in North America to private companies for establishing colonies. One such company, the VIRGINIA COMPANY OF LONDON, received an application for a patent* from the Pilgrims. The Pilgrims were PURITANS who disagreed with the teachings and policies of the Church of England. Most Puritans wanted to reform the Anglican* Church. The Pilgrims, however, believed they had to break away from it, and for this reason, they were sometimes called Separatists. Their views had brought them into conflict with church authorities and their neighbors in Scrooby, Yorkshire. The Pilgrims had emigrated to the Netherlands, but after several years, they had become dissatisfied with life there. A group of them wanted to move to North America to found a new community where they would find it easier to live according to their faith.

The Pilgrims received the patent they sought and decided to establish their colony on the northern part of the Virginia Company's land, far from the Anglican settlements in Virginia. To finance their voyage, they entered into an arrangement with a group of London merchants led by Thomas Weston. The Pilgrims agreed to farm, build houses, and fish for seven years. After that time, they would share any profits from the enterprise with the merchants.

Journey to a New World.
The Pilgrims set out in two ships, the *Speedwell* and the *Mayflower,* but the *Speedwell* soon developed leaks and had to return to England for repairs. For that reason, only the *Mayflower* set sail for North America from the port of Plymouth on September 16, 1620. The ship carried 101 people plus the crew. However, only 35 of these passengers were Pilgrims. The rest were people seeking opportunity in a new land.

After 66 days at sea, the *Mayflower* arrived in the "New World." However, the spot on which it landed was about 200 miles northeast of the intended

See map in British Colonies (vol. 1).

* *palisade* fence of stakes forming a defense

destination. Because this location was outside the area described by their patent, some of the passengers felt that the terms of the patent—including those that explained how the new colony should be governed—were no longer valid. To keep order, the Pilgrims' leaders drew up the MAYFLOWER COMPACT. Under this compact, the settlers agreed to choose the leaders of the colony and to obey the government established by those leaders. On November 21, 1620, all 41 free adult males on board signed the document.

Unable to find a suitable harbor, the Pilgrims sailed along the coast for another month before finally landing and founding the colony of New Plymouth. The site they chose seemed ideal. It had plenty of freshwater, cleared land, and no Indians in residence. The settlers built a crude palisade* for defense and a common warehouse for supplies, and each family constructed its own shelter.

The splendid site was vacant because recent outbreaks of disease— brought by earlier European visitors—had wiped out the previous inhabitants. The Indians' misfortune turned out to be a blessing for the Pilgrims. The epidemic had been so recent and so swift that the Indians' cornfields had not yet turned back into wilderness. The stores of corn they left behind helped the Pilgrims survive their first winter in North America. Although the first winter was actually mild, nearly half of the settlers died in the first few months.

The Rise and Decline of New Plymouth.

As the Pilgrims planted their first corn crop the following spring, two Native Americans visited the settlement. SQUANTO, who had learned English as the captive of an English sea captain, showed the settlers how to plant squash between the rows of corn and how to fertilize the land. He also helped the Pilgrims negotiate with Massasoit, the chief of the local WAMPANOAG tribe. The new settlers signed a treaty with the Wampanoag that allowed them to harvest their crops in safety. To celebrate God's favor in allowing them to survive in their new land, the

French explorer Samuel de Champlain sailed along the Massachusetts coast in 1605. He drew this map showing Indian settlements and numerous cornfields. About 15 years later, after most of the Indians had died from European diseases, the site became Plymouth colony.

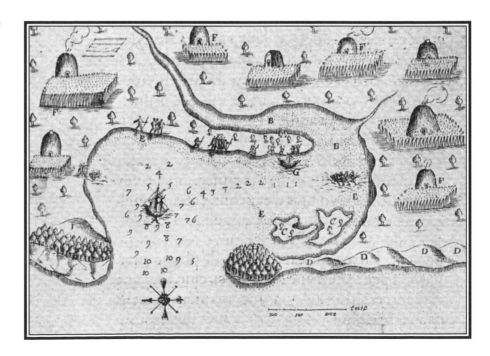

Pilgrims held a harvest festival and invited the Wampanoag—the first THANKSGIVING CELEBRATION.

New Plymouth continued to experience its share of difficulties. For the first nine years of its existence, the colony had no fully trained minister—a serious matter for a colony founded for religious purposes. In 1622 Thomas Weston arrived in Plymouth with a new batch of settlers, few of whom shared the Pilgrim's religious beliefs. These settlers were persuaded to move up the coast to begin their own settlement at Wessagusset. It lasted only a year. Three years later, a group led by Thomas Morton established another settlement nearby. The newcomers' lifestyle, which included drinking and dancing, offended the Puritans' strict morals. In 1628 the Pilgrims forced Morton and his companions to return to England.

The colony's biggest problem, however, was its failure to show a profit. The investors had hoped to make money from fishing and the FUR TRADE, but most of the Pilgrims devoted themselves to farming. By 1626 most of the original investors sold their shares and split the money with the settlers.

New Plymouth's prospects improved in the 1630s, when the larger and wealthier Massachusetts Bay Company established a colony to the north. Plymouth was able to sell livestock and grain to the new settlers, and the colony slowly began to grow. By 1637 its population had reached 550, and new Pilgrim settlements had been founded around Plymouth.

Plymouth never became very large, however. The colony's growth was limited by its failure to expand its community beyond Puritan Separatists or to develop any economic activity besides small farming. It was soon overshadowed by neighboring colonies. In 1691 the much larger Massachusetts Bay colony absorbed New Plymouth, which by then had about 7,500 inhabitants. (*See also* **Church and State; Separatists.**)

Rowdy Neighbors

The Pilgrims at Plymouth colony were always concerned about the morals of their neighbors—especially those of Thomas Morton. In 1625 Morton and a group of followers settled at Mount Wollaston (now Braintree) near Plymouth. Drinking was common, and the residents put up a maypole, which the Pilgrims considered an immoral pagan custom. Morton even began writing indecent poetry. The Pilgrims took no action, however, until Morton started selling arms to local Indians. Finally, the Pilgrim militia, led by Miles Standish, forced the group to return to England.

Pocahontas

ca. 1596–1617
Indian princess

See color plate 1, vol. 3.

Pocahontas, the daughter of the chief of the POWHATAN INDIANS, holds a well-established place in the stories of early colonial life. She is remembered now for her role in bringing about peaceful relations between her people and the English colonists who established JAMESTOWN COLONY in Virginia.

Pocahontas's father, called Powhatan by the English, ruled a good part of the tidewater area in present-day Virginia, including the land where Jamestown was built in 1607. Several months after the arrival of the English colonists, the Indians captured Captain John SMITH, the settlement's leader. According to tradition, Pocahontas begged her father to spare the Englishman's life. The accuracy of this story is uncertain—Pocahontas may only have "saved" Captain Smith from a symbolic execution designed to show the Powhatan chief's superiority. Upon Smith's release, the Indians and the colonists agreed to a truce.

Despite the agreement, clashes between the two cultures continued to occur. In 1613 the new leaders of Jamestown kidnapped Pocahontas and several other Indians to use as hostages in negotiations with Powhatan. During her stay in the settlement, Pocahontas learned English and converted to Christianity. She also met an English planter named John ROLFE, known for

his experiments with tobacco, who fell in love with her. They were married in 1614, and their union brought a temporary end to the conflict between the Indians and the colonists.

A year after her marriage, Pocahontas gave birth to a son, Thomas. In 1616 the Rolfe family, the governor of Virginia, and 12 Native Americans sailed for England on a goodwill tour. Treated like royalty, Pocahontas was introduced to the English king and queen. The VIRGINIA COMPANY OF LONDON used the visit to promote further colonization. Shortly before the family was to return to America, Pocahontas became ill with smallpox and died. She was buried at the St. George's Parish church in Gravesend, England.

Poetry

See *Literature*.

*The colonization of North America took place at a time of lively political thought in Europe. In the years between 1500 and 1800, political writers in Spain, France, the Netherlands, and England explored such topics as the origins and purpose of government, government organization, and the rights and responsibilities of rulers and citizens.

The colonization of North America introduced new issues for philosophers* to consider. They debated what gave Europeans the right to claim territory in North America and to exert control over the Indians. Of special concern to most political thinkers was the nature of the relationship between colonies and the countries that had founded them. In British North America, arguments over this issue contributed to the AMERICAN REVOLUTION.

* *philosopher* person who seeks wisdom and truth

Spanish Political Thought.   The 1500s were the golden age of Spanish political thought. Writers and university scholars examined ideas about how governments had come into being. One group believed that God had created the existing political structures. A second group based their thinking on what they called natural law. They claimed that individuals had originally lived in a state of freedom, equality, and independence. When people began to gather together in communities, they created a new kind of power that gave rulers the authority to make laws and administer justice. In becoming part of society, citizens had transferred sovereignty* over their lives to their ruler, who was above the law.

* *sovereignty* supreme power or authority

The goal of Spain's natural-law philosophers was to prove that their monarch was rightfully the absolute ruler of the state, free of control by the church or the pope. In their view, the power originally held by the people had been transferred to the monarch, giving the ruler total authority. This belief was the foundation of political life in the Spanish colonies, which were governed by officials who represented the monarch's will.

Spanish philosophers and authorities also debated the proper treatment of the Indians. Juan Ginés de Sepúlveda thought the Native Americans were fit only to be slaves. Bartolomé de LAS CASAS disagreed. Believing that the Indians possessed the power of reason and should be allowed to rule themselves, he argued that Spain had no right to take the Indians' land, property, and freedom.

183

Religion further complicated the matter. Almost all Spanish thinkers argued that it was the duty of Christians to take charge of non-Christians.

French Political Thought. The main feature of French political thought during the colonial period was its emphasis on absolutism—the concentration of all power in the hands of the monarch. Some philosophers believed that although the monarch was the supreme authority, his responsibilities included protecting his subjects' rights and seeking advice from councils that represented towns and regions. However, political disorder and civil war in France convinced many others that an absolute monarchy* was the only way to ensure order, unity, and peace in the country.

Leading French political writers of the late 1600s claimed that God had chosen the king to rule and that the king held the same place on earth that God held in the universe. To these people, the liberty of the monarch's subjects did not include individual rights or the power to take part in government. They favored a paternalistic government—one in which the king protected and ruled his subjects as a father protects and rules his children.

The French colonies in North America had a similar relationship with the monarchy. All control moved downward from the king or his representatives. Colonists had no assemblies or other ways of expressing their views or participating in government. France had lost its colonies in North America before the ideas of the French Enlightenment* took hold there. But Enlightenment philosophers such as Voltaire, Jean-Jacques Rousseau, and Baron Montesquieu had a major influence on British colonists in the late 1700s.

Dutch Political Thought. Dutch political thought was very different from the absolutism of the Spanish and French. The Netherlands, a loosely linked group of states with some republican* features, did not provide a good setting for ideas of glorified kingship or all-powerful monarchs.

In 1625 Hugo Grotius, the most famous Dutch political philosopher, published his theory about the rights of citizens in a society. He claimed that individuals voluntarily come together in political societies in order to live in peace, agreeing to respect each other's rights and property. Monarchs, he argued, should exist only for the good of the state. In justification of the Dutch seizure of Indian territory, Grotius argued that people can acquire property simply by making use of unoccupied land. To the Dutch—who had little understanding of the way Native Americans used the land—much of North America seemed to be "unoccupied."

Other Dutch political thinkers proposed such ideas as religious toleration* and government by assemblies of citizens. Colonists in New Netherland did not spend much time debating these ideas, though they did demand a greater role in managing their affairs. The company governing the colony reluctantly agreed.

English Political Thought. The Spanish, French, and Dutch colonies in North America produced little political thought of their own. In the British colonies, however, political theory was highly developed.

British America had a political system based on English tradition that included vigorous citizen participation in local government, elections, and institutions representing the people, such as law-making assemblies. The

* ***absolute monarchy*** rule by a king or queen who possesses unlimited power

* ***Enlightenment*** European intellectual movement of the 1600s and 1700s, based on faith in the power of reason and the idea that individuals have certain fundamental rights

* ***republican*** form of government in which the people elect government officials

* ***toleration*** acceptance of the right of individuals to follow their own religious beliefs

British colonies also had a more highly developed system of communication—including printing presses, NEWSPAPERS, LIBRARIES, and SCHOOLS—than the other colonies. As a result, political ideas spread quickly, and many people were involved in studying and discussing them. Finally, the population of the British colonies was larger, more prosperous, and better educated than the populations of the other colonies. Many people in British North America had the time and the ability to read political essays and books, not just from Britain but from all over Europe.

Political thought in the British colonies was like a complex fabric that included strands from many different sources. One of the fundamental threads in this fabric was the jurisprudential tradition—the importance of law as a way of limiting or controlling the power of the monarchy. This tradition grew out of English common law, which is a collection of judicial customs, decisions, and rules developed over centuries. The English believed that the common law protected the life, liberty, and property of citizens.

Another strand in colonial political thought came from the civic humanist tradition. Drawing on the writings of Aristotle and other ancient philosophers, civic humanists believed that the ideal state consisted of independent individuals who willingly and happily participated in self-government. Such a state could be achieved by a balanced government or constitution that shared power among the monarch, the nobles, and the ordinary people. The civic humanist tradition deeply influenced American patriots* during the 1760s and 1770s.

A third strand grew out of the liberal tradition. Inspired by advances in science during the 1600s, liberal thinkers hoped to develop a "science of man" that would organize human affairs on the basis of logic and natural principles. To philosophers in this tradition, the most important social unit was the individual. Each person was responsible for making his or her own judgments in matters such as religion and politics.

The leading English liberal philosopher was John Locke, who argued that people entered into political societies to protect their natural rights to life, liberty, and property. A government existed, in Locke's view, only to guarantee those rights to the individuals who voluntarily placed themselves under its authority. The government and the state had no authority and no reason for existence beyond individual rights. If a government violated those rights, its citizens were entitled to resist or even overthrow it. In the 1760s and 1770s, colonists drew on Locke's ideas in opposing Great Britain and claiming independence. Some of the wording of the DECLARATION OF INDEPENDENCE was based on Locke's 1690 book *Two Treatises on Government.*

A fourth strand in colonial political thought came from economics. Many of the economic writers of the time were involved in trade or manufacturing, and they sought to understand and describe the workings of the forces driving the new commercial economy. They viewed North America as a giant experiment in which people "improved" a wilderness by turning it into a civilized society. This way of thinking, which placed a high value on material goods and individual efforts, appealed to many ambitious Americans. Writers such as Daniel Defoe and Adam Smith were highly influential.

Another thread of colonial political thought came from Scotland, which had a long tradition of writings on the subject of human nature and government.

***patriot** American colonist who favored independence from Great Britain

Philosophers such as David Hume viewed history as the story of human progress from savagery to civilization. Unlike the liberals, who focused on the importance of the individual, the Scottish writers tended to emphasize the ties that bind societies together.

The final strand in the fabric of political thought grew out of the Enlightenment. It reflected a new interest in scientific discovery and in the belief that people could solve their own problems by using reason rather than by relying on religious belief. The most important Enlightenment figure in British colonial thought in the Revolutionary period was Charles-Louis de Secondat, Baron Montesquieu. His ideas about the separation of powers within a state played a leading role in the creation of the Constitution of the United States. Having won independence from Britain, American political leaders created a government where the executive, legislative, and judicial branches would share power. Their goal was to prevent any person or group from gaining control over the government.

As they laid the foundation for a new kind of state in what had been the British colonies, Americans drew upon the many traditions of European political thought and added a wealth of their own ideas and beliefs. (*See also* **Colonial Administration; Enlightenment: Influence in North America; Independence Movements.**)

Ponce de León, Juan

ca. 1460–1521
Spanish explorer

* *conquistador* Spanish explorer and conqueror

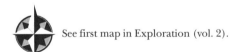

See first map in Exploration (vol. 2).

*T*oday most people know Juan Ponce de León as the Spanish explorer who searched in vain for a mythical spring called the "fountain of youth." However, he was also a skilled navigator and a capable administrator. He treated Native Americans with unusual kindness in an age when Spanish conquistadors* were noted for brutality toward the Indians.

As his name suggests, Ponce de León was born in the province of León in Spain. As a youth, he was a servant to the prince who later became King Ferdinand, one of the sponsors of the voyages of Christopher COLUMBUS. It is not known for certain when Ponce de León first came to America. Some historians believe that he sailed with Columbus on his second expedition, in 1493.

In 1502 Ponce de León arrived on the island of HISPANIOLA, where he became governor of the province of Higüey. In 1508 he explored the nearby island of Baringuén and claimed it for Spain, renaming it San Juan de PUERTO RICO. The following year, King Ferdinand named him governor of Puerto Rico.

At this time, Spain was entering the Age of EXPLORATION. Ambitious men were setting out in all directions, seeking new lands to bring into the Spanish empire. Ponce de León turned his attention northward, perhaps influenced by Indian legends about a place called Bimini that had a marvelous fountain whose waters could restore youth and health.

In 1513 the explorer sailed northwest with three ships and landed near what is now ST. AUGUSTINE, Florida. He called the place Tierra de La FLORIDA because he arrived on Easter Sunday—Pascua Florida in Spanish. Ponce de León then sailed south around the peninsula of Florida, passing a chain of islands now known as the Keys and heading north along Florida's western coast before returning to Puerto Rico. On the way back to Puerto Rico, he stopped at a group of tiny islands where he found sea turtles nesting. He

named the islands the Tortugas ("turtles" in Spanish). Today these islands contain a wildlife sanctuary that is home to sea turtles and many species of birds.

The following year, Ponce de León returned to Spain. Although he had found neither gold, nor wealthy cities, nor even a fountain of youth, the king rewarded him richly and appointed him governor of Bimini and Florida. But it was not until 1521 that the explorer set out on the expedition that was supposed to establish a Spanish colony in Florida. With about 200 men, he returned to the peninsula's western coast.

The exact site of the intended colony is not known, but it was probably on Sanibel Island, near present-day Fort Myers. The expedition proved unlucky for Ponce de León. Wounded in an attack by local Indians, the leader withdrew with his men to Cuba, where he died. Yet despite his failure to found a colony, Juan Ponce de León had added both Puerto Rico and Florida to Spain's American empire. (*See also* **Conquistador.**)

Pontiac, Chief

ca. 1720–1769
Ottawa Indian leader

*P*ontiac—also called Ponteach or Pondiac—became a symbol of Native American resistance to British expansion into frontier regions. The uprising he helped organize in the Ohio River valley occurred at the end of the FRENCH AND INDIAN WAR, the final struggle between France and Great Britain for control of North America.

After many years of warfare, Britain finally defeated the French in Canada in 1760. Indian leaders in the Ohio River valley feared that the end of

In 1763 Chief Pontiac led a force of French and Indian warriors in an attack on the British fort at Detroit. The assault was unsuccessful, and Pontiac made peace with the British three years later.

the conflict would encourage British settlers to stream over the Appalachian Mountains into their territory. Many tribes of the region decided to fight the British expansion.

Pontiac, a leader of the OTTAWA INDIANS, was one of many chiefs who actively opposed the British. Inspired by the teachings of Neolin, a DELAWARE INDIAN prophet, he stirred up support among other tribes to fight the British. In 1763 he helped lead a group of Indian warriors against the British fort at Detroit. Failing to capture the fort, he laid siege* to it for six months. The arrival of British reinforcements, however, forced the Indians to retreat.

At the same time that Pontiac and his men surrounded Fort Detroit, other groups of Native Americans rose up and began attacking British forts throughout the Ohio River valley. Europeans eventually gave the name Pontiac's Rebellion to the Indian uprising that swept the area. The Indians' resistance did lead to one victory. In an effort to bring peace to the region, the British issued the PROCLAMATION OF 1763, which placed a temporary ban on settlement by colonists of the lands west of the Appalachians.

Though important, Pontiac's siege of Fort Detroit was only one of many loosely connected Indian attacks against the British. Even during his own lifetime, Pontiac's power and courage were greatly exaggerated. In part this was due to several works by British authors—such as a 1766 play called *Ponteach, or The Savages of America*—that celebrated his deeds. After the loss at Fort Detroit, Pontiac moved westward into present-day Illinois, trying to win support for continued resistance to the British. He eventually made peace with the British in 1766. From then on, he favored a more peaceful attitude toward Britain, earning the hostility of many Native Americans in the area. He had lost all influence by 1769, when he was murdered by another Indian.

See *Books; Franklin, Benjamin.*

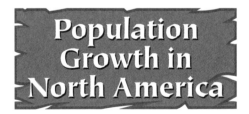
Population Growth in North America

*T*he number of people living in North America expanded at an astounding rate during the colonial period. Most of this growth occurred in the British colonies. The populations of New France* and the Spanish Borderlands* increased much more slowly and never reached the levels achieved in Britain's colonies. While the overall population of North America grew, the number of Native Americans declined drastically.

Decline of Indian Populations. No one knows exactly how many Native Americans lived in North America before the arrival of Europeans. Some scholars estimate that there were 4 to 5 million Indians; others believe that the number may have been closer to 10 or 12 million. The population was not distributed evenly across the continent. Settlements were more heavily concentrated in certain areas—particularly along the Pacific coast, in present-day Mexico, and east of the Mississippi River—than in the rest of North America.

Contact with Europeans, beginning in the late 1400s and early 1500s, had a devastating effect on Native Americans. The Europeans brought new

The population of the British mainland colonies grew dramatically during the colonial period, from about one thousand settlers in 1620 to more than 2.7 million a few years after the colonies declared their independence.

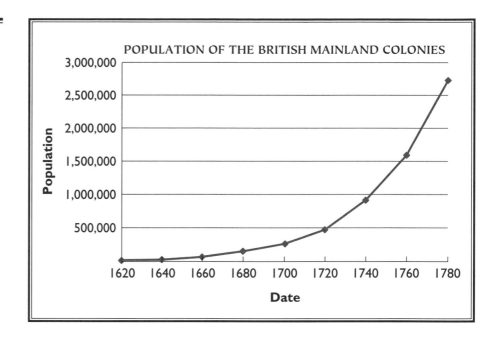

POPULATION OF THE BRITISH MAINLAND COLONIES

diseases, such as smallpox, that killed millions of Indians. Many Indians also died in warfare against the whites, while others were pushed out of their homelands and migrated to new regions. In the early 1600s, about 1 million Native Americans lived east of the Mississippi River. By the end of the colonial period, this number had declined to about 150,000.

As native populations declined, the number of Europeans soared. In 1700 about 250,000 non-Indian peoples lived in North America. Thereafter, this number doubled about every 25 years, reaching almost 3 million by 1780. The rapid population growth resulted from two factors: natural reproduction and immigration.

Natural Reproduction and Immigration. Natural reproduction—the birth of children—played an important role in the population growth of North America. Although life in the colonies was difficult, people there generally managed to eat better and live longer than Europeans did. This meant that more individuals reached adulthood, married, and raised families. In addition, colonists tended to marry at younger ages than people in Europe and to have more children. The combination of large family size and long life span contributed to the great increase in population.

The other major factor in population growth was immigration. Throughout the colonial period, large numbers of people arrived from Europe in search of greater freedom and better lives. Between the start of the colonial period and 1780, almost 1 million Europeans immigrated to North America. During that same period, more than 2 million blacks were brought to the colonies from Africa.

The vast majority of European immigrants settled in the British colonies. Far fewer people moved to the French and Spanish colonies, in part because the colonial policies of France and Spain did less to encourage immigration. By 1760, for example, New France had only about 85,000 colonists. The Spanish Borderlands had about 100,000 white settlers in 1800.

* **indentured servant** person who agreed to work a certain length of time in return for passage on a ship to the colonies

The immigrants to North America included people of many different backgrounds. Catholics, Protestants, and Jews came in search of religious freedom. Colonists from England, Germany, the Netherlands, France, Spain, and Portugal wanted land and opportunities that were lacking in their homelands. Many immigrants, particularly in the British colonies, were indentured servants*, who hoped to start new lives. Millions of black slaves were brought to North America against their will to provide labor for white colonists. Rich and poor, skilled and unskilled, free and slave—all contributed to the rapid population growth of North America in the colonial period.

Regional Variations.   Population growth varied in different regions and periods. In the 1600s, for example, the population grew faster in New England than in the Chesapeake region. The southern climate proved to be a breeding ground for disease, and the death rate was higher there than in New England. Men greatly outnumbered women in the Chesapeake area, while New England had large families and a more even balance of men and women. These factors resulted in higher rates of growth through natural reproduction in New England.

By the 1700s, the population of the southern colonies began to grow faster than that of New England. The native-born colonists had acquired resistance to disease, the number of men and women became more evenly balanced, and family size increased. People immigrated to the southern colonies at a much greater rate than to New England during this period. In addition, large numbers of black slaves were brought from Africa, contributing to a dramatic increase in the southern population in the 1700s.

By 1780 the American colonies had become the United States and included about 2.8 million people. Roughly 26 percent of them lived in New England and the same percentage in the middle states of New York, New Jersey, Pennsylvania, and Delaware. The number of people living in the Chesapeake region and the southern states had risen to about 48 percent of the total population. The population of the Spanish Borderlands and New France remained small and did not begin to grow significantly until well after the colonial period. (*See also* **Family; Immigration; Indentured Servants; Native Americans; Slave Trade.**)

* **strategic** of military importance
* **monopoly** exclusive right to engage in a certain kind of business

See map in New France (vol. 3).

*P*ort Royal was founded in 1605, two years before the JAMESTOWN COLONY of Virginia. Because of its strategic* location on the eastern coast of Canada, Port Royal became a focal point in the struggle between France and England for control of North America.

In 1603 the king of France granted Pierre du Gua, Sieur de Monts, a monopoly* on the rich FUR TRADE along the Atlantic coast of North America. Monts and his geographer, Samuel de CHAMPLAIN, set out to establish a base in the area. After many difficulties, they chose a site on the Annapolis Basin in present-day NOVA SCOTIA for their town of Port Royal. During the winter of 1606, settlers there performed *La Théâtre de Neptune en la Nouvelle-France,* probably the first play staged in North America. They also organized a social club, the Order of Good Cheer, to boost their morale.

For 100 years, control of Port Royal seesawed between the English and the French. In 1613 an English force from Virginia destroyed the settlement. French settlers rebuilt the town, only to have it captured by an expedition from New England in 1654. France regained control of Port Royal in 1670 and established it as the seat of government for the colony of Acadia. From this base, the French attacked ships traveling to and from New England.

English forces under Sir William Phips captured Port Royal in 1690 during KING WILLIAM'S WAR, but the Treaty of Ryswick restored it to the French seven years later. British colonists took the town back during QUEEN ANNE'S WAR. In 1713 the TREATY OF UTRECHT gave Port Royal—and all of Acadia—to Britain. The British renamed the town Annapolis Royal. It remained the center of government in Nova Scotia until 1749, when the British built the city of Halifax. (*See also* **Acadians; Drama; New France.**)

Portolá, Gaspar de

ca. 1720–1786
First Spanish governor of California

* **Franciscan** member of the Order of Friars Minor, a religious brotherhood

* **Jesuit** Roman Catholic religious order

* **presidio** Spanish fort built to protect mission settlements

Gaspar de Portolá led the expedition that established the first Spanish settlements in CALIFORNIA. Appointed military commander and governor of the region the Spanish called Alta, or Upper, California, he built some military bases that protected the MISSIONS founded by Franciscan* priests.

Born in Spain to a noble family, Portolá became an officer in the Spanish army and served in Italy and Portugal. In 1767 the Spanish crown sent Portolá to the province of Baja California (now part of Mexico). His first duty there was to carry out the government's order to expel the Jesuits* from the province. The following year, Portolá became the commander of an expedition to settle Alta California. Spain was eager to establish its claim to this region before it fell into the hands of Great Britain or Russia. The Spanish also wanted to protect their treasure ships sailing between Spain and Mexico.

Portolá's expedition, consisting of two land parties and two ships, set off from Baja California in 1769. Portolá's group, which marched overland, included Junípero SERRA, a Franciscan missionary. These Spaniards arrived at what is now San Diego in late June and founded a presidio* and a mission. Portolá then headed north with about 40 followers to look for Monterey Bay, a site visited and described by Spanish explorer Sebastian Vízcaino more than 150 years before. Portolá passed through Monterey without recognizing it and continued on to San Francisco Bay. But the following year his party returned to Monterey, where they established a mission and presidio to mark Spain's occupation of Alta California. Returning to Mexico, Portolá served as a military officer and governor of the city of Puebla until he went back to Spain in 1785. (*See also* **Presidios.**)

Portugal

Located on the western edge of the Iberian Peninsula and cut off from the rest of Europe by mountains, Portugal faces outward to the Atlantic Ocean. Throughout much of its history, this small country remained largely on the sidelines of European developments. In the 1400s, however, Portugal had its moment of glory when its mariners began exploring the coasts of Africa for trade opportunities and searching for a sea route to Asia. In the 1500s, the Portuguese established a colonial empire in Asia. Portugal's discoveries and achievements drew other European countries into a great competition of exploration and colonization.

Early History.   For much of the Middle Ages, Portugal was one of six Christian kingdoms that occupied the Iberian Peninsula. They all struggled to drive out the Moors* of northern Africa who had invaded the region in the 700s. Portugal also faced the challenge of remaining separate and independent when the other kingdoms began to merge to form Spain. By the 1100s, Portugal had succeeded in establishing a separate state, and by 1249 the Portuguese had expelled the Moors.

After the departure of the Moors, the country's trade, agriculture, and arts began to prosper. The Portuguese soon developed a strong monarchy and established the new capital city of Lisbon. Most of their territorial disputes—and occasional wars—with neighboring Spanish kingdoms had been settled. Portugal was about to emerge as one of the powers of Europe.

Conquest and Exploration.   Between 1385 and 1580, Portugal was ruled by the Avis dynasty*. Determined to enlarge their kingdom, these rulers launched a series of attacks against the Moors in northern Africa. Although they failed in an attempt to conquer the Moorish kingdom of Morocco in the early 1400s, their military campaign led Portuguese navigators on a series of voyages to the west and south that opened up new worlds.

The first result of Portugal's maritime* expeditions was the discovery and conquest of Madeira and the Azores, groups of islands in the eastern Atlantic. Then Portuguese ships sailed south along the coast of Africa, bringing home profitable cargoes of GOLD and slaves from western Africa. By the 1470s, Portugal's rulers came to regard maritime exploration as an important activity in its own right, not simply as a part of conquest.

During the first half of the 1400s, seagoing exploration received a huge boost from Prince Henry—"the Navigator"—who turned his estate in southern Portugal into a center for the study of geography and NAVIGATION. He encouraged shipbuilders to design new ships that could make long ocean voyages, collected maps and geographic texts, and invited scholars from many nations to visit and share their ideas.

Building a Colonial Empire.   Prince Henry established exploration as a serious mission in Portugal. But Portuguese explorers achieved their greatest triumphs under King João II (also known as John the Perfect). In addition to founding Portuguese colonies in western Africa, he sent mariners farther south along the African coast to the Congo River and beyond in search of a sea route to Asia.

In 1488 the Portuguese explorer Bartolomeu Dias sailed around the southern tip of Africa into the Indian Ocean. Ten years later the Portuguese navigator Vasco da Gama sailed all the way around Africa to India. These voyages and others paved the way for a colonial empire in Asia. By the mid-1500s, the Portuguese had established commercial bases in India, China, and the East Indies, and they controlled a prosperous trade between Asia and Europe.

* *Moors* North African Muslims

* *dynasty* succession of rulers from the same family or group

* *maritime* related to the sea or shipping

In addition to its widespread interests in Africa and Asia, Portugal was also active in the Americas. In 1500 a Portuguese fleet bound for India accidentally landed on the coast of Brazil, establishing Portugal's claim to the largest colony in South America. Around the same time, far to the north, Portuguese explorers reached what is now NEWFOUNDLAND and Labrador in eastern Canada. Portugal failed to found a colony in North America. But its fishermen—and those of other nations—were soon crossing the North Atlantic each year to fish in the waters off the coast of Canada.

Portugal's expeditions and colonization brought great wealth to the nation. Its leadership in exploration did not last long, however. When Spain, England, and the Netherlands emerged as major colonial powers, Portugal lost its supremacy at sea. By the 1600s, these colonial rivals had begun to chip away at Portugal's empire, particularly in Asia, where the Dutch gained control of most of the trade. Though weakened, Portugal held colonies in South America, Africa, and Asia for centuries. (*See also* **European Empires; Exploration, Age of; Slave Trade.**)

Postal Service

*C*reating postal systems was an important step in the development of the North American colonies. Reliable methods of sending and delivering mail helped link widely scattered people, allowing them to exchange information and promoting the growth of business.

Communication in the Colonial Era. In colonial times, letter writing was the chief means of communication among people. In the 1600s, however, finding a way to send a letter could be extremely difficult. North American colonists writing to friends, relatives, or business associates in Europe had to entrust their correspondence to sea captains, who carried the papers on their overseas trips. This method of mail delivery proved less than satisfactory because letters could easily be misplaced or damaged by water during the ship's long voyage. Worse yet, vessels could sink or be hijacked by pirates. Letters that did arrive safely took at least a month—usually longer—to reach their destination.

* *itinerant* traveling from place to place

Mail within the North American colonies had only a slightly easier journey. People depended on travelers or itinerant* merchants to deliver their letters. This meant that they had to find someone who was going to the right destination and hope that the letter carrier would be trustworthy. It might take weeks for a letter to arrive, as travelers frequently made many stops and detours along the route.

Early Attempts to Establish a Postal System. Looking for a more reliable and faster way to send mail, several British colonies began experimenting with official postal systems. In 1639 the Massachusetts General Assembly granted a Boston tavern owner the right to charge a fee for receiving and delivering mail. In 1657 the VIRGINIA HOUSE OF BURGESSES established "tobacco posts." Each plantation owner was responsible for passing official messages and letters on to the next plantation. In 1673 an intercolonial mail service between New York City and Boston was started, but it lasted only a few weeks.

Postal Service

In the British colonies, mail carriers usually traveled on horseback. It might take anywhere from a day to several weeks for a letter to reach its destination.

***patent** official document conferring a right or privilege

***Spanish Borderlands** northern part of New Spain, area now occupied by Florida, Texas, New Mexico, Arizona, and California

Royal Postal Systems. Despite the efforts of individual colonies, the delivery of mail remained disorganized and unreliable. Responding to the need for a centralized system, French officials devised a simple but effective postal service for NEW FRANCE. Postal carriers from France arrived in the spring, when travel was fairly easy, and delivered mail to specific merchants' shops. At each shop, a court clerk distributed the mail.

In the British colonies, the delivery of mail began to improve in 1691, when Parliament granted Thomas Neale a patent* to organize an intercolonial postal system. Neale was allowed to keep the profits from the system's operation in exchange for paying the government a small fee. Under the direction of Neale's deputy, Andrew Hamilton, post offices opened in New York City and Boston, and regular delivery service began between Philadelphia and New York City. By 1698 weekly mail delivery connected smaller towns such as Portsmouth, New Hampshire, and Newcastle, Delaware. Hamilton had little success in the southern colonies, however—primarily because the region's population was small and scattered. Suspicious of the system, many people refused to use it.

When Neale's patent ended in 1707, the British government stepped in and took charge of postal services in the American colonies. As part of the reorganization, deputies were appointed in each colony to oversee the delivery of mail. The royal postal system improved service between the northern and southern colonies.

Mail Delivery. In the Spanish Borderlands*, pack animals and wagon-train caravans carried the mail. In the British colonies, riders on horseback

traveled along a network of postal, or post, roads to deliver mail. The arrival of a post rider in a community caused great excitement.

Settlers living in areas that were more accessible by water than by land—such as Louisiana—received their mail and other goods by boat. In 1755 transatlantic mail delivery improved considerably when the British government began a direct packet service* between Falmouth, England, and New York City. By 1763 packet service had been extended to Boston and Charleston. Packet boats also traveled between colonial ports.

* **packet service** boats that carry mail and packages

Benjamin Franklin and Postal Reform.

In 1753 the British government appointed Benjamin FRANKLIN as one of two postmasters general of the colonies, a position he held until 1774. Franklin, who had been deputy postmaster at Philadelphia, started a series of reforms that made the royal postal service more dependable and less expensive. He also improved the speed and frequency of mail delivery, established new postal routes, and began overnight delivery between Philadelphia and New York City.

U.S Postal System.

The American colonies' rebellion against the British government extended to the postal service as well. Boycotted* by the colonists, the royal postal system stopped operating on Christmas Day, 1775. The next year, the SECOND CONTINENTAL CONGRESS appointed Franklin postmaster general of the new United States. (*See also* **Newspapers, Magazines, and Pamphlets.**)

* **boycott** to refuse to buy goods as a means of protest

Potawatomi Indians

* **clan** related families

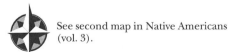

See second map in Native Americans (vol. 3).

An Algonquian-speaking people, the Potawatomi Indians were closely related to the OJIBWA and OTTAWA INDIANS. They originally lived in the area between Lake Michigan and Lake Huron, but attacks by the IROQUOIS in the 1630s and 1640s drove the tribe west to what is now Wisconsin. In the 1700s, the Potawatomi returned to their homeland and also spread to other parts of the Great Lakes region.

The Potawatomi lived like other tribes in the Great Lakes area. They grew corn, beans, squash, and other crops; hunted and fished; and gathered wild rice and other foods. Organized by clan*, they inhabited small villages. Their religious practices included the smoking of tobacco in sacred pipes and participation in the Grand Medicine Lodge society, an organization of healers.

French missionaries and fur traders first made contact with the Potawatomi in the early 1600s. The tribe soon established political and economic ties with NEW FRANCE. Some Potawatomi women married COUREURS DE BOIS (French woodsmen), and the children of these mixed-race unions—known as métis—often became leaders in the tribe. During the colonial conflicts between Britain and France, the Indians sometimes traveled east to take part in raids against English colonists in New England and New York.

In the late 1700s and early 1800s, the Potawatomi fought a series of wars in an attempt to stop American settlers from taking their lands. They joined the Ottawa leader, Chief PONTIAC, in his unsuccessful rebellion against the British colonists in 1763. During the American Revolution, the Potawatomi's loyalties were divided, with some supporting the British while others allied

themselves with the colonists. The tribe took part in rebellions against American settlers by the MIAMI INDIANS in 1790 to 1794, the SHAWNEE in 1809 to 1811, and the Sauk and FOX in 1832.

The Potawatomi finally were forced to surrender land to the United States and leave their homeland. Some remained in the Great Lakes region, but many migrated west and settled in Kansas and Oklahoma. (*See also* **Native Americans.**)

Poverty

People in colonial times had a somewhat different attitude toward poverty than do people of today. They generally believed that poverty was not a social problem to be solved but a natural and unavoidable part of life. Still, various communities developed ways of dealing with poverty and aiding the poor. Although poverty was less widespread in North America than in Europe in the 1700s, it increased in the next century, creating new problems in the countryside and in cities.

Treatment of the Poor.   The poor in the American colonies included several kinds of people. The poorest individuals—those who could not survive without help in the form of money, food, clothing, or shelter—were called paupers. Most often they were orphans, widows, the elderly, and the sick. Society generally regarded these people, sometimes called the "traditional poor" or the "worthy poor," with some sympathy because they were not expected to provide for themselves. Able-bodied individuals who could not work or would not work received less sympathy, though they might also be paupers.

* *Spanish Borderlands* northern part of New Spain, area now occupied by Florida, Texas, Arizona, New Mexico, and California

Little is known about poverty in the Spanish Borderlands*. In that region, religious organizations connected with the ROMAN CATHOLIC CHURCH gave aid to poor people, including Native Americans.

New France had little poverty. Because of the profitable FUR TRADE, the availability of land, and the shortage of labor, anyone able to work could earn a living. As in the Spanish colonies, the Catholic Church took care of those who could not work. During hard times, the government of New France set up special offices to help paupers in the major towns. Authorities in these offices collected donations for aid and found jobs for unemployed workers.

The English North American colonies modeled their treatment of the poor on the laws of England, where poverty was widespread during the 1600s and 1700s. English poor laws were based on the idea that people were supposed to care for their relatives, but the state took some responsibility for helping those who lacked family support. Local governments such as towns

* *parish* church district

* *apprentice* person placed in the care of a merchant or crafts worker to learn a profession

or parishes* enforced poor laws by collecting taxes to pay for assistance to the poor, forcing people to work, punishing those who did not work, finding positions as apprentices* for poor children, and even placing paupers in households that received fees for taking care of them.

In North America, as in England, many people thought that being poor was somehow related to a weakness in character. This attitude was especially strong in New England, where the PURITANS deeply believed that hard work was a virtue and laziness a sin. Puritan officials often complained about people who refused to work and accused them of creating their own troubles.

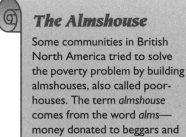

The Almshouse

Some communities in British North America tried to solve the poverty problem by building almshouses, also called poorhouses. The term *almshouse* comes from the word *alms*—money donated to beggars and other poor people. By the mid-1700s, a growing number of cities and rural communities had put their paupers into almshouses. But almshouses turned out to be more expensive to operate than local governments had expected, and many communities closed them down.

* *indigent* very poor person in need of public aid

* *vagrant* homeless wanderer

Colonial communities tried to keep the poor under control. Many followed the English practice of making those receiving public aid wear special badges, feeling that those who received help should be shamed. They also tried to prevent the desperately poor from becoming legal residents and therefore eligible for aid. Authorities warned indigents* away and sometimes whipped or jailed them if they did not leave. Occasionally, local governments shipped indigents out of their territory.

Poverty in the 1700s. The percentage of poor people in the American colonies rose during the 1700s because economic opportunity did not increase as rapidly as population. Large numbers of vagrants* appeared on American streets and roads, especially in the northeast. Many of them traveled around for years in search of work, shelter, meals, or charitable handouts. Among them were many women, including poor widows and deserted wives. Families moved together from one temporary or seasonal farm job to the next.

Urban areas saw a rise in poverty in the mid-1700s as their populations grew faster than the cities' ability to support them. Boston, for example, was home to many men who had been injured fighting in colonial wars and could not work, as well as many war widows and orphans without incomes. When the city fell on hard times, many citizens could not pay their taxes, and poverty soared.

Everywhere in the colonies, more women than men suffered poverty. Women were not considered suitable workers for many jobs, and when they did work, they received lower wages than men.

Most African American slaves lived in continuing poverty. White colonists did not usually think of slaves as poor people who needed aid because slaveholders were supposed to provide for them. Although blacks rarely starved, their masters usually gave them the worst and cheapest food, clothing, and shelter.

As the 1700s progressed, the rich grew richer while the poor grew poorer and more numerous. The growing discontent of the poor may have been one of many things that stirred up new political ideas in the colonies on the eve of the AMERICAN REVOLUTION.

Powhatan Indians

* *confederacy* alliance or league of peoples or states

See second map in Native Americans (vol. 3).

During the early colonial period, the Powhatan Indians lived in eastern Virginia. They formed a loose confederacy* of Algonquian-speaking tribes that included the Potomac, Rappahannock, and Pamunkey Indians. The Powhatan played an important role in the history of the JAMESTOWN COLONY, the first permanent English settlement in North America.

Each tribe in the Powhatan Confederacy had its own chief. A paramount, or supreme, chief ruled over all the tribes. In 1607 the paramount chief was Wahunsonacock. But the early English colonists called Wahunsonacock—and all the tribes under him—Powhatan because he came from a village of that name. Powhatan ruled some 30 chiefdoms. He had inherited control of a few tribes and gained power over the others through conquest and threats. He had many children by a number of wives. His most famous child was POCAHONTAS.

The Powhatan Indians lived in walled villages surrounded by outlying fields. Primarily farmers, they cultivated beans, pumpkins, roots, and MAIZE,

Powhatan Indians

In 1607 the Powhatan Indians captured Captain John Smith of the Jamestown colony and planned to put him to death. According to Smith, the chief's daughter Pocahontas pleaded on his behalf, and the Indians spared his life. This illustration accompanied Smith's account of the incident in *Generall Historie of Virginia* (1624).

or corn—which they stored on raised platforms. They also hunted for food and animal hides, fished, and gathered wild plant foods. The women farmed, prepared the food, and made household items, while the men hunted, fished, and fought in battle.

The Powhatan chiefs shared in the work of the village. They also collected tribute* such as corn, deerskins, and ornaments from the other villagers. In exchange for these gifts, the chiefs organized and protected the community's storehouses. They presided at ceremonial occasions—most notably the ripening of the first ears of corn—and they decided whether to take part in wars.

Kinship and extended family ties were important among the Powhatan. They had a matrilineal society, which meant that chiefs inherited their position primarily through their mother's family. Thus, when a chief died, his brother—or sister if he had no brothers—became chief. A chief's children ruled only when appointed.

* ***tribute*** payment made to a dominant power

When Chief Powhatan died in 1618, his brother Opechancanough succeeded him. Powhatan had eventually established peace with the Jamestown settlers, but Opechancanough wanted to drive them away. He led his people into two wars against the English—one in 1622 and a second in 1644. The colonists, who had grown stronger and more aggressive as the years went by, finally defeated the Indians. In 1646 the Powhatan Confederacy came to an end after English soldiers captured and killed Opechancanough. The position of paramount chief disappeared soon after.

Thousands of new colonists drove the weakened Powhatan off their lands. The Indians who survived were restricted to reservations. By the end of the 1600s, the Powhatan population—which had numbered about 10,000 at the time of the Europeans' arrival—had dwindled to only a few hundred.

Pregnancy and Birth

See *Family; Women, Roles of.*

Presbyterians

See *Protestant Churches.*

Presidios

*D*uring the colonial period, Spain built military outposts* known as presidios throughout the northern frontier region of its American empire. The presidios helped establish the nation's claims to these Spanish Borderlands* and protected its MISSIONS and settlements from attack by hostile Indians and rival European nations. The word *presidio* comes from the Latin *praesidium,* meaning "fortified place."

* **outpost** frontier settlement or military base

* **Spanish Borderlands** northern part of New Spain, area now occupied by Florida, Texas, New Mexico, Arizona, and California

Construction of the Presidio. Generally square or rectangular in shape, presidios were built from local material such as logs, stone, or adobe— sun-dried brick. Although stone was preferred, when available, it required skilled stonecutters and masons and considerable labor, so few stone presidios were constructed. High walls surrounded an inner courtyard of the presidio. Round towers called *torreones* stood on two opposite corners of the walls. Soldiers could fire at attackers through small holes in these walls. Most presidios had one main gate that locked from inside, although a few had a rear gate.

The inside of a presidio included such buildings as a guardhouse and jail, a chapel, a priest's house, officers' quarters, barracks for the troops, a kitchen and storehouses, and a carpenter's shop. The roofs of the buildings were high enough so that soldiers could stand on them and fire down over the outer walls.

Although presidios generally followed a basic pattern, some variations did exist. For example, the fort at Los Ades, in east Texas, was surrounded by a palisade* rather than a wall, and its *torreones* were diamond shaped rather than round. The presidios at SANTA FE and San Antonio had no walls, no towers, and no barracks. Instead, the main structures of these urban forts— the governor-captain's residence, the guardhouse, and the chapel—were

* **palisade** fence of stakes forming a defense

Presidios

This sketch by John Ross Browne shows Tubac, an Arizona presidio, in the mid-1800s. A wall surrounds the settlement, enclosing several buildings. The chapel is visible in the background.

built on the central plaza of the town, and the soldiers lived in huts nearby. The two presidios had different layouts because they were located in towns, not on the frontier.

Life in the Presidio. Soldiers stationed at the presidios had numerous responsibilities, including protecting the missions and escorting missionaries, merchants, and colonists. They were also charged with exploring the surrounding countryside and carrying the mail. Most soldiers brought their families with them or married Christian Indian women from the area. Building homes for their families around the presidios, they formed permanent settlements. These communities gradually attracted new residents, such as merchants seeking buyers for their goods and colonists looking for land to farm. The presidios also served as safe havens on the dangerous frontier, and travelers often camped near them.

The troops stationed in the presidios did not have an easy life. When the Marqués de Rubí, a Spanish official, inspected the northern frontier of NEW

200

Spain in the 1760s, he found the forts in terrible shape. Morale was low, and discipline and training were lacking. Soldiers often disobeyed their superiors. They had received no instruction in the use of their firearms, which in any case were frequently unusable. Many soldiers had fallen deeply in debt because they rarely received their pay on time. Moreover, officers made money off the troops by selling them poorly made goods at very high prices.

Rubí led an effort to reform the presidios in the Borderlands. He wanted to provide soldiers with working equipment, regular pay, and proper training. He also suggested reorganizing the presidios in a chain stretching from California to the Gulf of Mexico, which would allow faster communication among the troops at each fort. Most of his recommendations were accepted.

Effectiveness of the Presidios.   Despite the attempts at reform, Spanish presidio troops were never able to conquer the Native Americans of the Borderlands. Unlike European armies—which stopped to attack or capture forts—Indian warriors simply rode around them and raided civilian settlements. In addition, a Spanish soldier had so much equipment that he needed six horses to carry it on military campaigns. But the presidios were not large enough to hold all the soldiers' horses. The animals therefore had to be kept some distance away, making it much easier for the Indians to steal them. Without horses, the soldiers were unable to pursue the attacking Indians.

Despite their problems, the presidios did achieve some of Spain's goals, and no presidio was ever captured in a frontal assault by Indians. Recognizing the advantages of the presidio design, American traders and the U.S. Army later used them as models for the FORTS they built in the American Southwest. (*See also* **Architecture; Colonial Administration; Military Forces; Spanish Borderlands.**)

Press in Colonial America

* *broadside* large sheet of paper, printed on one side, that was handed around or posted on buildings and walls

* *Spanish Borderlands* northern part of New Spain, area now occupied by Florida, Texas, Arizona, New Mexico, and California

Colonists in British North America had a wide variety of printed materials available to them. The press—which refers both to the books, pamphlets, newspapers, and broadsides* produced on printing presses and the people who produce them—served as a means for the government and business to distribute information. It was also a way that religious and political groups could spread their message and a source of education and entertainment for the colonists.

In the mid-1700s, the press began to play a major role in shaping public and political life. During this time, the idea of freedom of the press took on new meaning and importance. Only the British had an active press in North America in colonial times, however. The Dutch and French colonies had no printing presses before they came under British control, and the Spanish Borderlands* imported reading material from Mexico.

The Press and Its Role.   The first printing press in the English colonies was run by Stephen Day of Massachusetts. *The Bay Psalm Book,* the first English book printed in North America, came from Day's press in 1640. The number of printers in the colonies grew steadily throughout the 1700s, from 6 in 1700 to more than 100 in 1776. In the 1600s and early 1700s, however,

Press in Colonial America

Newspaperman John Peter Zenger was arrested in the fall of 1734 for publishing criticisms of New York's governor. This drawing by Harry Fenn shows colonial officials burning copies of Zenger's *Weekly Journal* in front of the city hall on Wall Street.

American colonists still relied heavily on the English press. Booksellers sold works published in England as well as those produced in the colonies, and most newspapers carried stories about events in England or Europe. Colonial printers reproduced articles from London papers, which were already several months old by the time they reached American shores. Nobody expected the press to cover current or local events. Newspapers of the time contained poems and stories, and one printer filled his paper with articles copied from an encyclopedia.

By the late 1600s, however, a few writers, printers, and publishers began to report on current events. In 1685 Samuel Green, a Boston printer, copied stories of King Charles II's death from a London paper. After that, the press in Boston, Philadelphia, New York, and other cities produced news broadsides from time to time on major events. The first actual newspaper in the English colonies was *Publick Occurrences Both Forreign and Domestick,* printed in Boston in 1690. Published without the government's permission, this paper lasted for only one issue before authorities put a stop to it. No other newspapers appeared until the first issue of the successful *Boston News-Letter* came out in 1704.

In 1689 Samuel Green printed and distributed a statement in favor of changes in the government of Massachusetts. With this publication, the colonial press moved from recording the news to taking an active role in events. The press continued this trend toward greater involvement in public affairs in the 1720s and 1730s, when a few newspaper printers such as Benjamin FRANKLIN and his brother James published news, satiric* articles about current events, and letters on topics of local interest from people in the community.

Pamphlets did as much as newspapers—perhaps more—to create a press that was concerned with political issues. People criticized government officials in anonymous* pamphlets, and beginning in the 1740s, campaigners used pamphlets to inform and influence voters in local elections. In the 1760s, the colonial press became even more political. Colonists came to resent many British policies, and people were forced to take sides. Printers were no exception. Some print shops became active supporters of the patriot* cause.

The press gave a voice to the changes, new ideas, and opinions that swept through the colonies in the troubled years before the AMERICAN REVOLUTION. It allowed people to debate issues and rally support for their plans and programs. Between 1763 and 1776, the number of newspapers in the colonies doubled. Political pamphlets were even more important. Between 1764 and 1776, nearly 200 pamphlets appeared on the question of American independence, including the enormously popular *Common Sense* by Thomas PAINE. Newspaper publishers became involved in the issue as well. Some took the Loyalist* side, but more joined the patriots. Printers and publishers became major shapers of public opinion, not just artisans* who ran printing presses.

Freedom of the Press. For most of the colonial period, the British colonies did not really enjoy a "free press." At the time, the phrase "freedom of the press" meant that printers did not need the government's permission to publish anything. However, if they printed any material that criticized the government, they could be arrested for it. Writing that found fault with official policies was considered to be "seditious libel," and could be punished by imprisonment.

The best-known trial for seditious libel in colonial America was that of John Peter ZENGER, who criticized New York's governor in his newspaper. In 1735 Zenger went on trial and was found innocent. His victory has often been regarded as a triumph for freedom of the press. Although seditious libel remained a crime, publishers knew that colonial juries would not convict them as long as the public agreed with the opinions they printed. As opposition to British rule gained strength in the colonies, printers felt increasingly free to criticize government officials. In fact, the British accused colonial publishers of being "engines of sedition*" because they gave voice to patriot opinions.

Since the American Revolution, freedom of the press has taken on a new meaning—the freedom to print anything without fear of censorship or other interference by the government. The First Amendment to the United States Constitution, adopted in 1791, guarantees freedom of the press. (*See also* **Books; Literacy; Newspapers, Magazines, and Pamphlets.**)

* *satiric* referring to humor that criticizes or makes fun of something bad or foolish

* *anonymous* having no author's name

* *patriot* American colonist who favored independence from Great Britain

* *Loyalist* American colonist who remained loyal to Great Britain during the American Revolution

* *artisan* skilled crafts worker

* *sedition* conduct or language that leads people to disobey the laws of the state

Prison

See *Crime and Punishment.*

Privateers

* *maritime* related to the sea or shipping

*P*rivateering began in the 1500s, when the nations of Europe ventured out to explore and colonize other parts of the world. Determined to build empires, European powers often came into conflict with each other at sea as well as on land. This ongoing maritime* warfare created an opportunity for privateers—shipowners or captains who had permission from their government to attack, seize, or rob vessels belonging to enemy nations. In return, privateers kept the profits from ships or cargoes they seized.

In the early years, the line between privateering and piracy was thin. Privateers were supposed to carry a written commission—sometimes called a letter of marque—giving them the authority to attack ships. Privateers did not belong to their country's navy, nor did they sail in military ships. They used fast merchant vessels equipped with guns. After capturing an enemy vessel, a privateer brought it back to port. There a special court officially condemned it. The ship and its cargo were sold, and the profits were divided among the investors and the crew.

Many noted captains became privateers in the 1500s, during the age of American exploration. Their favorite targets were Spanish treasure fleets sailing from the Philippines and Mexico loaded with silver and gold. Sir Francis DRAKE preyed on Spanish ships in the mid-1500s, when England and Spain were at war.

In the following years, the possibility of acquiring riches attracted enormous numbers of privateers. During the FRENCH AND INDIAN WAR (1754–1763), perhaps as many as 11,000 American colonists took to the seas in the hope of capturing enemy ships—and becoming wealthy. Many privateers from the American colonies roamed the WEST INDIES, where four nations—Britain, Spain, France, and the Netherlands—had possessions in a small area. At any time, some of the nations were usually at war.

Patriotism as well as profits drew Americans such as maritime hero John Paul Jones to privateering during the AMERICAN REVOLUTION. American privateers carried on much of the fighting at sea, especially in the final years of the Revolution. They captured about 600 British vessels. By the mid-1800s, however, sea warfare was in the hands of national navies, and privateering had come to an end. (*See also* **Exploration, Age of; Pirates.**)

Proclamation of 1763

See map in British Colonies (vol. 1).

*B*etween 1754 and 1763, Britain and France fought the FRENCH AND INDIAN WAR for control of North America. In the treaty that ended the war, Britain gained a great deal of new territory, including the Ohio Valley. The British government issued the Proclamation of 1763 to regulate the settlement of this region and to pacify the Native Americans whose land had fallen into British hands.

In the mid-1700s, the land west of the APPALACHIAN MOUNTAINS was home to many groups of Native Americans, but France and Britain also laid

claim to the region. When the two nations went to war over it, many of the Indians joined forces with the French. France's defeat left its Indian allies in a crisis. British settlers were moving into their homelands, and the French could no longer aid them.

In May 1763, the Ottawa war chief PONTIAC led an assault on the British fort at Detroit. At nearly the same time, Indian forces attacked and destroyed other British posts in the region. Although the British soon regained control, the raids convinced them that they needed to establish peace with the Indians in the western territories. The Proclamation of 1763, issued in October, was the first step.

The proclamation established governments for Quebec and for East and West Florida, which had come under British control. It also reserved all the lands west of Quebec and the Appalachian Mountains and north of the Floridas for the use of the Indian population. No new settlement was allowed in this area without special permission from the king. Colonists could not buy land there, and all traders had to be licensed. The proclamation required any settlers already living in the region to leave.

The colonies resented the proclamation's limitation on westward expansion. Many people simply ignored the ruling and continued to settle west of the Appalachians. Although Britain eventually abandoned its efforts to enforce the Proclamation of 1763, the anger it stirred helped fuel the movement toward independence in the British colonies. (*See also* **Johnson, Sir William; Land Ownership; Treaty of Paris.**)

Proprietary Colonies

See *British Colonies.*

Protestant Churches

*M*ost of the people who settled in the British colonies of North America were Protestants. Coming from a variety of religious backgrounds, they established a number of distinctly different Protestant churches. These churches played a significant role in the cultural and political life of colonial America, and the influence of Protestantism remains strong today.

European Protestantism

* **doctrine** set of principles or beliefs accepted by a religious or political group

Protestantism arose in Europe in the early 1500s as a reaction to the doctrines* and practices of the ROMAN CATHOLIC CHURCH. The new religious movement spread rapidly throughout northern Europe—especially in Germany, England, the Netherlands, and Scandinavia—eventually dividing into many different sects, or groups.

The founder of the Protestant movement was Martin Luther, a German religious thinker who differed sharply with the Catholic Church on several important issues. Luther criticized the sale of indulgences—granting forgiveness for sins—by the clergy*. He also rejected the Catholic ideas that the pope was never wrong in matters of faith or morals and that the clergy were necessary to

* **clergy** ministers, priests, and other church officials

Protestant Churches

This article includes the following sections:

---

* **denomination** organized group of religious congregations

* **dissenter** person who disagrees with the beliefs and practices of the established church

---

lead believers to salvation. In Luther's view, the only true authority in religious matters was the Bible. In 1517 Luther nailed a document to the door of the cathedral in Wittenberg, Germany. Known as the Ninety-five Theses, it outlined his complaints against the Roman Catholic Church—and touched off a religious revolution that gave birth to the Protestant movement.

Although united in their opposition to Catholicism, early Protestants were divided over many other matters. Some of them believed that people could achieve salvation by doing good deeds and living according to Christian principles. Others argued that individuals had to experience a personal conversion to faith and dedicate their lives to God in order to win salvation. CALVINISTS—followers of John Calvin, the French minister who preached in Geneva—insisted that salvation was predetermined by God and that people could not change their destiny. Some Protestants thought that churches needed to have an ordained clergy—one approved by church officials. Others rejected the idea of any organization holding authority over individual congregations. Such differences of opinion split Protestants, creating various separate denominations* and sects.

European rulers in the countries affected by Protestantism became concerned about the different practices and beliefs that were developing within Protestantism. In an effort to control religious thought and organization, most of them gave approval and support to only one Protestant denomination—thus creating an official, established church. All other Protestant groups were banned by law, and individuals who followed the beliefs of those groups were punished. This policy prevented the spread of competing religious organizations. But instead of stamping out the banned religions, it drove them underground or forced their members to flee elsewhere.

Protestantism in North America

Many European Protestants immigrated to North America to escape persecution and gain the freedom to practice their faith. Once there, however, these same people often tried to limit the religious liberty of others. In some cases, they made their form of worship the only authorized one in the community, opposing any variation in the official church's positions. The PURITANS, for example, established their faith as the religion of Massachusetts and punished dissenters*.

Unlike Europe, however, North America was a vast and largely unsettled land. It was relatively easy for colonists to move away from authorities who tried to enforce their religious beliefs. Moreover, the British colonies attracted people of many faiths from many different nations. The size and ethnic makeup of the colonies ensured that religious pluralism—a variety of beliefs in one place—would take root in a way that was not possible in Europe.

Colonial Protestantism Before 1680. Although Protestant pluralism was established early in British North America, it did not occur at the same time or speed throughout the colonies. In New England, the dominance of the Puritans slowed, but did not prevent, the growth of pluralism. In the middle and southern colonies, the existence of various ethnic and religious groups, along

with weak church organization, kept any one religion from becoming dominant. As people with different beliefs continued to migrate to North America, they helped ensure that the colonies would be characterized by great religious diversity, or variety.

The Puritans of New England resisted pluralism. But the organization of their religion, known as Congregationalism, made orthodoxy* difficult. In the Congregationalist Church, ministers had control over their own congregations. Although church councils could debate matters of religious belief and practice, they did not have the power to enforce the policies they adopted. They did, however, have the authority of the colonial government behind them because churches were established by law and supported by taxes. Thus, religious dissenters could be punished or exiled. Rhode Island, founded by Puritan exiles, welcomed all Protestant faiths. Connecticut, on the other hand, remained almost untouched by Protestant diversity.

The middle and southern colonies included a greater variety of Protestant religions than New England did. In New Netherland (later New York), the Dutch Reformed Church existed alongside French HUGUENOTS, German Lutherans, Roman Catholics, and JEWS. Pennsylvania and New Jersey had English QUAKERS, Scottish Presbyterians, and Swedish Lutherans in addition to other English Protestants. Maryland, although originally founded as a Catholic colony, attracted many Protestant settlers. In Virginia the Anglican* Church was the official church, but it exercised little control over the religious life of the colony. The Carolinas had Protestant diversity, but religion played a much smaller role there than in other colonies.

Colonial Protestantism After 1680. Between 1680 and the mid-1770s, colonial Protestantism went through a dramatic change as a wave of European immigrants increased the membership of some groups and brought new Protestant sects to America. Before 1680 Protestantism was dominated by two denominations—Congregationalists in New England and Anglicans in the South. By the time of the American Revolution, other English Protestant sects—including Presbyterians, Baptists, and Quakers—had grown considerably. Non-English groups had expanded as well. As a result, colonial Protestantism became amazingly diverse.

The growth of population not only stimulated Protestant diversity. It also strengthened many existing churches. Early colonial congregations were usually small and isolated. Increased membership enabled many Protestant denominations to form strong church institutions that held greater authority over individual congregations and actively supported the faith. Dissent still existed, but it no longer posed as serious a threat to the survival of congregations.

In the mid-1700s, a religious revival known as the GREAT AWAKENING caused a great deal of popular enthusiasm for religion in the colonies. This revival both stimulated and undermined the stability of Protestant denominations. By attracting more people to religion, it helped increase church membership. Yet differences over religious belief and practice divided revivalists and more traditional church members. Such disagreements split congregations and denominations and sometimes led to the creation of new Protestant groups.

orthodoxy strict adherence to established traditions and beliefs

Anglican of the Church of England

African American Protestantism

Aside from certain rituals and customs, not a single African religious system survived the colonial period. Many African American slaves turned to Protestantism. Protestant churches treated slaves differently from white people, keeping them largely separate and allowing very little participation in church rituals. As a result of this separation, a distinctly African American Protestantism began to emerge after the colonial period. Shaped both by Protestant teachings and by practices remembered from Africa, it developed into a highly emotional faith. One of its outgrowths is the modern-day Pentecostal Church.

Continuing immigration and the emergence of new Protestant churches ensured that Protestantism would remain a powerful force in America. Moreover, the diversity of Protestant churches came to be something not only valued but also protected.

The Anglican Church

The Anglican Church was the official Church of England, supported and controlled by the crown. In many ways, it represented a cross between Protestantism and Catholicism. Although Anglicans rejected the authority of the pope in Rome, they continued to follow many practices of the Catholic Church, such as the use of traditional garments, elaborate rituals, and a structure that included bishops and archbishops. A movement to reform the Church of England began in the late 1500s. Those who demanded change wanted a "purer," more independent church. Known as Puritans, they faced persecution in England. The Anglicanism that came to North America in the early 1600s was shaped by the influence of these Puritan dissenters.

The Anglican Church in Virginia.
When the colony of Virginia was founded in the early 1600s, Anglicanism became its official religion. But church officials in England had almost no control over colonial congregations, and local conditions ensured that the Anglican Church in Virginia would be very different from the Church of England. Many early Anglican ministers in Virginia had been educated in England, then dominated by Puritans, and the colony had no colleges to train new clergy. Traditional priestly garments and church ornaments were in short supply. Furthermore, Virginia had no church courts or hierarchy* of religious officials to enforce policy. The shortage of Anglican clergy meant that ministers from other Protestant denominations often led Anglican congregations, exposing them to many religious influences.

Power in the colonial Anglican Church was held by the lay* members of congregations, who chose their own ministers. Organizations of lay members called vestries managed the everyday affairs of each church. Many vestries were dominated by wealthy landowners, and churches came to reflect the character of these leaders. Over time the poorer members of congregations began to drift away from the church, which seemed to serve the interests of the rich and powerful.

Anglican Success and Failure.
After 1700 Anglican leaders in the colonies launched a campaign to establish the denomination as the official religion throughout British America. Their effort met with resistance or indifference. The Puritans in New England feared that the spread of Anglicanism would bring a return to government authority over religion, which had driven them from England in the first place. In the middle colonies, religious diversity was too firmly rooted for Anglicanism to displace other faiths. Though Anglicans outnumbered other Protestant groups in the southern colonies, they faced a general lack of interest in religion there.

The Anglicans responded by forming religious organizations—such as the Anglican Society for the Promotion of Christian Knowledge in 1698 and

* **hierarchy** division of society or an institution into groups with higher and lower ranks

* **lay** not linked to the church by religious vows or clerical office

the Society for the Propagation of the Gospel in Foreign Parts in 1701—to spread their faith through missionary activity and by establishing religious libraries. They achieved some success. By 1775 there were more than 300 Anglican churches in the colonies, and about 10 percent of all colonists were Anglicans. In addition, the church had founded two COLLEGES—the College of William and Mary in Virginia and King's College (now Columbia University) in New York.

Despite these achievements, the Anglican Church failed to become the official church throughout British North America. The colonies were simply too big and too diverse. Many colonists saw no reason to change their religion. Moreover, the Anglican Church was unable to win over many poorer colonists because it was viewed as the church of the upper classes—rich merchants, large planters, and government officials. Finally, the Great Awakening shattered the idea of uniting Americans under the Anglican faith. The evangelical* nature of this religious revival and the passionate preaching of men such as George WHITEFIELD and Jonathan EDWARDS proved far more appealing to Americans than the formal rituals* of Anglican worship and the church's reliance on religious authority. The Anglican Church survived, but its influence declined. After the American Revolution, the church became known as the Episcopal Church to signify its break with Britain and the Church of England.

The Congregationalist Church

The Congregationalist Church was founded by Puritans who rejected the beliefs and practices of the Church of England and objected to its centralized control. Established as the official religion of the Massachusetts Bay colony, Congregationalism came to dominate the religious life of early New England.

The Congregationalists had a very loose system of church government. Churches were organized by groups of believers who made a covenant, or agreement, to worship together. Individual congregations recognized no authority beyond their own minister and council. Ministers, who were selected by the congregation, could serve just one congregation and had no power outside it. Although church councils could discuss religious doctrine and other issues, they could not tell congregations or individuals what to believe or how to worship.

During its earliest days, the Congregationalist Church faced challenges from many dissenters, including Roger WILLIAMS and Anne HUTCHINSON. Massachusetts authorities either prosecuted or exiled these individuals for opposing the established beliefs. Congregationalism also faced a threat from other Protestant groups that began to take root in New England. But colonial authorities used their power to support Congregationalism by taxing colonists to provide funds for its churches. Even so, groups such as the Baptists, Quakers, and Anglicans founded congregations in New England.

Before 1680 Congregationalism and Anglicanism were the two largest Protestant denominations in the British colonies, accounting for 90 percent of all churches. In New England, virtually every church was Congregationalist. By 1770 the arrival of other Protestant groups from Europe had reduced the Congregationalists to only about 20 percent of the churches in British

* **evangelical** Christian movement emphasizing the importance of personal faith in leading to salvation

* **ritual** ceremony that follows a set pattern

See color plate 2, vol. 3.

America. This did not, however, mean the end of Congregationalism as a powerful religious force. The privileges it enjoyed as an official church gave it many advantages in recruiting new members and in maintaining congregations in New England.

Outside New England, however, other denominations were growing much more rapidly than the Congregationalists. The arrival of large numbers of Presbyterians in America after 1680 led to a weakening of Congregationalism in the middle colonies, especially in New Jersey. Some Congregationalists there left their church to become Presbyterians. When the Anglicans made an effort to expand their denomination after 1700, they had a measure of success in New England. They won some converts among physicians, lawyers, and merchants, but the majority of Anglicans in Massachusetts came from the lower classes, especially people in seafaring trades, who were not welcome in Congregational churches.

The Great Awakening caused many Congregationalist churches in New England to divide into two groups—called Old Light and New Light—further weakening Congregationalism's dominance in the region. Never very strong outside New England, Congregationalism eventually become a minor Protestant denomination.

The Baptist Church

Though the Baptists in the colonies were not formally connected to Baptist congregations and institutions in England, they shared many of the same views. Central to their faith was the belief that baptism—and full membership in the church—should be restricted to adults who knowingly accepted God.

In 1639 Roger WILLIAMS founded the first Baptist church in colonial America. A Puritan dissenter from Massachusetts, Williams objected to the union of CHURCH AND STATE in that colony. Banished from Massachusetts because of his views, Williams went to Rhode Island and established a settlement at PROVIDENCE.

After only a few months, however, Williams withdrew from the Baptist congregation he had founded. The members had begun to argue over the issue of predestination—the belief that a person's salvation is determined by God before birth and that there is nothing individuals can do to change their spiritual destiny. By 1652 the dispute over predestination had split the Baptist congregation into two churches. A similar dispute divided the Baptists of the Rhode Island town of NEWPORT in 1656.

Baptists in Massachusetts experienced few of the internal disputes that troubled Rhode Island Baptists. Perhaps this was because of the opposition they faced as dissenters from the established Puritan faith. Between 1649 and 1680, several Baptist congregations were formed in Massachusetts, including one in Boston. These churches presented a challenge to the authority of the Congregationalists, drawing members away from the established church.

The first major immigration of Baptists to North America began in the late 1600s. Many Welsh and English Baptists arrived in New Jersey and Pennsylvania between 1680 and 1740, soon outnumbering the Baptists in

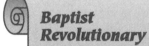

Baptist Revolutionary

During the period leading up to the American Revolution, Baptist leader Isaac Backus was a strong voice for the separation of church and state. In 1774 he led a delegation of Baptists to the First Continental Congress, where issues of liberty were being discussed, to speak out in favor of religious liberty. Drawing on the arguments of Roger Williams, he protested the establishment of the Congregationalist Church in Massachusetts. He did not succeed in convincing the other delegates at the time, but his views eventually became part of the United States Constitution.

New England. By 1740 there were more than 60 Baptist congregations in British America, most of them in the middle colonies.

The Great Awakening placed a strain on the Baptist Church, just as it disrupted other Protestant denominations. Congregations became divided over the message of evangelical preachers. Like the Congregationalists, the Baptists split into New Light and Old Light groups, with the New Lights supporting the evangelical message and the Old Lights rejecting it. Institutions such as the Philadelphia Baptist Association helped strengthen the church and were fairly successful in holding on to its membership. Even so, between 1740 and 1770, about half of all Baptists left the church for one reason or another. New members helped keep the Baptist Church from declining further during this period. It gained strength in the South, where, unlike other churches, it admitted black slaves into its congregations.

The Dutch Reformed Church

The Dutch Reformed Church, a branch of Calvinist Protestantism, first appeared in North America in 1628. By 1664 the church had established 13 congregations in New Netherland. But the English conquest of the colony that same year dramatically changed the fortunes of the Dutch Reformed Church.

The English agreed to allow Dutch colonists to continue to follow their own religion. At the same time, however, English authorities placed an Anglican minister in the Dutch Reformed congregation in Albany. At first the Dutch clergy protested this move, but they soon realized they had little choice but to accept it. Most Dutch merchants, concerned about their financial interests, also believed it was best to accept English customs and institutions.

One group within the Dutch Reformed Church, however, refused to accept the appointment of an Anglican minister and resented English interference in its church. Led by Jacob Leisler, these Dutch colonists rebelled against English officials in 1689. They received support in their uprising from the lower classes but not from Dutch traders and merchants or from the Dutch clergy. After the English regained control of the colony in 1691, they hanged Leisler and another leader of the revolt.

LEISLER'S REBELLION divided Dutch Reformed congregations between those who had supported and those who had opposed Leisler. Some congregations lost up to 90 percent of their members over the issue. These deep divisions remained, and by the early 1700s, Dutch Calvinism had split into two distinct churches.

One branch of the Dutch Reformed Church, consisting mainly of Leisler opponents, continued to seek favor with English authorities. Traditional in nature, this branch wanted to maintain Dutch customs and language and formal ritual in church services. The other branch became much more evangelical, emphasizing a personal and emotional religious faith. Many members of the evangelical branch took part in the religious revivals of the Great Awakening. They were also interested in gaining the right to make local decisions on church matters, a right granted by church officials in the Netherlands in 1747.

The evangelical branch of the Dutch Reformed Church was the first to embrace the English language and customs in its services, largely as a result

Remember: Words in small capital letters have separate entries, and the index at the end of Volume 4 will guide you to more information on many topics.

of its involvement with English denominations in the revival movement. The other branch of the Dutch Reformed Church resisted the use of English until 1763. It finally began hiring English-speaking preachers because the children could no longer understand Dutch.

In the years leading up to the American Revolution, the divisions within the Dutch Reformed Church hardened. Members of the traditional church generally remained loyal to the British, while the congregations of the evangelical church overwhelmingly supported the patriots*. After the Revolution, the Dutch Reformed Churches in America gained complete independence from church authorities in the Netherlands. They also resolved some of their differences and reunited in 1784 to form the Reformed Dutch Churches of New York and New Jersey.

The Presbyterian Church

The Presbyterian Church, a branch of Calvinist Protestantism, developed in England and Scotland. In 1680 no more than a handful of Presbyterian congregations existed in the British colonies. Thereafter, their numbers increased more rapidly as a result of both immigration and proselytizing—spreading the faith and gaining new members.

By 1740 the number of Presbyterian congregations in the colonies had reached more than 130. Some of them were formed by English settlers in places such as Boston, New York City, and Charleston. A few, including several churches in New Jersey, were established by Congregationalists who became Presbyterians.

Many of the Presbyterian immigrants to the colonies were "Scotch-Irish"—Scottish people who had settled in Ireland in the 1600s on lands seized by the English crown. The Scotch-Irish immigrants settled primarily in New Jersey, Pennsylvania, and the backcountry of the Carolinas. Others who arrived directly from Scotland came as Presbyterians, Anglicans, and Quakers. By the 1740s, however, Presbyterianism had become the dominant religion among the Scottish population, and being Scottish usually meant being Presbyterian as well.

In 1706 colonial Presbyterians established an organization, the Presbytery of Philadelphia, to serve as the governing body for the faith. Ten years later, there were enough Presbyterian congregations in the colonies to justify the formation of a higher church institution, called the Synod of Philadelphia. The synod divided congregations into regional presbyteries, each with authority over church properties and ministers within their region. The synod and presbyteries provided stability to the Presbyterian Church. They settled disputes among members and between congregations, ordained ministers, established qualifications for entrance into the clergy, and assigned ministers to congregations.

However, the religious revivals of the Great Awakening created divisions within Presbyterianism just as they did among other denominations. In 1745 the Synod of Philadelphia split between those in favor of and those opposed to revivalism. Those in favor founded the Synod of New York, which demanded strict obedience from ministers and firmly disciplined them for offenses.

* **patriot** American colonist who supported independence from Britain

The First Presbyterian Church in Newburyport, Massachusetts, is the burial site of revivalist minister George Whitefield. Preachers like Whitefield stirred up enthusiasm for religion among Presbyterians. But they also created divisions that caused the church's governing body to split in 1745.

Faced with the expansion of other Protestant denominations, the Presbyterian synods reunited in 1758 and worked to create and fill the demand for new congregations and ministers. The church sent ministers on preaching tours throughout the colonies, resulting in a doubling of congregations by the time of the American Revolution.

The Lutheran Church

The Lutheran Church originated in Germany and spread to parts of Scandinavia. In the mid-1600s, Swedish immigrants established some Lutheran congregations in the Delaware River valley. The real growth of the church, however, occurred after 1710, when a dramatic increase in the number of GERMAN IMMIGRANTS made Lutheranism a major religion in British America, particularly in the middle colonies. By 1740 there were at least 85 Lutheran churches in the American colonies, over half of them in Pennsylvania. The

Remember: *Consult the index at the end of Volume 4 to find more information on many topics.*

remaining congregations were scattered from Georgia to New York. Only New England lacked a Lutheran church.

Lutheran congregations faced a number of difficulties, including poor organization and lack of money. Most Lutheran ministers came to the colonies on their own rather than being sent by church authorities in Germany. Once in the colonies, they found themselves at the mercy of congregations unwilling to provide financial support. In Germantown, Pennsylvania, for example, settlers seldom attended Lutheran churches and gave them little money.

Competition from other German religious sects eventually led to changes in the Lutheran Church. Many Lutherans feared the influence of these sects and began working to strengthen their religion. By the 1740s, institutions such as the Lutheran Ministerium of Pennsylvania were helping to bring order and stability to colonial Lutheranism.

German Sects

Many German-speaking immigrants who came to America in the late 1600s and the 1700s were members of small Protestant sects that had broken away from the major Protestant denominations. These groups found that they could practice their religions in the frontier regions of the colonies without fear of persecution or interference by others.

The first German immigrants to arrive in Pennsylvania in 1683 were a group of former Lutherans who had recently become Mennonites. The Mennonite Church, which was established in Switzerland in the early 1500s, rejected worldly concerns and stressed simplicity in life and religious practices. Some of these settlers, led by a Mennonite named Johann Kelpius, founded a religious community in 1685 in which everyone shared their possessions in common.

The Amish were a branch of the Mennonite movement. Founded in Germany in the 1690s, the Amish had strict ideas about the way their members should dress, behave, and live. The first Amish immigrants arrived in the colonies in the 1720s, but most came in the 1760s. Like other German immigrants, they settled in Pennsylvania, primarily in Lancaster County, west of Philadelphia. The Amish were noted for their "old-fashioned" ways, which made them distinctive and often disliked by others. Some Amish communities continue to preserve this lifestyle today in eastern Pennsylvania and the Finger Lakes region of New York.

The Moravians—members of the Church of the United Brethren—were an evangelical religious sect founded in Europe in the late 1400s. They came to be noted for their focus on the sufferings of Christ, their belief that individuals could become free from all tendency toward sin, and their interest in emotional preaching. The first Moravian settlers in North America arrived in Georgia in 1736. Within several years, they had established communities in Pennsylvania and North Carolina. During the 1740s, the Moravians tried to unite various German Protestant sects into a single group called the Congregation of God in the Spirit. They were unsuccessful, and by the 1750s, it became clear that the Moravians would be just one of many German denominations in the colonies.

The Methodist Church

The Methodist Church had barely started to take shape in colonial America before the American Revolution. But in the 1800s and 1900s, the church had a sweeping effect on the development of American religion.

Founded in the 1730s by the English evangelist John Wesley and his brother Charles, Methodism was a reform movement within the Church of England. The Wesleys rejected the doctrine of predestination—the belief that God determines whether an individual will go to heaven or hell and that nothing can be done to alter that decision. Instead, they preached that individuals have the ability to achieve salvation through their devotion to God and personal religious experience. Methodist views attracted attention in the British colonies through the distribution of John Wesley's books, which became popular long before the arrival of any Methodist ministers. Their ideas gained acceptance in the 1740s and 1750s, during the Great Awakening.

Methodism remained an informal movement through the mid-1760s. The first Methodist congregation in the colonies was founded in New York City in 1766. By 1776 only eight congregations had been established, most of them in Maryland and Virginia. The advance of the Methodist Church ended abruptly that same year. John Wesley actively supported Britain in the struggle over American independence, and he sent all but one Methodist missionary back to Britain at the outbreak of the Revolution. This position almost led to the disappearance of Methodism in America because the religion lost many of its converts.

The one missionary left in the colonies, Francis Asbury, almost single-handedly saved American Methodism. His support for colonial independence helped restore the denomination's reputation and win back some converts. The success of the Methodist Church in the 1800s was due to a rebirth of the religion after the American Revolution. (*See also* **Acts of Toleration; African American Culture; Deism; Freedom of Religion; Missions and Missionaries; Music and Dance; Religious Life in European Colonies; Separatists.**)

Providence, Rhode Island

* *dissenter* person who disagrees with the beliefs and practices of the established church

* *doctrine* set of principles or beliefs accepted by a religious or political group

* *providence* divine guidance

* *charter* written grant from a ruler conferring certain rights and privileges

*T*he capital of the colony of RHODE ISLAND, Providence was founded by religious dissenters* who fled Massachusetts to escape persecution. The settlement became a haven for religious freedom as well as a center of colonial commerce.

In 1636 PURITAN leaders in Massachusetts banished the preacher Roger WILLIAMS from the colony because of disagreements with him over religious policy and doctrine*. Williams and several of his supporters moved to the Narragansett Bay area, where they bought land from the NARRAGANSETT INDIANS. There they established a settlement, calling it Providence because of "God's merciful providence*" in giving them a new home.

In 1637 Williams and the other settlers drew up a covenant, or agreement, that guaranteed religious freedom and provided for majority rule in nonreligious matters. Under a charter* granted by the English king in 1644, Providence united with the neighboring settlements of Portsmouth and NEWPORT.

These three communities—known as Providence Plantations—formed the beginnings of the colony of Rhode Island.

Providence suffered Indian attacks during King Philip's War in the late 1670s, but after that the town grew steadily. Commerce and trade became increasingly important in the 1700s, turning Providence into a thriving seaport. Trade with the WEST INDIES brought great wealth to local merchants, who built fine houses in Providence. In 1770 Rhode Island College (now Brown University) moved to the town.

Providence played an active role in the Revolutionary period. In 1772 residents burned a British ship that had been sent to enforce British trade laws. The Rhode Island Independence Act, signed in Providence in May 1776, approved a break with Britain two months before the Declaration of Independence. During the Revolution, American and French troops were stationed in the city.

See second map in Native Americans (vol. 3).

*T*he Pueblo Indians consist of various Native American communities in ARIZONA and NEW MEXICO that share certain cultural traditions. Their name comes from the Spanish word *pueblo,* meaning "village." In the years following the Spanish conquest of the region, the Pueblo Indians managed to hold on to many of their traditions. The ZUNI and HOPI INDIANS are among the best-known Pueblo groups.

Early History. Scholars believe that the Pueblo Indians are descended from the Anasazi, an ancient people who built huge apartment-like buildings with hundreds of rooms throughout the canyon lands and plateau regions of present-day Colorado, Utah, Arizona, and New Mexico. For reasons not fully understood, the Anasazi abandoned these dwellings sometime before the 1300s. By the time the Spanish arrived in the Southwest, the Anasazi's descendants were living in communities along the Rio Grande in New Mexico and in isolated locations in western New Mexico and northern Arizona.

The earliest contact with Europeans occurred in 1539, when the Spanish explorer Marcos de Niza arrived in Zuni territory. Niza marveled at the Indian settlements, and his reports of the region inspired stories of a group of fabulously rich villages known as the SEVEN CITIES OF CÍBOLA. Explorer Francisco de CORONADO came to Pueblo territory in 1540 in search of those cities, and other expeditions followed. In 1598 Juan de OÑATE arrived with missionaries and colonists and established the colony of New Mexico. The Pueblo Indians were friendly to the Spanish at first. However, relations eventually grew strained as the newcomers began to threaten Pueblo ways of living and religion.

Pueblo Culture. Pueblo villages contained freestanding houses and large, multistory structures—some as high as five stories—that sheltered many families. Made of stone and adobe, a sun-dried brick, the buildings generally had no doors. The Indians used ladders to reach the upper floors and entered rooms through holes in the roofs—an arrangement that made the villages easier to defend against enemies. Pueblo communities also contained underground rooms

This print shows women of the Zuni tribe—one of several groups of Pueblo Indians—grinding corn. The original drawing, by R. H. Kern, was published in the 1800s in a report of an official expedition conducted by the United States government.

See color plate 3, vol. 2.

* *artisan* skilled crafts worker

* *clan* related families

called kivas, which served as meeting places and as the site of ceremonial and religious rituals.

The Pueblo had mastered the skills needed to survive in a mostly desert environment. They learned to build reservoirs to store water and irrigation channels to bring the water to their fields. An agricultural people, they grew corn, squash, beans, melons, and other crops. They also hunted deer and small game and gathered various wild foods. The Indians raised cotton and wove it into fabric for clothing and blankets. Their artisans* crafted fine pottery, baskets, and jewelry.

The Pueblo Indians had a complex religion. They worshipped the forces of nature and believed that many supernatural spirits roamed the earth and sky. During intricate ceremonies and rituals, the members of secret religious societies impersonated these spirits by wearing elaborate costumes and masks. Among the Hopi and Zuni, the masks, the costumes, and the spirits they represented were known as kachinas.

Although the Pueblo shared a common culture, there were differences among the various groups. In the Indian villages along the Rio Grande, social organization was based on membership in clans* traced through both women and men. Among the Indians farther west, including the Hopi and Zuni, clan membership was traced only through women. Politically, each Pueblo village was independent and had its own leaders. The authority of these leaders came from membership in the local religious societies.

Spanish Impact on the Indians.

When the Spanish began to colonize New Mexico, the lives of the Pueblo Indians changed. The Spanish introduced animals—horses, sheep, goats, and cattle—that became part of the Pueblo economy and crafts such as blacksmithing and woodworking.

tribute payment made to a dominant power

Spanish colonization had harmful effects on the Pueblo as well. The colonists brought European diseases, which killed many Indians. They forced the Indians to work as laborers for them and to pay tribute*, usually by giving up a portion of their crops. The Spanish also tried to make the Pueblo convert to Christianity and to abandon their traditional beliefs. Indians who tried to resist were harshly punished. The Indians of New Mexico eventually rebelled against Spanish oppression*. In the PUEBLO REVOLT of 1680, they killed many colonists and missionaries and forced the remaining white settlers to flee to the south.

oppression unjust or cruel exercise of authority

The Spanish regained control of New Mexico in 1696 and renewed their efforts to colonize the region. This time, though, they treated the Indians less harshly. They showed more respect for Pueblo culture, allowing the Indians to maintain many of their traditions. In addition, the Spanish crown offered land grants to Pueblo villages, which gave the Indians more control over their own affairs.

Maintaining Pueblo Culture.

The Pueblo remained under Spanish colonial rule until 1821, when Mexico gained its independence from Spain and took over control of Pueblo lands in New Mexico and Arizona. In 1848 Mexico ceded* those regions to the United States, and the Indians came under the authority of the American government. Throughout the 1700s and 1800s, the Pueblo had fairly peaceful relations with the white people who settled near their territory or traveled through it.

cede to yield or surrender

The Pueblo Indians have maintained much of their traditional culture up to the present day, in part because of their geographical isolation. Today some groups continue to live in the same places they occupied when the Spaniards arrived. One village in New Mexico, Acoma pueblo, is thought to be the oldest continuously inhabited community north of Mexico. (*See also* **Encomiendas; Missions and Missionaries; Native Americans; Religions, Native American; Spanish Borderlands.**)

Pueblo Revolt (1680)

tribute payment made to a dominant power

The Pueblo Revolt was a Native American uprising that took place in NEW MEXICO in 1680. Pushed to the breaking point by Spanish policies, the PUEBLO INDIANS killed several hundred white settlers and drove the rest out of the territory. The Indians hoped to regain the way of life they had known before Europeans invaded their homeland.

Spain began colonizing New Mexico in the late 1500s. By 1680 the colony had about 2,500 whites, including soldiers, missionaries, and settlers. Under the Spanish system of ENCOMIENDAS, the colonists had the right to demand labor and tribute* from the Indians. Treated little better than slaves, the Pueblo suffered greatly and resented Spanish rule.

The seeds of the revolt, however, lay mainly in the Europeans' attitude toward the Indian religion. The Spaniards believed that the Pueblo beliefs and

religious ceremonies were evil, the work of the devil. They not only wanted to convert the Indians to Christianity but also hoped to wipe out all traces of Pueblo religious beliefs. Missionaries destroyed sacred objects and shrines and harshly punished those who continued to take part in native religious ceremonies. In 1675 Spanish authorities arrested 47 Pueblo religious leaders on charges of sorcery*. Four of the men were hanged; the rest were whipped in public.

* **sorcery** witchcraft

One of those whipped was a man named Popé. After his release, Popé began making plans to strike back at the Spanish and to restore Indian rule and customs. He secretly preached his ideas and gained an increasingly large group of followers. By 1680 Popé and other rebels were ready to act, and they set a date for an uprising. Although the Spanish learned of the coming attack from some Indian allies, it was too late to avoid the conflict.

The Pueblo Revolt began on August 10, 1680. Pueblo Indians throughout New Mexico attacked Spanish colonists, killing about 400 settlers and 21 missionaries and destroying missions and property. The surviving Spaniards took refuge in SANTA FE, the colonial capital. On August 15, the Indians surrounded the town and held it in siege* for nine days. Short of food and water, the colonial governor and surviving colonists finally decided to make a break and run. Seeing their enemies retreating, the Indians left them alone, and the terrified Spanish fled from New Mexico.

* **siege** prolonged effort by armed troops to force the surrender of a town or fort by surrounding it and cutting it off from aid

The Pueblo Revolt was one of the most successful Indian rebellions in North America. Yet the Pueblo's triumph did not last. In 1692 Spanish troops began reconquering New Mexico, and Spain regained control of the region four years later. At the same time, however, the revolt had a long-lasting impact. The Spanish ended the system of *encomiendas* and treated the Indians less harshly. They also allowed them to keep many of their religious ceremonies. (*See also* **Missions and Missionaries; Native Americans; Religions, Native American; Spanish Borderlands.**)

Puerto Rico

Puerto Rico, which means "rich port" in Spanish, is a large island in the WEST INDIES that was a Spanish colony for more than 400 years. During the early days of Spanish rule, the island served as a base on the sea route between Europe and Spain's other colonies in North and Central America.

Christopher COLUMBUS discovered Puerto Rico during his second voyage to the Americas, in 1493. But colonization did not begin until 1508, when Juan PONCE DE LEÓN took possession of the island. The Spaniards quickly conquered the Taino Indians living there, forcing them to work as slaves. Hard labor and disease eventually killed most of the islands' Indian population.

At first the Spanish concentrated on mining GOLD in Puerto Rico, but after exhausting the gold supply, they turned to agriculture. By the early 1500s, they had established large sugar PLANTATIONS, using Indians and later African slaves to work the fields. TOBACCO became an important cash crop* in the 1600s, as did coffee in the 1700s.

* **cash crop** crop grown primarily for profit

During the late 1500s and the 1600s, Spanish treasure ships stopped at Puerto Rico on their way from Mexico to Spain. These vessels attracted

Punishment

* **privateer** privately owned ship authorized by the government to attack and capture enemy vessels; also the ship's master

* **cede** to yield or surrender

numerous Dutch, French, and English pirates and privateers*, including Sir Francis DRAKE, who attempted to raid the port city of San Juan in 1595. Spain responded by building several large fortresses to defend the island.

Much of Puerto Rico's trade in the 1700s consisted of SMUGGLING. In 1804, however, Spain officially opened the island's ports to foreign trade, and the economy began to grow. Resentment of Spanish rule also grew, and Puerto Rican colonists staged several unsuccessful revolts in the 1800s.

A movement for independence arose in the late 1800s, and in February 1898, Spain granted Puerto Rico self-government in many matters. A few months later, however, war erupted between Spain and the United States. U.S. troops occupied Puerto Rico during the short-lived Spanish-American War, and Spain ceded* the island to the United States at the war's end. (*See also* **European Empires; Exploration, Age of; Slavery.**)

Punishment

See *Crime and Punishment.*

Puritans

* **ritual** ceremony that follows a set pattern

* **vestment** special garment worn by those conducting religious services
* **clergy** ministers, priests, and other church officials

*T*he Puritans were a Protestant group that emerged in England in the 1500s. They disliked the elaborate rituals* of the Anglican Church, the nation's official church, and sought to "purify" it. Leaving their homeland to find freedom to worship in their own way, Puritan immigrants founded the first English colonies in New England.

The Origins of Puritanism. In the mid-1500s, England's King Henry VIII broke away from the ROMAN CATHOLIC CHURCH and established the Church of England, or Anglican Church. The English monarch became head of the new church, replacing the pope. But the English church held on to many Catholic traditions, including some elaborate ceremonies, the special vestments* of the priests, and the sign of the cross. It also retained much of the organizational structure of the Catholic Church. The clergy* was divided into levels from deacons to priests, bishops, and archbishops, all answering to a supreme authority—the king.

Many English Protestants strongly disapproved of the lingering imprint of the Catholic Church on Anglicanism and called for reform. They wanted to do away with many of the rituals of the Catholic Church. They also rejected the idea of a central church authority, whether the pope or the English monarch. These people came to be known as Puritans because of their desire to purify the Anglican Church of all traces of Catholic influence. Though they preferred to call themselves "the godly," they later accepted the name *Puritan.*

Social problems in England also played a role in the growth of Puritanism. At the time, many small farmers were abandoning the countryside and moving to cities because new laws on land rights left them without any fields. Some people believed these changes would destroy traditional ways of life and threaten the order of English society. They gathered around Puritan preachers who spoke of bringing more discipline to daily life.

Puritan John Endecott served as leader of the Massachusetts Bay colony during the time the first colonists spent at Naumkeag, or Salem, before moving to Boston. Later, as the colony's governor, Endecott gained a reputation for stern efficiency and intolerance of other religions.

The Puritans' desire to reform society often led to clashes with their neighbors. Their drive to change the church led to persecution by the government. Believing that reforming English society and its church was a hopeless cause, some Puritans—appropriately called Separatists—separated from Anglicanism altogether. A group of these Separatists, later known as the PILGRIMS, left their homeland for the Netherlands before immigrating to New England and founding the PLYMOUTH COLONY in 1620.

Most Puritans rejected separatism, focusing instead on spreading their views and trying to change the church from within. During the reigns of King JAMES I (1603–1625) and Charles I (1625–1649), however, the Puritans' hopes for reform grew dimmer, and persecution by the government increased. Many Puritans began to look to North America, where they would be able to establish a new society far from the corruption of the Anglican Church and the harassment of non-Puritan neighbors. Their mission, as they saw it, was to build a godly "city upon a hill," which would serve as an example to the English churches.

Puritan Beliefs.

The Puritans' religion was based mainly on CALVINIST principles. According to their beliefs, God determines what will happen and then makes it come to pass through his will. He established a "covenant of grace" with the first man, Adam, and promised him salvation if he obeyed God's laws. However, Adam chose to sin, breaking the covenant. The Puritans believed that all humans inherited Adam's inability to understand God's plan—an imperfection they called "original sin." Humans, therefore, could never discover the will of God through the use of reason and must rely on faith alone. After Adam's fall, God established a new "covenant of grace" by sending his son, Jesus Christ, to sacrifice himself for the sins of humans. By accepting Christ as their savior, individuals could achieve salvation.

Puritans combined this idea of the covenant with a belief in predestination—the idea that God has already decided which people will go to heaven and which to hell. Therefore, salvation cannot be achieved through good works or pure thoughts and cannot be controlled by the individual. Those who are members of the "elect"—the ones God has chosen to go to heaven—will eventually come to Christ and be saved. Those who are not among the "elect" can do nothing to bring about salvation. The idea of predestination helped explain to believers why some people lived godly lives while others did evil. It also guaranteed that God would never abandon those who accepted his covenant.

The Spread of Puritanism.

In 1629 a group of investors founded the Massachusetts Bay colony as a haven for Puritans. A year later several wealthy Puritans organized the Providence Company, which established several settlements on islands in the Caribbean. By 1642 about 80,000 people had left England for these new colonies. In North America, the Puritans also settled in VIRGINIA and MARYLAND, but they never had as strong an influence on society or culture there as they did in New England.

In New England, the Puritans adopted a form of organization in which each church congregation was independent from others. Each chose its own ministers and recognized no central church authority. Under this system, called

Quakers

* **lay** not linked to the church by religious vows or clerical office

Congregationalism, the lay* members of each town founded the local churches and played an important role in running them. This arrangement, combined with the fact that only church members could vote, kept discipline in "godly"— that is, Puritan—hands, and ensured a high degree of cooperation between the church and government authorities. Those who strayed too far from Puritan practices were quickly disciplined by the colony's leadership. For example, Roger WILLIAMS was banished from MASSACHUSETTS in 1635 for, among other things, denying the government's authority to punish religious offenses.

Puritan influence over political affairs in Massachusetts began to decline when King William III granted a new charter in 1691 that gave the vote to all property holders. Although the Congregationalist Church still had the power to tax all residents, the state was forced to tolerate other faiths and could no longer impose religious discipline on all colonists. At the same time, a new generation, born in North America, failed to adopt the Puritan faith as completely as those who had emigrated from England. Into this situation came powerful preachers such as Jonathan EDWARDS and George WHITEFIELD. They touched off the GREAT AWAKENING, a religious revival that swept New England in the early 1740s. Like the earliest Puritan ministers in England, Whitefield and other revivalists traveled the countryside, drawing large crowds to sermons that often attacked the local clergy.

The Great Awakening stirred up religious feeling and increased the number of conversions, but it also split the Puritans. Those who supported the revival—called the New Lights—founded their own denominations* or joined others, such as the Baptists. By the late 1700s, the influence of Puritanism on New England had weakened considerably.

* **denomination** organized group of religious congregations

Despite its decline, Puritanism had a significant impact on American society and culture. Because of the Puritan influence, New England had a much higher degree of social and political stability than the other English colonies in North America. The Puritans' emphasis on education led them to establish many SCHOOLS and COLLEGES in New England during the colonial period, contributing to a high literacy rate. The persecution they had experienced before fleeing England taught them to mistrust the power of monarchs. This may help explain the leading role New Englanders took in fighting for colonial rights against British power in the years leading up to the American Revolution. Many of the Puritans' ideals—such as belief in hard work, the importance of the family, and their mission to serve as an example to others—continue to be identified as traditional American values. (*See also* **Church and State; Freedom of Religion; Hutchinson, Anne; Protestant Churches; Religious Life in European Colonies; Salem Witchcraft Trials; Separatists; Winthrop, John.**)

Quakers

* **ritual** ceremony that follows a set pattern
* **Anglican** of the Church of England

*T*he Quakers, or members of the Society of Friends, originated in England in the mid-1600s. They believed that a person did not need a minister or church rituals* to reach God. Their views were condemned by the Anglican* Church. Many Quakers left England for the North American colonies, where their beliefs continued to cause problems with religious and government authorities.

Instead of formal religious services led by a minister, the Quakers held meetings at which any person could speak who felt moved to do so. This picture of a Quaker meeting dates from sometime in the 1700s.

* *sect* religious group

The Roots of Quakerism. In the mid-1600s, many English Protestants had become dissatisfied with the Anglican Church. A group of people, known as PURITANS, wanted to reform it. The Puritan movement soon divided into a number of groups with different ideas about the way to worship to achieve salvation. Some people, who called themselves Seekers, decided that none of these sects* was really inspired by God. They began to meet, waiting in silence for inner guidance from the Holy Spirit.

George Fox was associated with the Seekers. In the late 1640s, he began wandering the English countryside, preaching about an inner light through which any person could come to know the Holy Spirit. Fox began attracting followers, drawing perhaps 30,000 to 40,000 people to his movement by 1660. They became known as Quakers because they trembled when they were under the influence of the Holy Spirit.

Quakers behaved in ways that clearly separated them from other members of English society. They dressed simply, accepted women as the equals of men, and did not recognize class differences. They would not, for example, take off their hats to show respect to people who held a higher rank in the social structure because they thought all people were equal in the sight of God. They also refused to take oaths—because this would imply that they did not

Quakers

War Relief

One of the greatest challenges Quakers faced in colonial times was meeting the demands of the society they lived in, while following their belief in nonviolence. They came up with some creative solutions. In 1740, when Britain and France were at war, Pennsylvania's Quaker-led assembly refused to pay for a military expedition against the French. Instead, it offered a sum of money to be used specifically for the purchase of bread, meat, and flour. During the American Revolution, the Quakers were criticized for refusing to fight for independence from Britain. In response, they set up a large-scale war relief program for collecting money, clothing, and food.

speak truthfully at other times—and believed strongly in pacifism*. Moreover, they rejected church authority or organization. The Quakers' ideas challenged the established church and society of England and led to their persecution by English authorities. In the 1660s, thousands of members of the Society of Friends were jailed, and about 500 died in prison. William PENN, a leading English Quaker, was sent to prison four times for stating his beliefs publicly.

Quakerism in North America.   Even before they were widely persecuted in England, Quakers—also known as Friends—had immigrated to America to spread their faith. The first arrived in Massachusetts in 1656, but they were not welcomed by the Puritan leaders there. In the mid-1600s, colonial officials punished Quakers for challenging the established orthodoxy* by whippings, imprisonment, deportation, and even hanging. Quaker settlers driven out of Massachusetts found refuge in surrounding colonies. By 1670 a majority of residents of neighboring Rhode Island were Friends. They also spread to other colonies, including New York, Virginia, and the Carolinas. The Quakers' greatest successes came in remote areas that had no established churches. Because their religion did not need ordained clergy* or prayer books, it could take root and grow on the FRONTIER, where such things were in short supply.

Quakerism became firmly established in North America with the founding of the colonies of East and West Jersey and PENNSYLVANIA. A group of Friends established West Jersey in 1675, basing its government on Quaker beliefs. Six years later, Pennsylvania was founded by William Penn. A friend of King Charles II, Penn received a royal grant for the colony. It became a haven for Quakers and adopted a government based on the religion's principles. But the colony also welcomed people of other faiths and soon had one of the most diverse populations in North America. In keeping with the Quakers' pacifist views, Pennsylvania's constitution did not provide for the creation of a militia*. It also extended the right to vote to any Christian male over 21 who either owned a certain amount of property or paid a personal tax. The colony passed laws to provide for the poor and, at Penn's insistence, generally treated the Indians fairly, buying land from them rather than simply taking it.

The Friends prospered in Pennsylvania, coming to control not only the government but also the economic and social leadership of the colony. This influential position led prominent Quakers to abandon their rejection of worldly concerns in the hope that they might exercise some control over colonial society. They developed a more formal organization, including monthly, quarterly, and yearly meetings to deal with issues of everyday life, such as education and marriage. They wrote the Book of Discipline, which listed penalties for those who failed to follow the Quakers' strict code of behavior.

Britain's colonial wars with France and Spain severely tested the Quakers' principles and made them rethink their role in society. The Pennsylvania assembly, dominated by Quakers, refused to pass bills to raise money or troops that would support these conflicts. But as non-Quakers gained more power in the colony, Pennsylvania eventually abandoned its pacifist position. After the colony formed a militia, many Friends stopped paying taxes. Most of those who sat in the assembly resigned.

During and after the AMERICAN REVOLUTION, the Quakers' views caused them to clash with their fellow colonists. Many Quakers were fined or jailed for refusing to serve in the army or to pay taxes for the war. The Society of Friends also set itself apart by its opposition to SLAVERY. By taking firm stands on issues of freedom and equality, the Quakers contributed to the development of important principles that became part of the new American nation. (*See also* **Antislavery Movement; Church and State; Freedom of Religion; Protestant Churches.**)

Quartering Acts

*I*n 1765 and 1774, the British PARLIAMENT passed laws known as the Quartering Acts, which concerned the housing, or quartering, of British troops in the colonies. The American colonists greatly resented these laws and did what they could to resist them.

After the FRENCH AND INDIAN WAR, large numbers of British troops remained in North America. Parliament passed a law that shifted part of the cost of maintaining these troops to the colonies. The American Mutiny Act of 1765, known as the Quartering Act, required the colonies to provide British soldiers with lodging. Parliament worded the law carefully to prohibit stationing soldiers in colonists' homes. Local officials were supposed to house troops in barracks or inns. If such accommodations were not available, colonial governments had to place soldiers in vacant buildings and provide them with firewood, candles, bedding, and cooking utensils, all free of charge.

Colonists resented the law. They argued that it placed an unfair financial burden on communities that housed troops. Some colonies, such as Virginia, had no British soldiers to quarter. But New York, as the main port for the arrival and departure of soldiers, had to provide housing for many troops. Efforts of New Yorkers to resist the law led Parliament to pass the New York Restraining Act of 1767, which barred New York's colonial assembly from meeting until the colony agreed to obey the Quartering Act. But the Restraining Act never took effect because New York complied with the law.

In 1771 New Jersey refused to pay its share of the housing costs, and Britain withdrew its troops from the colony. Authorities hoped this action would demonstrate the benefits of having an army unit present. Soldiers not only helped maintain order, but they also boosted the economy by spending their pay locally. Britain's strategy worked. Other colonies quickly agreed to pay their contributions, and problems with the Quartering Act disappeared in most places.

The colonists of Massachusetts, however, continued to resist the law. In 1768 the city of Boston housed British troops in Castle William, a fort on an island in Boston harbor. When Britain stationed more troops in Boston after the BOSTON TEA PARTY in 1773, it wanted to make sure the soldiers would be located right in the city, close to any political activity. Parliament passed a new Quartering Act that placed the royal governor rather than local officials in charge of arranging lodgings for soldiers. This law was one of the four INTOLERABLE ACTS designed to strengthen royal control in Massachusetts.

Like the earlier law, the Quartering Act of 1774 did not allow British troops to be housed in private homes. Its goal was to force the colonists to

Quebec

* **patriot** American colonist who supported independence from Britain

give soldiers access to vacant buildings. But Massachusetts patriots* convinced the owners of such buildings to delay repairs so that soldiers could not be lodged in them. As a result, the British troops had to camp out on Boston Common until November 1774.

While opposition to the original Quartering Act had been confined primarily to Massachusetts, the Intolerable Acts angered other colonies as well. They responded by calling the FIRST CONTINENTAL CONGRESS, which passed a resolution to disobey the acts. Increasing resistance to these and other British policies contributed to the growing movement for independence. (*See also* **Independence Movements; Military Forces.**)

Quebec

See color plate 6, vol. 1.

*L*ocated on the ST. LAWRENCE RIVER in southeastern CANADA, Quebec became the first permanent French settlement in North America. The town also served as the capital of NEW FRANCE. Important battles took place in Quebec during the struggles between France and Britain for control of the continent and during the American Revolutionary War.

The French explorer Jacques CARTIER was the first European to lay claim to Quebec. Sailing up the St. Lawrence in 1535 in search of gold and a passage to China, Cartier noticed a number of Indian villages along the river. One of these, called Stadacona, became the site of Quebec many years later.

Samuel de CHAMPLAIN, another French explorer, and Pierre du Gua, Sieur de Monts, a French shipowner and merchant, established the town in 1608. Three years earlier the two men had founded PORT ROYAL on the western coast of present-day Nova Scotia. Quebec proved to be a better site for a fortress and trading post because it was located farther inland and on a high cliff. It was also close to furs and fur-trading Indians. Champlain named the settlement Quebec from the Indian word *Kebec,* meaning "place where river narrows."

Quebec grew slowly, mainly because the COMPANY OF ONE HUNDRED ASSOCIATES, the trading company that governed the colony, failed to send settlers. In 1663 New France returned to royal control. The French king sent Jean-Baptiste Talon to be its new administrator, and Quebec was made the colony's capital. The town soon began to prosper, developing into the principal center for trade, government, and religion in New France. By 1700 Quebec had 1,900 inhabitants.

The British made several attempts to gain control of the town. They captured Quebec in 1629 but returned it to France three years later as part of a treaty settlement. In 1690 Sir William Phips, governor of Massachusetts, led an expedition to conquer Canada. After quickly defeating the French at Port Royal, Phips was turned back at Quebec by the French governor Louis Frontenac. In 1711 a British fleet on its way to Quebec crashed on reefs in the St. Lawrence during a storm.

The Battle of Quebec—also called the Battle of the Plains of Abraham—was fought during the FRENCH AND INDIAN WAR, the last of the series of wars between Great Britain and France for control of North America. In 1759, a year after the fall of the French fort at LOUISBOURG, the British general James Wolfe received orders to capture Quebec. Wolfe's forces sailed up

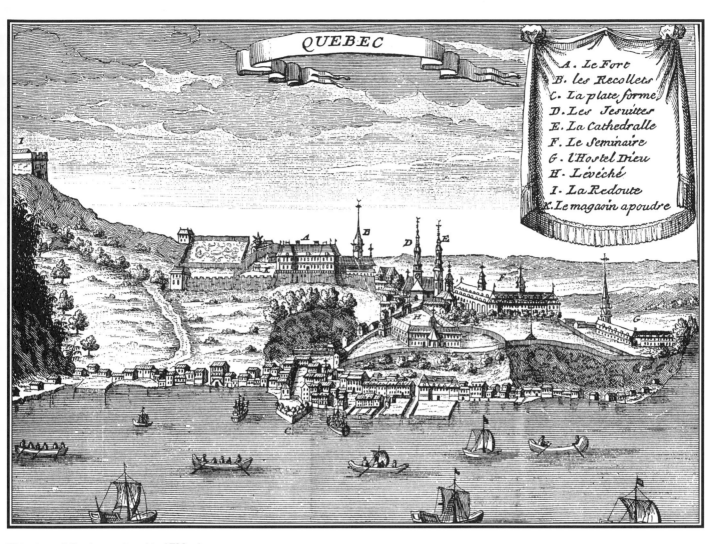

This view of Quebec, printed in 1722, shows the St. Lawrence River in the foreground, the fortress at the far left, and the tall spires of the cathedral and other religious buildings.

the St. Lawrence River and landed on the Ile d'Orleans (Island of Orleans) below Quebec.

Over a period of two months, Wolfe made attempt after attempt to capture the city. Finally, on a cloudy, moonless night, a small group of British soldiers overpowered a French guard. The British were able to cross the river safely and scale the cliffs during the night. The next morning, September 13, 1759, the French and British forces met in battle on the Plains of Abraham outside Quebec. The French surrendered five days later. Both General Wolfe and the French commander General Louis-Joseph de Montcalm lost their lives in the fighting. After the fall of Quebec, the British went on to capture MONTREAL. France's dream of an empire in the "New World" had come to an end.

At the beginning of the AMERICAN REVOLUTION, in December 1775, patriot* troops led by Benedict ARNOLD and Richard Montgomery attacked Quebec. They hoped to convince Canadian colonists to join them in rebellion against Britain. The Canadians refused, and the small American force was crushed. The remaining Americans retreated after British reinforcements arrived in the spring of 1776.

* **patriot** American colonist who supported independence from Britain

227

Quebec Act (1774)

* **civil law** body of law that regulates and protects the rights of individuals

* **autocratic** ruling with absolute power and authority

*T*he Quebec Act was one of the so-called INTOLERABLE ACTS. Passed by Parliament in the first half of 1774, it angered American colonists and contributed to the movement for independence. At the same time, however, the law established religious and legal rights for the French inhabitants of British Canada.

After defeating the French in the FRENCH AND INDIAN WAR in 1763, Great Britain gained control of Canada. The British then faced the problem of governing this former French colony. To win the support of the French-speaking population, Parliament passed the Quebec Act. The act created a centralized government for the colony, with a royal governor and an appointed—rather than an elected—council. The Quebec Act restored French civil law* and gave Catholic French Canadians complete religious freedom. It also extended the boundaries of Quebec to include the lands of the Ohio Valley.

The Quebec Act infuriated the colonists in Britain's American colonies. They felt that Parliament's failure to create an elected assembly was a step toward autocratic* rule. American colonists were also outraged by Quebec's new boundaries, which blocked further westward expansion of several colonies. Protestants—particularly those in New England—strongly objected to the act's recognition of Catholicism.

Passage of the Quebec Act and other Intolerable Acts prompted the colonists to organize the FIRST CONTINENTAL CONGRESS to discuss a response to British actions. In September and October 1774, the congress passed the Suffolk Resolves, which condemned the Quebec Act and urged colonists to actively resist British policies. (*See also* **Canada; Independence Movements.**)

Queen Anne's War (1702–1713)

* **prestige** high standing and respect in the eyes of others
* **succession** transferring authority on the death of a ruler to the next ruler

*Q*ueen Anne's War was part of a long struggle between France and England. From the late 1600s to the mid-1700s, the two nations were often at war in Europe. Their wars reached across the Atlantic Ocean to their colonies in North America, pitting French and English colonists and their Indian allies against each other. France and England both hoped to expand their overseas empires and gain power and prestige* at the expense of the other.

Queen Anne's War began in Europe, where it was called the War of the Spanish Succession*. After the death of King Charles II of SPAIN in 1700, King Louis XIV of FRANCE, who had married into the Spanish royal family, managed to get his grandson named king of Spain. Other European powers feared that France would gain control of Spain's huge empire in Europe and the Americas. To prevent this, England, the Netherlands, and the Holy Roman Empire joined together and declared war on France. English colonists in North America called the conflict Queen Anne's War because it began soon after Queen Anne came to the throne of England.

The European war dragged on for years, with a death toll in the hundreds of thousands. In the Americas, most of the fighting took place in the West Indies, the Carolinas, and New England. English colonists attacked the Spanish town of ST. AUGUSTINE in Florida in 1702 and later drove off a fleet of French and Spanish ships that tried to invade CHARLESTON.

French and Indian raiding parties from Canada struck the first blow in New England, attacking frontier settlements in 1703. The following year they destroyed the town of Deerfield, Massachusetts. Colonists from Massachusetts responded by striking at French forts in PORT ROYAL and QUEBEC, just as they had done in an earlier conflict. With the help of a large British force, they captured Port Royal in 1710, but the attack on Quebec ended in disaster, with nine ships and 900 men lost in heavy fog and gales at sea.

France's North American colony survived the war but lost much of its territory in the peace settlement of 1713, known as the TREATY OF UTRECHT. Britain gained control of Newfoundland, the Hudson Bay area, and Acadia, which it renamed NOVA SCOTIA. Britain emerged from the war stronger than ever, France weaker. (*See also* **European Empires.**)